KU-517-740

Public Space, Media Space

Public Space, Media Space

Edited by

Chris Berry
King's College London, UK

Janet Harbord
Queen Mary, University of London, UK

Rachel Moore
Goldsmiths, University of London, UK

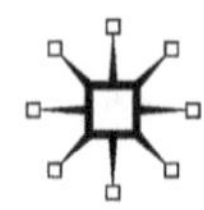

First published 2013 by
PALGRAVE MACMILLAN

Palgrave Macmillan in the UK is an imprint of Macmillan Publishers Limited, registered in England, company number 785998, of Houndmills, Basingstoke, Hampshire RG21 6XS.

Palgrave Macmillan in the US is a division of St Martin's Press LLC, 175 Fifth Avenue, New York, NY 10010.

Palgrave Macmillan is the global academic imprint of the above companies and has companies and representatives throughout the world.

Palgrave® and Macmillan® are registered trademarks in the United States, the United Kingdom, Europe and other countries.

ISBN 978–1–137–02775–7

This book is printed on paper suitable for recycling and made from fully managed and sustained forest sources. Logging, pulping and manufacturing processes are expected to conform to the environmental regulations of the country of origin.

A catalogue record for this book is available from the British Library.

A catalog record for this book is available from the Library of Congress.

Contents

Figures

Acknowledgments

The editors would like to acknowledge the support of a Leverhulme Trust Programme Grant for the Goldsmiths Leverhulme Media Research Centre, which hosted the symposium that led to this collection, as well as the research conducted by the editors and written about in this volume. We are also grateful to our editorial assistant, Corey Kai Nelson Schultz, without whose hard work we would have been unable to put this book together, and to the contributors to the volume for their thought-provoking chapters and cooperation throughout the editorial process. Finally, Felicity Plester and Catherine Mitchell at Palgrave have been enthusiastic and helpful editors, guiding us through the sometimes choppy waters of putting together an edited collection.

Every effort has been made to trace all copyright holders, but if any have been inadvertently overlooked, the publisher will be pleased to make the necessary arrangements at the first opportunity.

Contributors

Mona Abaza obtained her PhD in 1990 in sociology from the University of Bielefeld, Germany. She is currently Professor of Sociology at the American University in Cairo. From 2009 to 2011 she was Visiting Professor of Islamology in the Department of Theology, Lund University. She was a visiting scholar in Singapore at the Institute for South East Asian Studies (1990–1992), Kuala Lumpur (1995–1996), Paris (1994), Berlin (Wissenschaftskolleg 1996–1997), Leiden (2002–2003), Wassenaar (2006–2007) and Bellagio (Rockefeller Foundation 2005). Her books include *Twentieth Century Egyptian Art: The Private Collection of Sherwet Shafei* (2011), *The Changing Consumer Culture of Modern Egypt: Cairo's Urban Reshaping* (2006), *Debates on Islam and Knowledge in Malaysia and Egypt: Shifting Worlds* (2002) and *Islamic Education, Perceptions and Exchanges: Indonesian Students in Cairo* (1994).

Chris Berry is Professor of Film Studies at King's College London. Prior to his current appointment, he taught at La Trobe University in Melbourne; the University of California, Berkeley; and Goldsmiths, University of London. His publications include *Cinema and the National: China on Screen* (with Mary Farquhar, 2006), *Postsocialist Cinema in Post-Mao China: The Cultural Revolution after the Cultural Revolution* (2004), *The New Chinese Documentary Film Movement: For the Public Record* (edited with Lu Xinyu and Lisa Rofel, 2010), *Electronic Elsewheres: Media, Technology, and Social Space* (edited with Kim Soyoung and Lynn Spigel, 2010) and *Cultural Studies and Cultural Industries in Northeast Asia: What a Difference a Region Makes* (edited with Nicola Liscutin and Jonathan D. Mackintosh, 2009).

Michael Bull is a reader in media at the University of Sussex. He is the author of *Sounding Out the City: Personal Stereos and the Management of Everyday Life* (2000) and *Sound Moves: iPod Culture and Urban Experience* (2007). He and Les Back co-edited *The Auditory Culture Reader* (2003) and he is a founding editor of the journal *Senses and Society*. He is Director of the Centre for Material Digital Culture at Sussex and a core member of the European think tank Future Trends Forum, based in Madrid. He is currently writing a monograph on the history of sonic connections.

Francesco Casetti is Professor of Film and Media at Yale University. He is the author of *Inside the Gaze: The Fiction Film and its Spectator* (1999), *Theories of Cinema, 1945–1995* (1999) and *Eye of the Century: Film, Experience, Modernity* (2008). He has been Visiting Professor at the University of Paris 3, University of Iowa and University of California, Berkeley. Casetti and Jane Gaines were the co-founders of the Permanent Seminar on Histories of Film Theories. He is the General Editor of the series "Spettacolo e Comunicazione". He has taught for 30 years in Italy, where he served as President of the Association of Film and Television Teachers.

Beatriz Colomina is an architectural historian and theorist who has written extensively on questions of architecture and media. Her books include *Privacy and Publicity: Modern Architecture as Mass Media* (1994), which was awarded the 1995 International Book Award by the American Institute of Architects, *Sexuality and Space* (1992), which was awarded the 1993 International Book Award by the American Institute of Architects, and *Architectureproduction* (1988). She was selected to be a juror for the Venice Biennale (2010), and in the architectural competition for the new headquarters of Corporación Andina de Fomento in Caracas, Venezuela. She is the Founding Director of the Program in Media and Modernity at Princeton University. In 2006–2007 she curated, with PhD students, the exhibition "Clip/Stamp/Fold: The Radical Architecture of Little Magazines 196X-197X" at the Storefront for Art and Architecture in New York, and the Canadian Centre for Architecture in Montreal. The exhibition continues to travel around the world, most recently in the Museum of Design of Barcelona and the Colegio de Arquitectos de Murcia.

Anne M. Cronin is a senior lecturer in sociology at Lancaster University. She has published *Advertising and Consumer Citizenship* (2000), *Advertising Myths* (2004), *Advertising, Commercial Spaces and the Urban* (2010) and *Consuming the Entrepreneurial City* (co-edited with Kevin Hetherington, 2008). She is currently working on a project on friendship and spatiality.

Tamsin Dillon is Director of Art on the Underground. She is committed to an innovative and challenging practice, developing opportunities for artists to create new work, and for diverse audiences to experience art in contexts both within and beyond the confines of the museum and gallery. Since 2003, she has developed Art on the Underground to deliver high-quality art projects with world-class artists through a range of project strands. Dillon was at Chisenhale Gallery, London, from 2000 to 2002 and prior to that worked in a range of institutions and contexts, including Whitechapel Gallery, London; Capp Street Project, San Francisco; Chelsea and Westminster Hospital, London; and Norbury Park, Surrey. She has taught and lectured at a range of cultural and educational institutions, including the Royal College of Art, Chelsea College of Art and the Camberwell College of Art.

Helen Grace established the MA Programme in Visual Culture Studies in the Department of Cultural and Religious Studies, Chinese University of Hong Kong and is currently Visiting Professor at the National Central University in Taiwan as well as Research Affiliate, Sydney College of the Arts and Associate, Department of Gender and Cultural Studies, University of Sydney. She is an award-winning filmmaker, photographer and new media producer, and her work is included in *A Different Temporality: Aspects of Australian Feminist Art Practice, 1975–1985*, Monash University Art Museum, 2011. Her recent works include *Speculation: The October Series*, (Articulate Project Space, Sydney, June–July-2012); *IPO: Emotional Economies* (John Batten Gallery, Hong Kong, May 2009); *Train of Thought* (Kiasma Museum of Contemporary Art, Helsinki, 2006). She is the author of the CD-ROM, *Before Utopia: A Non-Official Prehistory of the Present* (2000). She co-authored *Home/World: Space, Community and Marginality in Sydney's West* (1997) and edited *Aesthesia and the Economy of the Senses* (1996)). Her current research is on ubiquitous media and user-created content, focusing on camera phone images in Hong Kong and China.

Janet Harbord is Professor of Film Studies at Queen Mary, University of London. She is the author of several books on film and philosophies of screen technologies in the digital age. She has been the recipient of collaborative grants from the EPSRC and AHRC for the project "MediaCity: Social Trends" (2009), and the Leverhulme-funded "Tracking the Moving Image: Screens in Public Space in Cairo, London and Shanghai" (2009–2011). Her current project is a book on Giorgio Agamben and film entitled *Ex-centric Cinema*.

Zlatan Krajina worked as an associate lecturer in media and communications at Goldsmiths, University of London, and is currently based at the University of Zagreb, where he teaches postgraduate modules on "media cities" and media audiences. His work explores issues concerning screen technologies, social space, mobility and experience.

Marysia Lewandowska is a Polish-born artist based in London since 1985 who, through her collaborative projects, has explored the public function of media archives, collections and exhibitions. She collaborated with Neil Cummings between 1995 and 2008. Research has played a central part in all of her projects, which include the book *The Value of Things* (2000), and "Capital" (2001), which inaugurated the "Contemporary Interventions" series at Tate Modern (2001). The "Enthusiasm" project was shown at the CCA (Warsaw), Whitechapel Gallery (London), Kunst Werke (Berlin) and the Tapies Foundation (Barcelona) in 2005–2006. The film *Museum Futures: Distributed* was shown at the Moderna Museet (Stockholm) in 2008, and *Tender Museum* was shown at the Muzeum Sztuki (Lodz) in 2009. Intellectual property was a focus of a recent project entitled "How Public Is the Public Museum?" commissioned by the Moderna Museet (Stockholm) in 2010. Questions of ownership and the art world are the subject of the forthcoming book *Undoing Property*, to be published in 2013.

Rachel Moore teaches in the Media and Communications Department at Goldsmiths, University of London. She received a John Simon Guggenheim Fellowship for her current project, "In the Film Archive of Natural-History," which investigates the use of old movies and footage in current artistic practice, a portion of which was published as "Love Machines" in *Film Studies 4*. She is the author of *Hollis Frampton: (Nostalgia)* (2006), *Savage Theory: Cinema as Modern Magic* (2000), as well as articles on Patrick Keiller (*LUXonline*), James Benning and Kenneth Anger (*Afterall*). She is a member of the Leverhulme "Spaces of Media" project investigating the use of screens in urban spaces today.

Lisa Parks is Professor of Film and Media Studies at the University of California, Santa Barbara. Her research explores uses of TV, satellite and computer technologies in transnational contexts. She is the author of *Cultures in Orbit: Satellites and the Televisual* (2005) and co-editor of *Planet TV* (2003), *Undead TV* (2007) and *Down to Earth: Satellite Technologies, Industries and Cultures* (2012). She is currently working on two new books: *Coverage: Media Space and Security after 9/11* and *Mixed Signals: Media Infrastructures and Cultural Geographies*.

Introduction

Chris Berry, Janet Harbord and Rachel Moore

The physical public space of the city is back on the agenda. Not so long ago, Rem Koolhaas wrote that "the street is dead" and "The Generic City is what is left after large sections of urban life crossed over to cyberspace" (Koolhaas, 1995, pp. 1253, 1250). Whilst an evacuation of physical space is both anticipated and confirmed in his commentary, the situation today presents us with a less clear division of online and offline worlds. After the 2011 Arab Spring, followed by the August riots in several cities of the UK, we can say with certainty that media, space and event are thoroughly imbricated. Public space is almost by definition contested, or at least negotiated, space in that no one person or company can unequivocally own and control it. Yet the privatized regulation of public space, or the current hybrid formation of privately owned public space, encroaches on such rights to contest and negotiate. What we understand as media networks and media domains are not to be imagined simply as counter-forums to regulated public space or prosthetic adjuncts to what occurs in cities; rather, they are part of the material and experiential formation of what now constitutes life in public spaces.

While "the event," both politically and philosophically, features largely in the contemporary re-focusing of public space, it is to the everyday and the habitual that we must turn to find its dynamic form, which today is inseparable from media. This collection, focusing primarily on the quotidian urban experience of public space in many of the world's cities, draws from and engages with previous work situated within a number of disciplines and sub-fields. Both pairings of "public space" and "media space," we may note, are situated at the intersection of a number of concerns, demanding different methods of research and frameworks of analysis. Perhaps the most prolific of approaches has emerged from political media analysis, where the role of social and network media in supplementing a demand for democracy in public space is critically debated. Whilst, for example, Zizi Papacharissi in *A Private Sphere: Democracy in a Digital Age* argues that the Internet has created a virtual public sphere accessed from the private space of the home or office, Matthew Hindman's *The Myth of Digital Democracy* challenges optimistic accounts of new media and public participation, as does James Curran, Natalie Fenton and Des Freedman's *Misunderstanding the Internet* (Hindman, 2009; Papacharissi, 2010; Curran *et al.*, 2012). The question of how social and network media create effects also subtends Lieh Lievrouw's *Alternative and Activist New Media* (2011), and *Blogistan* (2010), Annabelle Sreberny and Gholam Khiabany's analysis of web 2.0 in Iran (Sreberny and Khiabany, 2010; Lievrouw, 2011).

If political approaches are drawn to social and network media, to pursue questions of publicness and democracy in particular, these are connected to a larger field of research that considers the relationship between specific individual media and specific public spaces. The site of the movie theater as an alternative public sphere was the subject of Miriam Hansen's *Babel and Babylon*, an historical account of how early twentieth-century cinema provided a participatory domain for migrant communities (Hansen, 1994). More recently, the tracing of TV across public sites, ranging from the doctor's waiting room to the airport, characterizes Anna McCarthy's *Ambient Television* (McCarthy, 2001). The effect of TV outside of the home is dependent on what she calls the "site specificity" of its disposition rather than its particular program content. And the sounds of media in public space are the subject of Charles Hirschkind's *The Ethical Soundscape* (2006), an examination of cassette sermons and the possibility of counter-publics in Mubarak's Egypt. The methodological problem that public space and public media present is then one of boundary – the difficulty of defining the spatial or conceptual edges to research. As these projects illustrate, either the singularity of the object has held the critical focus in a variety of contexts, or a site has provided the bounded space within which a number of media can be seen to operate.

The stable form of media objects and the boundaries of public space are, of course, radically under pressure. To take but one example of media object mutation, cameras (representation devices) become embedded in phones (devices for transmission), whilst the logic of regional, national and, to a certain extent, temporal boundaries is undercut by mobile networks of connectivity. The complexity of this situation is addressed from a geographic perspective by Nick Couldry and Anna McCarthy in *Media Space: Place, Scale and Culture in a Media Age* (2004), and Lynn Spigel, Soyoung Kim and Chris Berry in *Electronic Elsewheres: Media, Technology and the Experience of Social Space* (Couldry and McCarthy, 2004; Berry *et al.*, 2010). If the extensive horizon of media connection is revealed in its unexpected forms in these edited collections, it is important to note how the notion of domestic space connecting to public space is transformed with the arrival of new generations of media in the home. In *Home Territories*, David Morley looks at the mediated formation of the homeland as well as the domestic home, whilst Lynn Spigel, in "Designing the Smart House: Posthuman Domesticity and Conspicuous Consumption", explores the promise of continuous communication between media devices in the home and its occupants as they move around in the external world (Morley, 2000; Spigel, 2010).

In foregrounding the everyday, this anthology gives emphasis to the habituated practices and enactments with media to produce the multifaceted subject of public space. To be clear about our understanding of the terms public, space and the everyday, it is worth outlining their key features and capacities before moving on to a discussion of the essays themselves.

Public

In a recent consideration of the term, Alistair Hannay distinguishes between "the public" and "a public," the latter referring to an audience, gathering or following (Hannay, 2005, pp. 26–32). On the one hand, "public" can simply mean "outside the home" or "outside private space." It can refer not only to the streets and squares of the town, but also to other privately or state-owned spaces that are accessible to the general citizenry, ranging from shopping malls to train stations. On the other hand, "the public" is often understood to refer to a very particular political formation associated with liberal and bourgeois democracy, whereby private individuals come together to discuss and deliberate upon "public affairs," or matters of common interest. This is what is sometimes spoken of as the "public sphere."[1] Whichever understanding of "public" is at work, negotiations of public space and public activities are most commonly imagined as face-to-face activities: jostling for space on crowded sidewalks, holding meetings and demonstrations, and the pleasures and perils of shopping all involve bodily encounter.

Further still, a rationally defined idea of public space is challenged by the dream-like experiences of the city, familiar to us through modernist writing. The stream of consciousness that inflected the city as psyche and vice versa is now conjoined in the contemporary moment to the experiential discourses of embodiment (Grosz, 1995; Blackman, 2008). Public space is a corporeal affair and, in the reciprocal feedback mechanism through which spaces and bodies are co-constituting, "environments actively produce the bodies of their inhabitants" (Grosz, 1995, p. 109). This is evident in the many ways in which we respond to media. It draws our attention (literally turning heads), or inscribes pathways by attracting or repelling us with images or sounds, or in suggestively affecting our appetite. Embodiment, as it is rehearsed in these public spaces, is the practice of subconscious and semi-conscious habituation, not simply a delegation of meaning to the body. We may well recall Gregory Bateson's warning that the "Anglo-Saxon epistemological tendency [is] to reify or attribute to the body all mental phenomena which are peripheral to consciousness" (Bateson, 1972, p. 320). Instead, a host of ephemeral sensual factors bring states of consciousness and the body together, and it is in this light that we consider our habituation to public spaces.

The importance of the discourses of embodiment and mental phenomena for any understanding of public space, as it is constituted with and through media space, lies not least in its departure from the rationalist project attributed to Habermas. In his theorization of publicness, the media has played a role in the constitution of the public sphere at least since the eighteenth century. Habermas famously contrasted face-to-face communication in the coffee shop with the manipulation of public interaction by mass media in *The Structural Transformation of the Public Sphere*, first published in the original German in 1962 and translated into English in 1989. The role of the press is also crucial to Benedict Anderson's theories on the nation-state, elaborated in *Imagined Communities* (Anderson, 1983), which can be considered as another kind of public space. In each of these cases there is a profound ambivalence about the role of the media, regarded as representational devices, enablers of public consciousness and participation, or, as in Habermas, an impediment to direct face-to-face communication, idealized in such images as the Greek agora. Whilst the public sphere is not necessarily (and perhaps never has been) an empirical public space, it exists as a phantom of a past ideal that is imposed on the present.

Many of the essays here articulate a conceptual and experiential model of public space that runs counter to Habermas' rationalism. Thought processes and identity are the product of interactions between the individual and the crowd, tactile technologies and visual spectacle, bodily movement and media narration. These interactions have a rhythmic quality, whereby states of being or qualities of subjectivity are fluid, changing as their relations to the field of operation changes. Nonetheless, the subject establishes a marked vector through the city however contingent that might be (see Lefebvre, 1992). The public is thus subsumed under a number of contingencies, not least of which is space.

Space

The presence of media in public space has transformed our understanding of both "space" and "publicness" (Eckardt *et al.*, 2008). The traditional idea of space as "enclosure"[2] has become fundamentally problematized by the presence of media distributing and redirecting data flows that transverse the boundaries of an enclosure. A more thorough critique of the concept of space, from the philosophy of Deleuze and Guattari to the geography of Edward Soja, has corroded the traditional notion of space as the blank backdrop to human activity (Deleuze and Guattari, 1984, 1988; Soja, 1989). Space as heterogeneous matter, comprised of diverse things and qualities, has become a philosophical concept worked upon in media and cultural geography, and in discourses of architecture and urban design (Hensel *et al.*, 2009). The significant value of thinking space through heterogeneity is twofold. First, heterogeneity posits difference as difference, not as a deviation from a standard model (the town square, the badly lit alley) but instead as a proliferation of variegated spaces that overlap and transmute. Second, heterogeneous space is produced (rather than already existing) or, more explicitly, performed. The activities, events, small acts and transmissions in public space are a production of the environment, as Lefebvre argues forcefully in *The Production of Space*, which otherwise would not exist (Lefebvre, 1991). Space, in other words, is an imminent field of relations that are in constant flux as bodies, material forms and images come into contact.

We can posit media as components and constituent forms in the production of the spatial as a field of mobile relations. In a less abstract formulation, we can see this enactment of the spatial in the sphere of orbital space in the contemporary moment. The production of the orbital as space is a practice that has remained robustly resistant to official accounts of mapping (Parks, Chapter 3 in this volume) but is nonetheless the product of claims of ownership, the installation of satellite objects and infrastructures, and the processes of data exchange and image flow. Space emerges through practices that become consolidated in representational forms, such as televisual and filmic images or diagrammatic models. The unending need for space to be continuously reproduced also needs to be understood here, a point that opens onto the possibilities of contestation; space is never finally fixed but only stabilized at certain historical moments. If it is the case, as has been argued, that enactments of space inevitably involve media, then what we understand by "media" in this scenario also demands consideration. In Vilem Flusser's prophetic work, the definition of media in a post-photographic world is articulated as mobile units of data whose definition has been prescribed by programmers (Flusser, 1989/2002). This is not a media of chemical images but a protean form of code that can be reconfigured as image, sound or noise. It is a media that contributes to the "atmosphere" of an environment in multiple ways. The affective capacity of media in public space is one of the least visible and yet most significant features of its presence. Media (as news streams, broken "white noise" screens, recorded image loops, montages, ambient sound and multi-screen live relays) create moods, tones and reminiscences, as discrete as the humidity and volume of the air and yet as charged as the weather. Interacting with the particular conditions of a location, the meaning and experience of media is not knowable in advance; images, sounds and words are all changed by the contexts in which they appear.

The everyday

That screens are, as public entities, part of everyday life is obvious, and yet it is precisely the self-evident nature of the everyday that invites challenge. As Michel de Certeau writes in his introduction to *The Practice of Everyday Life*, the task is to make a discussion possible, in his case a discussion of " 'ways of operating' or doing things." His project was to make into an object of investigation what we otherwise understand as background activities to the "main business" of life (de Certeau, 1984, p. xi). The everyday is elusive, he notes, and we may add to that the untraceable immateriality of public media and their effects, which make for methodological problems. Yet it is not only the transient nature of public media that produces the difficulty of how to get hold of the subject, or indeed how to make it a subject of enquiry. This difficulty of transience is doubled in the recognition that our relation to the everyday (as domestic or public environment) barely registers as a conscious engagement. How then might we find out about our experience of public media when we are hardly aware of what we do as we move through public space?

Public space more than often functions as a space between the virtual and the real, between labor and leisure, between work and home. In urban public space, the technology that sends us off into virtual worlds and the embodied experience of physical and mental meandering all but collide, forming a mise-en-scène that is all montage. Cross-cutting between the technological voices, signs, billboards, iPods, faces, moving bodies and architectural façades characterizes our movement through the city. The technological and the embodied become just so many reified strips of perception whose arrangement is all but arbitrary. Long ago in his early considerations of the city, Walter Benjamin saw the reification of experience as either "a source of threat and insecurity or as the occasion for inventive response" (Caygill, 1998, p. 131). The environments that touch on our urban everyday extend now to the omnipresence of the virtual; because of this, labor can be seen to invade every moment of waking life. While technology and the virtual provide mechanisms for avoiding the "ambiguous and inauthentic experience of blockage which resists our comprehension" (ibid.), that is to say our daily montage, our labor practices today filter through in characteristically opaque ways.

While we are always betwixt and between those categories, nonetheless to step out in public is to risk the experience of the everyday. Despite the aggression of advertising and the privatizing devices that mitigate their effect, public spaces still hold the promise of the chance and contingency associated with embodied experience. We now turn to the essays to sketch how the intersections of publicness, space and the everyday are manifest in this volume.

The essays

At least four themes emerge across the essays included here. First, there is the question of how new media and new uses in urban public space are reshaping the dimensions of urban public space. Second, the public spaces in question are also places with particular historical, political and social configurations, defining the way in which media operate in these places. Third, patterns of labor and leisure, both in the making and consumption of media technologies, are changing and these changes put new pressures on media in public space. Finally, the subjective experience of everyday life and the urban environment is one in which people are at least temporarily away from home. This too affects the deployment of media in public space and the responses of individuals to them. The topics of the essays are spaces and devices both large and small, whose study here alerts us to the ongoing processes by which what was once remarkable becomes everyday.

Shaping space

First, there is the question of media and the characteristics of urban public space. Until recently, the media that characterized urban public space were less frequently connected to "electronic elsewheres" (Berry *et al.*, 2010). Billboards, traffic signs, neon advertising and so forth might have arrived from elsewhere and might have beckoned to us with the delights of another place, but, once installed, their primary connections were to the site where they were located and the people in it. Now wireless technology and the media that use it have changed that situation, crossing and breaking down the boundaries of urban public space as surely as they do domestic space. Urban public space is connected to every other wireless-mediated space through the numerous mobile phones in people's pockets that facilitate everything from "flash mob" dance happenings to the marches and demonstrations in Cairo that form the context of Mona Abaza's essay (Chapter 4). The same mobile phones link up with closed circuit television (CCTV) cameras, cash registers, stored value cards of various kinds and other networked media to create a culture of surveillance that tracks us across the public and private spaces of our lives (Laidler, 2008). Traffic lights and signs are also modulated remotely according to changing traffic conditions, and moving image screens display TV programming and advertising images beamed down from satellites.

This newly connected quality of urban public space and its historical antecedents is the primary focus of three essays in this volume. In "Multi-screen Architecture" (Chapter 2), Beatriz Colomina examines how, in 1959, Charles and Ray Eames produced one of the first information spaces in their exhibit, *Glimpses of the USA*, produced for the American National Exhibition in Moscow. A multi-screen filmic "performance" of the American quotidian, the exhibit broke with the linear narrative of film by presenting what Colomina calls a mosaic of information. Despite the ideological linearity of the display, emphasizing the productivity of a nation, *Glimpses* evidences the role that architects played in creating multi-media environments. Similarly, in tracing the genealogy of public screens through the history of cinema and TV theory, Francesco Casetti argues that these screens are symptomatic of an ontological change. In "What is a Screen Nowadays?" (Chapter 1) he asserts that screens are no longer surfaces on which we project events that happened before in order to "represent" them; rather, they are sites where images circulate as signals in the air and are momentarily made visible to us. In a phrase that vividly captures the new connected and networked quality of urban public space today, he writes: "media have become devices for the 'interception' of information that saturates social and virtual spaces: they have become 'lightning rods,' if you will, onto which the electricity in the air is discharged."

The air is, in a sense, the subject of Lisa Parks' essay, "Mapping Orbit: Towards a Vertical Public Space" (Chapter 3). Although nothing in urban public space draws our attention to the realm of the satellite, its new, networked quality is entirely dependent upon satellite communications. Parks analyzes efforts to map satellite orbits and the space in which they operate as a discourse of competing possibilities for imagining and conceptualizing this space. By throwing the spotlight on this occluded realm of the satellites, she draws our attention to a host of new and unresolved conceptual and practical issues generated by orbital space. Not only does wireless networking connect public spaces to each other but also, Parks argues, their space now extends upwards to the realm of the satellites. Who owns this "vertical public space"? How should it be governed, given that it certainly exceeds the individual nation-state? By opening up questions about the vertical dimensions of urban public space, she challenges us to re-think what we want and can hope for from urban public space.

Spaces as place

The second theme that runs through many essays is public space as place – that is, sites that occupy historical, political and social ground. The distinction between space and place has been debated in scholarship since at least the time of Yi-Fu Tuan's *Space and Place* (1977). As the preceding discussion indicates, space is no longer understood as somehow inert or pre-human but as constituted through social relationships. Koolhaas' comment on the "Generic City" echoes a broad field of argument about the quality of post-modern and global city spaces, and reminds us that these qualities are produced and enforced rather than natural (Koolhaas, 1995). Another theorist whose arguments are particularly relevant here is Guy Debord. In his *Society of the Spectacle*, originally published in French in 1967, he proposes two modes of spectacle, both of which operated by occluding history (Debord, 1994). These were the dispersed spectacle of the market capitalist economies, epitomized by the consumerism of postwar America, and the concentrated spectacle, epitomized by the personality cults of both Hitler's fascism and Stalin's communism. Two decades later, and not long before his suicide in 1994, he published the French edition of *Comments on the Society of the Spectacle* (Debord, 1998). Here he proposes the concept of the integrated spectacle, which combines the qualities of the two earlier forms.

Debord writes: "When the spectacle was concentrated, the greater part of surrounding society escaped it; when diffuse, a small part; today, no part. The spectacle has spread itself to the point where it now permeates all reality" (Debord, 1994, p. 9). While his interpretation differs from that of Koolhaas, both of these visions of the city rest on the erasure of all trace of place, rendering a globally smooth space of flow and consumption (and occluded production). Yet, the implication of some of the essays here is that this may be a step too far. While the dream of consumption as the only form of endorsed aspiration may indeed animate many of the attempts to shape urban public space today, the media technologies deployed in the effort to realize them have to be installed in specific places with their own histories, habits, cultures, politics and more.

Nowhere is this more apparent than in Mona Abaza's remarkable "Cairo Diary: Space-Wars, Public Visibility and the Transformation of Public Space in Post-Revolutionary Egypt" (Chapter 4). She witnesses a year in which citizens have struggled with the authorities over access to, and control of, not only the streets but also the walls that line them. These have been canvases for a vibrant media culture of graffiti, frequently white-washed by the authorities, only to be redrawn later. Combined with the use of online media, mobile phones and photography to mobilize, record, inspire and circulate, the result is a transformed urban public space whose local specificity has, at least for the time being, overwhelmed the blanket of consumerism.

Less dramatically but not less insistently, in an essay on the patterns of moving image screen use in Shanghai, Chris Berry's "Shanghai's Public Screen Culture: Local and Coeval" (Chapter 5) shows how these are taken up in locally specific uses. Site specificity here refers to the particular topography of the buildings, the patterns of their usages and the customs of the users in Shanghai. Moreover, the demands generated by such factors ensure that the installation and deployment of the screens in each public space under consideration are unique. In noting the prevalence of relatively small moving image signs in liminal spaces, for example, Berry recalls a long lineage of public signage going back to inscribed characters on mountainsides and, more recently, the blackboard culture of the Mao era. If Abaza and Berry's essays speak very directly to the uniqueness of place, contra the dream of smooth and homogenized flow animating neoliberal globalization, place specificity is also a significant dimension of a number of other essays in this volume.

Labor

Commuting, of course, is the task of the laborer, a task which new technologies have been deployed to both ameliorate and disturb. These devices – mobile phones, iPods and iPads, for example – have clearly divided labor trajectories. On the one hand, their development and branding are the product of "immaterial labor," while their manufacture belongs to a super-Fordist mode of production. Immaterial labor refers to the labor that produces cultural value and is characterized by its lack of boundaries in worker's lives, wherein the worker is finally self-employed and working, in so far as they are thinking all the time. That time is not paid for by the hour but rather by its value, which is difficult to assess. Rachel Moore makes the argument that London's St. Pancras Station is built for the immaterial laborer and looks for ways in which it might offer her solace in "In Transit: Between Labor and Leisure in London's St. Pancras International" (Chapter 7).

Super-Fordist labor takes up most of its workers' waking hours, although they are paid for these hours, however poorly. Super-Fordism was once meant to refer to Fordist manufacture on a grand scale made possible by robots. In practice, the manufacture of computer components and mobile devices in China, for instance, turns people into machines. It does this by controlling both their waking and sleeping hours such that they work 15 hours a day at the factory where they also sleep, dormitory style. These two forms of labor are both hidden, necessarily so, as Helen Grace sees it in "iPhone Girl: Assembly, Assemblages and Affect in the Life of an Image" (Chapter 6).

The effacement of labor is, of course, nothing new. The power it stores – so buried within its shiny product – emerges in its fetishized, branded afterlife as a consumer good, in this case as an iPhone in which a worker has secreted her image, an image that is first released by its surprised consumer and later becomes a viral Internet phenomenon. Effaced labor is normally part of the fetishized character of the commodity; in this case, however, when the laborer introduced herself personally, the fetish value of the product was surpassed when her image (albeit in virtual form) took on a social life of its own.

Siegfried Kracauer maintained that the ways in which we labor and the distractions such as cinema to which we attend are all of a piece. Formally, the legs of the famous Tiller Girls formed undulating surface patterns that matched the arms uniformly at work on the assembly line, shot for shot. These patterns are part of what he called a "mass ornament," whose surface splendor was the place in which one had to look for meaning, rather than at the dancers or individual workers. Thus, this essay looks now to the diffuse distribution of the image and the life it took on, rather than to the girl herself, in order to understand the current labor situation and our position in it.

Away from home

To step out in public means to risk experiencing things that are beyond the modicum of control one can maintain in the home environment. Advertisers call this "Out-of-Home" (OOH). This refers, in advertising terms, to the many media mechanisms available to reach consumers when they are not at home. Yet falling victim to the onslaught of advertising screens is hardly the experience one has in mind as one enters the urban everyday. Indeed, the proliferation of devices to create one's own microenvironment would suggest that we are almost immune to their advances. Despite the aggression of advertising, privatizing devices mitigate its effect, demonstrating how the experience of public space is continuously negotiated.

Marysia Lewandowska's contribution, "Direct Address: A Brechtian Proposal for an Alternative Working Method" (Chapter 9) alerts us to the fact that in the eyes of those who control the screens we encounter in public, we are just so many moving targets. Set against other visions of what it means to enter a public, it is no wonder that screens, billboards and graffiti feature large in the efforts of various urban citizens to influence the shape of public experience. Artists' interventions into the quotidian public domain are addressed in three very different contexts. Janet Harbord's interview with Tamsin Dillon, director of Art on the Underground, outlines the ambitions of various site-specific ventures of Transport for London over the years, and the more recent importance of screens, in "Encountering Screen Art on the London Underground" (Chapter 8). This is a very different conception of a public from the idea that an advertiser might have, continuing a near century-long tradition of commissioning artworks to embellish passengers' underground journeys.

Other ways of negotiating the OOH experience fall to the subject itself. Moving to the world of advertising of branded products made by the iPhone girl, Anne M. Cronin and Zlatan Krajina discuss how people treat posters and screens in the course of working through an average day. Based on empirical research consisting of observation and interviews, Cronin explores the many different mediatizations that occur in people's engagement with outdoor advertising (Chapter 12), while Krajina discusses the way in which those engagements are habituated during people's underground commutes (Chapter 10). Cronin's "Publics and Publicity: Outdoor Advertising and Urban Space" argues that we see billboards differently from the way their producers presume we will do. Krajina's empirically based study of the many ways in which underground commuters use advertisements to divert or direct attention, "Domesticating the Screen-Scenography: Situational Uses of Images and Technologies in the Tunnels of the London Underground," yields creative and unexpected results. Michael Bull's "Privatizing Urban Space in the Mediated World of iPod Users" (Chapter 11) addresses the privatization of public space through the iPod's ability to create a personalized world for the urban subject, which fills the empty spaces, times and values that the contemporary environment tends to foster. These essays document alternative strategies, as well as creative addresses by citizens official and otherwise to the subject when they are away from home and in *Public Space, Media Space*.

Notes

1. For a full discussion of the public sphere, see Calhoun (1992).
2. For a defense of space as the enclosure of chronological and historical time, preserved against the ravages of an instantaneous real time of media, see Virilio (1997, pp. 381–390).

Bibliography

Allen, John (1999) "Worlds within Worlds", in Massey, Doreen, Allen, John and Pile, Steve (eds.) *City Worlds* (London and New York: Open University Press).

Anderson, Benedict (1983) *Imagined Communities: Reflections on the Origins and Spread of Nationalism* (London: Verso).

Augé, Marc (1995) *Non-Places: An Introduction to Supermodernity* (London: Verso).

Bateson, Gregory (1972) *Steps to an Ecology of Mind* (Chicago and London: University of Chicago Press).

Berry, Chris, Kim, Soyoung and Spigel, Lynn (eds.) (2010) *Electronic Elsewheres: Media, Technology and the Experience of Social Space* (Minneapolis: University of Minnesota Press).

Blackman, Lisa (2008) *The Body* (Oxford and New York: Berg).

Bull, Michael (2000) *Sounding Out the City: Personal Stereos and the Management of Everyday Life* (London: Berg).

Calhoun, Craig J. (ed.) (1992) *Habermas and the Public Sphere* (Cambridge: MIT Press).

Caygill, Howard (1998) *The Colour of Experience* (London and New York: Routledge).

de Certeau, Michel (1984) *The Practice of Everyday Life*, Steven Rendall (trans.) (Berkeley: University of California Press).
Couldry, Nick and McCarthy, Anna (2004) *Media Space: Place, Scale and Culture in a Media Age* (London: Comedia).
Cronin, Anne (2010) *Advertising, Commercial Spaces, and the Urban* (Houndmills: Palgrave Macmillan).
Curran, James, Fenton, Natalie and Freedman, Des (2012) *Misunderstanding the Internet* (New York: Routledge).
Debord, Guy (1994) *Society of the Spectacle*, Donald Nicholson-Smith (trans.) (New York: Zone).
Debord, Guy (1998) *Comments on Society of the Spectacle*, Malcolm Imrie (trans.) (London: Verso).
Deleuze, Gilles and Guattari, Felix (1984) *Anti-Oedipus: Capitalism and Schizophrenia*, Brian Massumi (trans.) (London: Athlone).
Deleuze, Gilles and Guattari, Felix (1988) *A Thousand Plateaus: Capitalism and Schizophrenia*, Brian Massumi (trans.) (London: Athlone).
Eckardt, Frank, Geelhaar, Jens, Colini, Laura, Willis, Katherine S., Chorianopoulos, Konstantinos and Hennig, Ralf (eds.) (2008) "Introduction", in *Mediacity Situations, Practices and Encounters* (Berlin: Frank & Timme).
Flusser, Vilem (2002/1989) *Vilem Flusser: Writings*, Strohl, Andreas (ed.), Erik Eisel (trans.) (Minneapolis and London: University of Minnesota Press).
Grosz, Elizabeth (1995) *Space, Time and Perversion: Essays on the Politics of Bodies* (New York and London: Routledge).
Habermas, Jürgen (1989) *The Structural Transformation of the Public Sphere*, Thomas Burger and Frederick Lawrence (trans.) (Cambridge: MIT Press).
Hadj-Moussa, Ratiba (2010) "The Undecidable and the Irreversible: Satellite Television in the Algerian Public Arena", in Berry, Chris, Kim, Soyoung and Spigel, Lynn (eds.) *Electronic Elsewheres: Media, Technology and the Experience of Social Space* (Minneapolis: University of Minnesota Press).
Hannay, Alistair (2005) *On the Public* (New York: Routledge).
Hansen, Miriam (1994) *Babel and Babylon: Spectatorship in American Silent Film* (Cambridge: Harvard University Press).
Hensel, Michael, Hight, Christopher and Menges, Achim (eds.) (2009) *Space Reader: Heterogeneous Space in Architecture* (Chichester: Wiley Publications).
Hindman, Matthew (2009) *The Myth of Digital Democracy* (Princeton: Princeton University Press).
Hirschkind, Charles (2006) *The Ethical Soundscape: Cassette Sermons and Islamic Counterpublics* (New York: Columbia University Press).
Koolhaas, Rem (1995) "The Generic City", in Koolhaas, Rem, Mau, Bruce, Sigler, Jennifer and Werlemann, Hans (eds.) *S, M, L, XL* (New York: Monacelli).
Laidler, Keith (2008) *Surveillance Unlimited: How We've Become the Most Watched People on Earth* (Cambridge: Icon Books).
Lefebvre, Henri (1991) *The Production of Space*, Donald Nicholson Smith (trans.) (Cambridge: Blackwell).
Lefebvre, Henri (1992) *Rhythmanalysis: Space, Time and Everyday Life* (London: Continuum).
Lievrouw, Lieh (2011) *Alternative and Activist New Media* (Cambridge: Polity).
McCarthy, Anna (2001) *Ambient Television: Visual Culture and Public Space* (Durham: Duke University Press).

Morley, David (2000) *Home Territories: Media, Mobility and Identity* (New York: Routledge).
Papacharissi, Zizi (2010) *A Private Sphere: Democracy in a Digital Age* (Cambridge: Polity).
Sassen, Saskia (2003) "Reading the City in a Global Digital Age: Between Topographic Representation and Spatialized Power Projects", in Krause, Linda and Petro, Patrice (eds.) *Global Cities: Cinema, Architecture and Urbanism in a Digital Age* (New Brunswick: Rutgers University Press).
Soja, Edward (1989) *Postmodern Geographies: the Reassertion of Space in Critical Social Thought* (New York: Verso).
Spigel, Lynn (1992) *Make Room for TV: Television and the Family Ideal in Post-War America* (Chicago: University of Chicago Press).
Spigel, Lynn (2010) "Designing the Smart House: Posthuman Domesticity and Conspicuous Consumption", in Berry, Chris, Kim, Soyoung and Spigel, Lynn (eds.) *Electronic Elsewheres: Media, Technology and the Experience of Social Space* (Minneapolis: University of Minnesota Press).
Sreberny, Annabelle and Khiabany, Gholam (2010) *Blogistan: The Internet and Politics in Iran* (London: I.B. Tauris).
Tuan, Yi-Fu (1977) *Space and Place* (Minneapolis: University of Minnesota Press).
Virilio, Paul (1997) "The Overexposed City", in Leach, Neil (ed.) *Rethinking Architecture: A Reader in Cultural Theory* (London: Routledge).

1

What Is a Screen Nowadays?

Francesco Casetti

Mike Figgis' film *Timecode* recounts 93 minutes in the life of a group of people living in Los Angeles (*Timecode*, 2000). The duration of the movie and of the events it relates coincide: the story is captured in one long take without intervals or cuts. Most surprising is the possibility of following more than one situation simultaneously: it was shot with four different digital cameras, and all four takes are presented contemporaneously, on one screen divided into four sections. Sometimes the plotlines of the various characters intersect with one another more or less haphazardly, and when this happens the camera that has been following one of the characters may shift to another character and follow him or her instead. At other points the plotlines converge, and we discover retrospectively the correlations. More often, however, the events proceed in parallel, without intersecting, but also without excluding the possibility of eventually crossing paths. We watch the stories in the four adjacent sections of the split screen, jumping from one to another, attempting to establish connections, selecting what seems to be the central point, at the mercy of the flow of images.

This is not the first time that cinema has experimented with the split screen (Hagener, 2009, pp. 145–155). However, there is something new in Figgis' film: something quite different from the traditional desire to enlarge visible space or to juxtapose contemporaneous events that take place in separate spaces. His screen, divided into four, evokes the new kinds of screens that already constituted a familiar presence at the beginning of this millennium. It reminds us of the mosaic structure of the television screen, inside of which many conduits of communication coexist. It suggests the computer screen, with all the available applications in view, or the television monitors placed one next to the other that display images from surveillance cameras in the security centers of office buildings and malls. It also reminds us of the conglomeration of screens in the great media-facades of many cities, such as New York's Times Square. *Timecode* suggests that the movie screen no longer stands by itself; on the contrary, due to outside influences its very nature is changing. We can on longer observe it as we did before, nor can we expect that it will offer us the same kind of images as it used to.

I shall attempt here to think about how the proliferation of screens has led to a general transformation of their nature. They are no longer surfaces on which reality is relived, so to speak. Rather, they have become transit hubs for the images that circulate in our social space. They serve to capture these images, to make them momentarily available for somebody somewhere – perhaps even in order to rework them – before they embark again on their journey. Therefore screens function as the junctions of a complex circuit, characterized both by a continuous flow and by localized processes of configuration or reconfiguration of the circulating images.

This transformation of the screen is actually the symptom of a more general media transformation. The advent of the network and of digital technology has led us out of an era in which media operated as instruments for exploring the world and for facilitating dialogue between people – that is, as instruments of mediation vis-à-vis reality and other people. Media have become devices for the "interception" of information that saturates social and virtual spaces: they have become "lightning rods," if you will, onto which the electricity in the air is discharged. In this context, cinema has also found itself questioning its own identity, discovering perhaps a new destiny, but also exploring how it may still be useful and productive.

The cinematic screen

What exactly was the screen? The term has an intriguing history. In the fourteenth century the Italian word *schermo* denoted something that protects against outside agents, and that therefore presents an obstacle to direct sight.[1] Along this line, the term also indicated someone who serves to mask the interests of another person, as in the Dantean formulation *donna schermo* or "screen woman."[2] The English term "screen" also referred to a protective surface in the sixteenth and seventeenth centuries, especially against fire or air.[3] However, "screen" (or "skren") also indicated smaller devices, used to hide oneself from others' glances, such as fans, or partitions of a mostly decorative nature.[4] At the beginning of the nineteenth century, the term began to enter into the sphere of entertainment: in the phantasmagoria, "screen", *schermo* and *écran* designated the semi-transparent surface onto the back of which a series of images were projected so that the screen now served to open our gaze to something hidden. This association with the instruments of spectacle was strengthened with the introduction of the shadow play (which the West had already imported from the East in the seventeenth century), and moreover with the magic lantern, from which the projection is cast from in front of the screen rather than from behind it (see Huhtamo, 2004). Contemporaneously, "screen", at least in English, acquired yet another aspect: during the Victorian age it referred to those surfaces on which figures and cut-outs were pasted, forming both a private collection of images and a small public exposition.[5] It is from this rich background that the term arrives, in various languages, at the turn of the twentieth century to indicate the white curtain onto which filmic images are projected, finding its most widespread meaning in this connection to the cinema.

The route traveled by the word is instructive. It demonstrates a slippage of meaning: from a surface that covers and protects, to one that allows us to glimpse images projected from behind, to one that gathers representations of new worlds, to one that can contain figures that reflect our personality. The major metaphors employed by classical film theories for the cinematic screen encapsulate this entire history. The first metaphor is that of the window: the screen is a breech in the barrier that keeps us separated from reality, thanks to which we re-establish contact with the world. The obstacle between us and the outside is represented primarily by the walls of the movie theater; however, the most powerful impediments are the cultural filters that do not allow us to look directly at reality. Among these filters there are our habits and prejudices, as Jean Epstein underlined back in 1921 (Epstein, 1984, pp. 235–241), or the massive presence of writing and the press, which make the human being readable but not visible, as stated by Béla Balázs in 1924 (Balázs, 2010). Therefore, the screen should be understood as a laceration that allows us to see reality directly, again and anew. One of the first occurrences of the metaphor of the window is found in an Italian reflection by Tullio Panteo, which highlights the immediacy of the gaze: "[At the cinema] what matters is feeling calmly as if one is an indifferent spectator, as if at the window, of whom neither intelligence of judgment, nor the exertion of observation, nor the nuisance of investigation is required" (Panteo, 1908). But the metaphor of the window found particularly fertile ground in the realist theories of cinema, including André Bazin's (Bazin, 1967). In fact, these theories are all characterized by a desire to reactivate a direct gaze on things, and by the knowledge that, in order to do so, one must overcome resistance, obstacles and impediments. In this light, cinema literally offers to the world the possibility of a redemption.[6]

The second major metaphor is that of the frame: the screen is a surface within which appear figures capable of depicting *the*, or at least *a*, world.[7] Here we are no longer dealing with a direct gaze on things but rather with a representation of them. This leads to the emergence of new aspects: in particular, the content of the image, from a simple datum, becomes a construct at the root of which is a work of mise-en-scène. Nevertheless, a representation does not cease to speak to us about reality; every time an understanding of the laws of nature is applied to a representation (something that true artists always do eventually), it also ends up revealing to us the dynamics and composition of reality. This explains why the metaphor was utilized most of all by formalist theorists of cinema, who were well aware that an image within a frame is just an image. Nevertheless, if well designed, it is capable of fully restoring to us the sense of the world in which we live. For just such a consideration of the screen, an exemplary approach is Sergei Eisenstein's (see his contributions from "The Dynamic Square", to "The Principles of Film Form", to *Nonindifferent Nature* (Eisenstein, 1931a, b, 1987)).

The third major metaphor is that of the mirror: the screen is a device that restores to us a reflection of the world, including a reflection of ourselves. This metaphor had already emerged in earlier cinematic theories. Giovanni Papini suggested in 1907 that "sitting before the white screen in a motion picture theater we have the impression that we are watching true events, as if we were watching through a mirror following the action hurtling through space" (Papini, 1907, pp. 1–2). Yet the metaphor of the mirror finds its most fully developed elaboration in the psychoanalytic approach, which asserts that spectators may identify with the film's protagonists and with the gaze (of the director, of the camera, of a transcendental subject, of the gaze as such?) that captures them on the stage. Film's spectators see a world to which they yield themselves, but they also see a point of view regarding this world with which they associate themselves. In this sense, they see themselves seeing. I should add that the mirror reunites that which the two preceding metaphors held apart: the former underlined the possibility of perceiving things directly, while the latter highlighted the necessity of passing through their representation. This third metaphor posits a reflection that allows us to see things as they are, and ultimately offers up only an image of them.

These three major metaphors, which, among others, Elsaesser and Hagener retrace usefully (Elsaesser and Hagener, 2010), share one important trait: they all identify the screen as the place in which reality offers itself to spectators – in all its immediacy, consistency and availability (see also Altman, 1976, pp. 260–264; Sobchack, 1992, pp. 14–15). At the cinema we have access to the world; through its cinematic representation, we may sense its structure and its possibilities, and thanks to the process of identification, we can make the world ours. It should not be surprising then that the first theories of cinema often speak of an "epiphany": on the screen, reality reveals itself in all its density to eyes ready to witness it. Antonello Gerbi writes: "Submerged by the sounds, we are ready to receive the new Epiphany. Are we buried in the deep or hovering among the stars? I don't know: certainly we are very close to the heart of the cinema" (Gerbi, 1926, p. 842). These references to epiphany often lead early theories of cinema to assume a religious tone: cinema is a miracle, and to experience it means participating in a rite. To quote Gerbi again,

> This piece of crude canvas... is reborn as an altarpiece for the liturgies of the new times. From the uniform rows of spectators (or of the faithful? Or of wandering lovers?) not even the light murmur of a prayer rises up: this perfect adoration is carried out, following the teachings of all of those learned in mysticism, in perfect silence.
>
> (Gerbi, pp. 840–841)

On a more secular note, the three metaphors mentioned above allow us to glimpse an idea of the cinema as media. Marshall McLuhan suggests that media form the nervous system of a society: "we have already extended our senses and our nerves by the various media" (McLuhan, 2001, pp. 3–4). If his claim is correct, the movie screen is essentially a terminus from which we gather data from outside (window), as well as an organ with which we re-elaborate data (frame), and a device for self-regulation and self-recognition (mirror).

Beyond cinema

The television screen differs from the movie screen: it is small rather than large; it is made from glass as opposed to canvas; it is fluorescent rather than reflective; and the world it hosts is broadcasted live rather than recorded. However, in its early years, this screen recalled the same major metaphors mentioned above: it was a window, even if the walls it faced were those of the home instead of a public space; it was a frame, even if its components were arranged differently; and it was a mirror, even though it was more reflective of a society than of an individual. Already in 1937, Rudolf Arnheim underlined the conceptual continuity between cinema and television:

> Television will not only reproduce the world like cinema – its images will be colored and perhaps even plastic – but it will render this reproduction even more fascinating by making us take part, not in events which have simply been recorded and conserved, but in far-away events at the very moment in which they occur.
>
> (Arnheim, 1937, p. 271)[8]

More recently, in her historical reconstruction of the early television, Lynn Spigel highlights how the television set functioned as a home theater (Spigel, 2010, pp. 55–92). In its initial stages, television apparently did not alter a well-consolidated system of concepts.

Nevertheless, there arose a new metaphor which came to join the others, and which in some ways signaled a new direction. Television, it was often said, was like a fireplace in front of which the family gathers. This metaphor not only emphasizes the continuity of consolidated habits (today we would say the processes of domestication of a medium) but also indicates that this screen brings the outside world into the domestic space – radiating it like firelight, and endowing it with the continuity of a warmth that permeates the home. Indeed, the epiphany becomes the everyday: it persists within reach, so to speak. This radical availability of the world, and its transformation into a flow of images onto which viewers can continually graft themselves, would eventually come to be a decisive characteristic of new screens.

A greater sense of novelty came on the scene in the 1960s with the appearance of multi-screens. One such form of installation consists of the simultaneous projection of a film onto multiple surfaces. The New York World's Fair of 1964–1965 provided more than one example of this. For instance, there was Charles Eames' spectacle, which involved 14 projectors and 9 different screens.[9] This structure was then immediately reinterpreted in an experimental key by Andy Warhol, in particular in his *Chelsea Girls*, in which the arrangement and synchronization of at least two screens was much freer (Warhol, 1966). Another form of installation – the video-wall – was created by stacking up a series of video devices. This too took its first steps in the 1960s, offering spectators greater immersion in the images. Nam June Paik provided an almost immediate artistic reinterpretation of it with his *TV Cello* (1964) – a series of television sets stacked on one another in the form of a cello.

With the introduction of the multi-screen installation, the traditional screen seemed to signal openly that it felt constrained within its traditional confines. The time had come for it to grow, to multiply, to spread out, and this moment arrived in the 1980s and 1990s. It was precisely during these two decades that a series of extensions became common (the connection of the television set to the VCR and to the videogame console, for instance).[10] Moreover, it was primarily during this 20-year span that the screen began to constitute an essential part of new media, following a trajectory which will surely continue into the next decades. Examples of this process are the increasing presence of the computer in daily life[11] and the great success of the French Minitel – an amalgamation of the telephone and the video-screen.[12] The introduction of the portable DVD player allowed for the personal consumption of videos outside the walls of the domestic space.[13] Cellphones began to become a fixture of everyday experience with the first of the four (and counting) generations of mobile telephone technology.[14] Electronic organizers started replacing paper diaries.[15] Tablets began developing along a path that would lead to incredibly successful products, such as the Kindle and the iPad.[16] And, finally, media-facades started taking their place as a characteristic feature of many urban spaces, before acquiring the capability, as they now have, of interacting with passers-by. Indeed, media have become media-screens.

This screen explosion, which is still affecting us today, has led us to a true turning point. We find ourselves surrounded by unprecedented technological innovations: surfaces made of liquid crystals, of plasma, of LEDs, and as flexible as a piece of paper. And since they are increasingly interconnected, they are able to communicate with one another. This watershed represents a conceptual transformation as much as it does a technological fact: it is the very idea of a screen that is changing, as Lev Manovich has already suggested (Manovich, 2000, pp. 94–115). There are three aspects that I consider crucial. First, the great diffusion of screens allows media content to multiply the occasions on which it may present itself (in order to watch a film, we are no longer confined to the movie theater). Second, the fact that these screens are often connected allows for the retrieval of content independent of the situation or location in which the users find themselves (in order to watch a film, we can download it where and when we like). Finally, and more radically, the ubiquity of these screens makes possible the living or reliving of media experience in new environments and on new devices (we can feel like spectators, even by watching a film in a train on a portable DVD player). In short, this screen explosion has resulted in a diffusion of content on many platforms (spreadability), an interconnection of reception points (networking) and a reactivation of experiences in many situations (relocation).

This new situation, which seems to have now arrived at a maturation point, has literally led the screen to assume a new nature. It no longer represents the site of an epiphany of the real; rather, it is a surface across which travel the images that circulate through social space. The information that surrounds us condenses on the screen, lingers for a moment, interacts with the surrounding environment and then takes off for other points in a kind of continuous movement.

New metaphors for the screen

To better understand this new situation, let us attempt once again an exercise in terminological recognition by asking: What are the key words that communicate what a screen is nowadays? There is no doubt that the old metaphors no longer work, so we must discover which other terms have supplanted them.

The first term is undoubtedly "monitor": the screen increasingly serves to inspect the world around us, to analyze and verify it – in essence, to keep it under control. The window which once restored our contact with the world has become a peep-hole through which to scrutinize reality, in the likely event that it may be hiding something dangerous.

The screen as monitor is first of all what we find in the large surveillance centers and in the security offices of apartment buildings and commercial complexes. A series of viewers form a kind of wall, which allows for the constant surveillance of every room and corridor, and, above all, every entrance/exit and every point of the external perimeter. Who is it that performs the surveillance? In many cases, members of the security staff view the monitors. However, in many 24-hour, closed-circuit systems, the images gathered by the cameras are simply recorded; there is no one watching, unless the footage is reviewed later, but only "after" something has happened. The security monitor does not necessarily imply a gaze.[17]

Such a situation takes us inevitably back to Bentham's Panopticon, which Foucault chose as the emblem of the disciplinary society (Foucault, 1979). While the Panopticon was designed so that only one individual was required to keep an eye on the entire building, in the case of security cameras, everything is observed but there are no longer any observers. Put another way, no one is looking since the end goal is not to observe (or to make known that one is being observed) but simply to gather data to be mined in case the need arises.

This same contradiction is found in an even more paradoxical form in the other example of the screen as monitor: the global positioning system (GPS). This is also an instrument used to keep territory under observation, in order to avoid possible inconveniences and to take advantage of possible opportunities. We use it to stay on track and to arrive quickly at our destination; to avoid running out of gas and to locate the nearest service station; to avoid dying of hunger and to find a decent restaurant in the vicinity. The GPS may seem to represent the return of the observer – after all, its small screen is always in front of the driver's eyes – but the gaze it elicits differs significantly from that traditionally linked to a screen. It is an intermittent gaze, activated only – and most often – in moments of need; and it is a gaze with multiple focal points, aimed both at the maps supplied by the kit and at the surrounding reality, which continues to be visible through the windshield and windows of the vehicle. These windows do still exist. In short, it is a gaze that is largely independent of the device. In this light, the GPS confirms the fact that although monitors are in constant need of new information, they do not always require an eye to scrutinize and observe them.

The second term that defines contemporary screens – replacing the metaphor of the frame, which nowadays exhibits clear limitations – is "bulletin board", or even "blackboard." In fact, in the screens that surround us, we encounter less and less frequently representations capable of restoring the texture of the world, and more and more frequently figures that function as memoranda, as signposts and, above all, as instructions for behavior.

Let us consider screens found in waiting rooms, in stations and in modes of public transport. Various messages pass across these surfaces: film and video clips, advertisements, tourism documentaries and so on. Their objective is not to offer an external reality or to alleviate the sense of oppression brought on by the closed environment in which we find ourselves confined. Rather, they are intended to help us pass the time and prepare for future actions: they inform us of the approach of a train (to the station), of whose turn it is (in the waiting room), of the weather at a destination (in an airport), of the beauty of tourist destinations (in a ticket office) and of exercises to do in order to avoid discomfort (on an airplane). More than fragments of the world, they are instructions for behavior.

The same may be said for the videos in shops and malls, which display the goods for sale on the counters and shelves. Again, what is important is not what these videos depict: the merchandise is right next to them, in plain sight. What really counts is the information that accompanies the depiction of the merchandise: we see how it is used, how much it costs, where it comes from, why it is convenient and which lifestyle it matches. It is according to this information – often evocative and emotional – that we adjust our behavior – that is, to either purchase or not to purchase the merchandise. The presence of these videos acts as a sort of veil on reality: we have ceased to look at things via their representation; we look instead at a set of directives aimed at us.

In seeming contrast to this, many homepages of institutional websites function in a similar manner. I am thinking, for example, of those of schools or universities. These relate academic life to a profusion of attractive images: they reveal a whole world to the eyes of the reader. However, these illustrations act as bridges to boxes or links that offer detailed information aimed at the various users of the site: students, professors, families and administrators. A possible life experience is transformed into a series of announcements.

Videogames offer perhaps the clearest example of the screen as bulletin board or blackboard. The image that they present consists essentially of a group of figures of variable value upon which the player must act. Their value is defined by a score that appears in an accompanying box or that flashes near a character in the game. The players choose their moves based on these values, deciding whether to confront the character, to move to another portion of the landscape, to acquire new abilities and so on. The player's moves will determine changes in value: either the value of a specific character or of the total gains or losses. This score will in turn determine new moves. Therefore the essence of the game does not lie in recognizing characters that appear on the screen: attention is concentrated above all on a set of values and on a menu of possible lines of action. The players do not find pleasure in contemplating a representation; rather they move within a forest of instructions. I would add that in many of these games – those called "shoot 'em all" – the essence of the action consists in destroying that which appears before the player. This means that the world that is represented here is not only completely abstract, reduced as it is to numeric values, but also essentially destined for decomposition. What a perfect example of the tendency of the bulletin board to disassociate itself from reality, in order to create space for a flow of information. (This does not mean that what they present is not reality: it is simply not mere physical reality. Rather, it is an entity that causes facts, possible actions, comments, values and so on to overlap. In this respect, "augmented reality" is exemplary: when

I point my cellphone in front of me, I see on the screen a piece of urban landscape made up of actual buildings, supplemented by indications that help me to move within the city, as well as information about edifices belonging to the past that have since disappeared, and projects for future construction.)

The third way to better describe a contemporary screen – as an alternative to the traditional metaphor of the mirror, now obsolete – is to think of it as a "mailbox" or "scrapbook." Spectators now struggle to identify with a character or story; they prefer instead to construct images of themselves in the first person, by assembling photos, texts and comments often lifted from elsewhere and trusting these heterogeneous materials to a blog or putting them in circulation on a social network. Therefore more than identifying with someone or something else, they cut, paste, compose and send.

I mentioned blogs: the personal homepage is the first example of the screen as scrapbook. Blogs are literally mosaics of texts and figures, which accumulate day after day, narrating the life of the blogger. This is a particular kind of self-presentation: the materials that form it are only partly self-produced; often they are recuperated from elsewhere, and once they are posted on the internet they are further recyclable in order to narrate other lives. The resulting portrait is true to life, but in its dismantling and reassembling, it could also apply to anyone. This means, paradoxically, that the flow of data, news and quotations is almost more important than the representation of subjectivity: the "I" is born of the personal use of what the user finds.

In the social networks typical of web 2.0, such as Tumblr, this condition returns in an even more radical way. Thanks to the presence of a feed reader, the page is loaded with content lifted from elsewhere until it forms a kind of newspaper that contains what the user reads or in which the user is interested. The posts of other bloggers appear on the user's dashboard, and they may sometimes – though not always – add comments or corrections. This results in an enormous accumulation of citations, references and sources with a relative paucity of the user's own interventions. The user's personality continues to manifest itself within this accumulation, but this manifestation comes about as the result of a type of link to which they connect themselves, much more so than as the result of what they say directly. Precisely because of this, their voice is ultimately nothing more than a montage of others' voices – almost as if to radicalize the fundamentally dialogic and heteroglossic nature of our discourse, highlighted by Mikhail Bakhtin 80 years ago (Bakhtin, 1981).

Even when this voice is made direct, the situation is not much altered. *Twitter* and *Facebook* (the initial page – or wall – of which is also reminiscent of the bulletin board) represent interesting examples. There is more space here for an exchange of opinions; however, any personal intervention is restricted to a few possibilities (in *Facebook*: "like", "comment" and "share"). Furthermore, this intervention is limited in space and therefore often devoid of much meaning (it is difficult to imagine that a click on the "Like button" can really reveal a personality). The user's intervention depends on the material that is currently available (they speak through what they find). Finally, it reflects thoughts and opinions that are strictly dependent on the subject touched upon in a discussion: once the subject changes, nothing hinders the emergence of other orientations, except a kind of loyalty to the objects that are "collected" and that lead each "friend" to offer obsessively what is expected of them.

In conclusion, these social networks are typified by a kind of self-presentation that is based on an arrangement of material, often borrowed from others, and linked closely to contingency – or simply guided by obsession. The same arrangement may also be reassembled in order to represent other personalities (perhaps of the same individual: there is no shortage of people who live a plurality of virtual lives under different nicknames). If it evolves, it may follow a course of personal transformation ("today I am not who I was yesterday"); but often, at least it seems to me, it simply follows the progression of circumstances ("I am who I am depending on the day"). These characteristics highlight the limits of these self-presentations: their value lies in how they are displayed, not in what they say; and while they have value for an individual, this is neither exclusive nor permanent. In light of this, we could say that in the very moment in which the social network participant presents a self-portrait, they open the door to their own dissolution. More decisively, what is lost is the traditional process of identification: the social network participant no longer finds completed stories in which to project themselves; they live in the midst of a continuous flow of data, available to them for every eventuality; they adapt their life to the material that they can gather; and they make of their life a bricolage.

From the screen to the display

Monitor, bulletin board (or blackboard) and scrapbook (or mailbox): these new keywords indicate just how distant the new screens are from the old. If it is true that we continue to deal with a rectangular surface on which figures in movement appear, it is also true that this surface no longer implies a reality, an envision, a recognition. This new screen is linked to a continuous flow of data but it is not necessarily coupled to an attentive gaze, to a world that asks to be witnessed or to a subject that is reflected in what it sees. There is a connection and a disconnection: a set of figures becomes perpetually available here where we are, but it does not necessarily lead us to a stable reference, an assured addressee and a full identification.

The concept of a "display" may help to better render an idea of this new entity.[18] The display shows, but only in the sense that it places at our disposition or makes accessible. It exhibits, but does not uncover. It offers, but does not commit. In other words, a display does not involve its images in the dialectic between visible and invisible (like a window used to do), between surfaces and structure (like a frame) or between appropriation and dispossession (like a mirror). The display simply "makes present" images. It places them in front of us, in case we may want to make use of them. It hands them to us, if you will.

The display is fully realized in the form of the touch screen. Here the eye is connected to the fingers, and it is they that signal if the observer is paying attention and what kind of attention they are paying. Touch solicits the arrival of images but, even more so, it guides their flow: it associates them, it downloads them and it often deletes them; it enlarges them, moves them around and stacks them. While it is the eye that supervises the operations, it is also the hand that guides them. It is the hand that calls to the images and seizes them (Flusser, 2010, pp. 23–32).

We are beyond the old situation in which spectators were immersed in a world that surprised them and held their attention from the screen. Now, spectators surprise and grab hold of the images that scurry before them, images that are not necessarily capable of restituting an empirical reality; rather, they are oriented toward supplying data and information. They are not even addressed directly to anyone in particular: it is their flow more than their capture that defines them. Finally, they are tied more closely to the hand than to the eye: it is only when they are "touched" that they find their place and define their value. The display screen makes these images present. It is here that they exit the flow and come to a halt. It is here that they become simultaneously available and practicable. We literally extract them from the screen, according to a logic that mixes push and pull.[19]

In short, we cannot look out of a display screen, nor can we fill our eyes with it, nor can we lean out of it. Instead we ask of it, as at an information window. We work on it, as at a table. We wait by it, as at a bus stop. And we find ourselves in front of something that stays with us for just as long as is necessary.

Naturally, not all the screens that surround us enter fully under the rubric of the display screen. There are still moments in which the reality around us is represented to an interested and engaged observer. This may happen on the very same devices that normally seem to negate the possibility of an epiphany. Google Earth, though it offers me maps and not territories, can lead me to rediscover the pleasure of taking a walk; Photoshop, though it offers me an image of how I would like to be, may obligate me to face myself again; a videogame, though it gives me the opportunity to abandon the world, may also give me the scripts and the characters to construct another one. Computers, cellphones and tablets are still widely used for diffusing documentations and investigations, for fostering public discussions and for constructing effective communities (as documents, for example, Paola Voci's *China on Video: Smaller-Screen Realities*, 2010). Indeed, there is still room for direct testimony that reconnects us to an exploration and to a dialog.

Although the contemporary media landscape is multi-faceted, current tendencies are moving toward the display: a surface on which we find – when we find it – a reality that goes beyond empirical data, from the moment in which samples, information and elements of possibility are mixed together; and a surface on which a gaze is trained – when there is one – that goes beyond the traditional poles of contemplation and analysis, from the moment in which it is accompanied by the manipulation of what is being observed. The epoch of the window, the frame and the mirror is largely coming to an end.

A new scenario?

This transformation of the screen is symptomatic of a larger transformation, which involves media in their totality. Media have long been conceived of as means of mediation between us and the world and between us and others: they serve to supply information and share it among subjects. In this sense they appeared as instruments of transmission and dialog. This kind of idea prevails in models such as that proposed by Harold Lasswell in the 1940s (Lasswell, 1948, pp. 37–52), but it persists in the subtext of Marshall McLuhan's reformulations of the 1960s (McLuhan, 2001) and Raymond Williams' of the 1970s (Williams, 1974), in which the emphasis is placed, respectively, on medias' abilities to extend our senses and to elaborate cultural models. We have now entered into a new dimension. Let us take, for example, GPS or Wii, or even tablets and smartphones: these are primarily devices that serve to access information and services. Thanks to them, we "recuperate" a series of data – perhaps without meaning to, but anytime and anywhere. Put another way, we "intercept" elements that are present in social (and virtual) space, and we utilize them in the situation in which we find ourselves, whatever it may be, only to store them away. In essence, we capture, modify and release.

This characteristic is recognizable in all contemporary media, which invite us to "secure" something that is "available," and which is made available again after we have used it, perhaps transformed by our intervention. We are no longer in the sphere of a proper communicative exchange; there are no hand-offs or confrontations, transitions or transactions. There is a circulation of information in which we must immerse ourselves, and media are the essential components of this circulation. They function as nexuses of interconnected circuits. They store data so that we may avail ourselves of them. They permit us to modify the situation in which we find ourselves, and they help us to construct new situations with data. They allow us to adapt what we find. And, finally, they relaunch these same data, after they have been used and adapted, within these various circuits. In short, media are places in which information in unremitting movement is downloaded and then uploaded to continue on its trajectory.

Such an orientation may be confirmed in the growing success of applications such as feed readers: programs aimed both at supplying users with a continuous stream of fresh data and at aggregating these data among themselves. Another confirmation may be found in practices such as web harvesting: research in the forest of data that arrive or that may arrive, in order to comb through them, keep them in view and eventually stow them away. In both cases, the objective is to acquire, assemble and archive the information that is circulating, in order to then make it available to whomever might be connected.

I do not know if we can call this "communication" precisely. I repeat: we are no longer primarily dealing with messages addressed to specific individuals or encounters between people. Of course, there still exists the space for announcements and dialogs but, above all, there is an enormous mass of data that circulates through the air, so to speak, and that occasionally halts and then takes off again.[20] Media are the instruments of a slackening of speed – as well as of an acceleration – of this perpetual motion. Thanks to them, we can "block" something here in front of us, to then "relaunch" it – which is to say, we download it and then upload it. In so doing, we place ourselves at a transit point, rendering our experience that of an ephemeral place.

The same goes – and above all – for visual media. Contrary to a long tradition of "realism," the image is no longer engendered by facts; rather, it is born of an amalgamation of elements that are concretized according to the circumstances. And even when the image is the product of a live recording, it remains part of an information flow that makes it available for new combinations and new circumstances. The image is an aggregate of provisory data and an entity in continuous movement, responsive to momentary needs, ongoing discourses and up-to-the-minute rhetoric. It is not important whence the image comes, but rather that it circulates and that it can pause somewhere to then take off again.

Vilém Flusser has offered an effective portrait of this situation: written ahead of its time, and in a somewhat prophetic tone, it is proving to be consistent with what is effectively happening. He begins with the observation that the reality that surrounds us has crumbled into fragments: "The world in which [people] find themselves can no longer be counted and explained: it has disintegrated into particles – photons, quanta, electromagnetic particles... Even their own consciousness, their thoughts, desires, values, have disintegrated into particles, into bits of information, a mass that can be calculated" (2010, p. 31). This state does not prevent us from forming an image of the world; however, this image can no longer be based on a depiction capable of tracing the contours of things (an *Imagination* in German). Rather, it must emerge from a calculated montage of fragments, from an "envision" (an *Einbildungskraft* in German). "The whirling particles around us and in us must be gathered onto surfaces; they must be envisioned" (ibid., p. 31). This is what constitutes media: they block the whirlwind of data and they recompose them into new figures. They accomplish this mechanically, following pre-programmed automatisms, from which it is difficult to depart. And they do so blindly, offering up various combinations, some of which are completely unpredictable. This is another reason why the images they supply (which Flusser calls "technical images," to distinguish them from traditional ones)[21] no longer constitute evidence, strictly speaking. Nevertheless, what media present to us continues to concern reality: only it is not an already formed world, rather it is a world in formation, and it does not contain exclusively factual elements, rather it also – and above all – contains elements of possibility: "The production of technical images occurs in a field of possibilities: in and of themselves, the particles are nothing but possibilities from which something accidentally emerges" (ibid., p. 16). In light of this, technical images, although they cannot be considered either true or false, bring us closer to things. They allow us to emerge from the abstraction into which the world is flung; they return to us some meaning; they lend themselves to some project.[22] They continue to speak to us, but from inside a continual and unstable wandering.

I would add that the effectiveness of these images depends on how and where they appear. Above all, the situation is decisive – a situation that the images find and simultaneously shape. It is one thing if images materialize on my computer, only for me, in an interstice of my daily life; it is quite another if they are displayed on a public screen in front of a crowd gathered for an event. Similarly, it is one thing if images reference distant events, which I follow, perhaps even with great concentration, but disinterestedly; while it is quite another if they refer to my surroundings, in which I can, or perhaps must, intervene. And finally, it is one thing if images remain trapped in a schema or formula on a screen; while it is quite another if theirs is simply a temporary stopover, open to ulterior developments. I am thinking, for instance, of the images of the Arab Spring: it makes quite a bit of difference whether they reappeared on the screens of Times Square for the benefit of curious passers-by, or on the smartphones of the crowd gathered in Tahrir Square. In essence, if it is true that the destiny of these images is to be permanently in transit, it is also of essential importance when and where they land. Their force, meaning and even their political value are determined in great part by their location.

We no longer find ourselves faced with an exchange but a circulation; no longer in front of a merely factual reality but a reality born of a recombination of information packets. We are dealing with a whirlwind of data, which occasionally pauses only to reconstitute itself and set off again; but also with presences that manifest themselves here before us, and therefore can still communicate to us about the world. This is precisely the media landscape that we must now confront – and the display screen is its perfect emblem.

The cinema, again: from temple to portal

Is there still space for cinema in this new landscape? Can it find real hospitality on the display screen? And can it, in turn, teach us something?

Cinema undoubtedly represents a point of resistance with respect to the process that I have attempted to describe in the preceding pages, for at least three good reasons. First, cinema is still largely the prisoner of a tradition that sees it as the closest art to reality. Cinema continues to be –

both in the collective imaginary and in the intentions of its authors – a trace of the world: its images, even when they serve to narrate fiction, continue to possess a strong documentary value. Second, cinema still carries with it the dream of an organic unity. The stories that it offers are aimed at constructing structured worlds which are dense and coherent: for as much as a film makes space for randomness, what it shows us always reveals a strong consistency. Third, cinema is still based on a system of broadcasting. Films are distributed along pre-established routes and arrive at predetermined points. It is true that it is becoming increasingly easy to find films everywhere – and recuperate them through legal and illegal practices – but it has not yet become a "whirlwind" of images, as has happened online for other types of products.

The weight of a tradition of realism, the strength of narration and the directionality of distribution – cinema seems to channel images and conduct them toward a reference, toward a text, toward a well established addressee—in an era inclined to leave the circulation of data open. However, this characteristic does not confine cinema to the margins of the great media transformation currently underway. On the contrary, it proves useful by demonstrating some contradictions in the contemporary panorama.

First, even if we do not trust images as we did in the past, there still exists a need for truth. It emerges from many small, personal artifacts posted on *YouTube*, whether they are the documentation of a childish prank or the cellphone camera footage of some historical event. The same need has inspired such strange sites as *Photoshop Disasters*, motivated by the desire to point out the distortions perpetrated by Photoshop users, mostly in advertisements. Second, even if the "grand narratives" have vanished (in coincidence with the post-modern condition, according to Lyotard, 1984), the need for stories is still vital. We see evidence of this in the flourishing genre of neo-epics in the mold of Tolkien and superhero films, in which the vicissitudes of the characters wind along seemingly infinite paths. And we also see it in the pleasure that the creators of personal homepages and blogs take in narrating their lives. It emerges too from videogames, both those fantastical in nature (the parameters of which are basically "realistic") and those inspired by history (in which a past verdict may be reversed, as long as the new narration remains consistent). Third, even if circuits are always open, there still exists the need for an actual, concrete, effective reception. This need is evidenced in the desire to feel involved in what one watches that emerges from some particularly politically engaged areas of social networks, or from the systematic count of viewers and their comments that accompany the videos posted on *YouTube*, or from the conversion of virtual contacts into actual encounters, often stubbornly hoped for and celebrated on *Facebook*. Even in the era of technical images, a need for authenticity, for stories and for encounters continues to assert itself. Cinema, in its battle to maintain a relationship with reality, with narration and with its spectator, can become the witness to these necessities.

On the other hand, cinema participates fully in the era in which it lives. It too is now permeated by the logic of the display. It is no coincidence that the worlds represented on the screen are increasingly fluid, or that the stories are increasingly inconsequential or that the settings are often unstable and the scenes are increasingly composed of collages and mosaics. Nor is it a coincidence that cinema now regularly lifts narratives and figures from other media, while simultaneously offering to other media its own stories and figures, in a kind of continuous exchange. Finally, it is no coincidence that cinema is in constant search of new environments and devices on which to transfer itself, from city squares to my smartphone. Cinema increasingly lives through forms and situations that are unsteady, provisional and contingent,[23] and that reconfigure themselves for a moment and then take off again along new trajectories.

Here, cinema drops its claim to "channeling" images; instead, it limits itself to "localizing" them, supplying them with some modalities of stylistic or narrative reorganization, and especially with a place in which to offer them to someone's gaze. In other words, it gives the images a definite – but not definitive – "how" and "where": a "how" and "where" that delineate the situation within which the images can operate, while also allowing them to conserve all their mobility and potential. Localization does exactly this: it arrests circulating images for a moment; it makes them converse with a context that they, in pausing, create around themselves; and it gives them meaning through this conversation, without, however, eradicating other possibilities for meaning.

Cinema's capacity to supply images with a stop-over – as opposed to a final destination – gives it a new and enhanced role with respect to other sites of vision. On the one hand, cinema reminds us that images can still materialize in concrete environments, in front of an audience, in precise circumstances – even now, when viewing is mostly individual, often casual, and tends to take place in a neutral space and time. On the other hand, cinema teaches us that images are not easily imprisoned: their appearance is necessary if we want them to speak to us, but it is also always temporary. Therefore, places of vision are now conceived of as unstably structured environments, characterized by temporary gatherings and fleeting images. This is true of spaces where films are screened, and also, by extension, of all the spaces in which the presence of a screen leads to the formation of a spectator community – and perhaps even for all the public spaces in which images are in play. We increasingly find more sites that allow for circulating data to acquire a weight and a value, thanks to the link to a territory; however, these sites are formed and dismantled according to the circulation of data. Though they are real spaces, they tend to function like a kind of portal in which images in flux are made to converge, and thanks to which one may make contact with the data whirling through the air.

If cinema today does want to function as an example, this is the only lesson that it can give us. We still need public spaces in which to welcome and experience images. However, these spaces can no longer exist as temples dedicated to a pre-established rite, as Ricciotto Canudo described movie theaters at the beginning of the last century (Canudo, 1908, p. 3; 1988, pp. 58–66). Nor can they continue to host a docile audience, ready to abandon itself to what it sees, as successive theories often described.[24] They can only be meeting points between images and spectators, both of whom are in transit. It would be useful here to recall Sigfried Kracauer's farsighted definition of the cinema as a "shelter for the homeless" (Kracauer, 1930, 1998, pp. 88–95). Today's shelter is simply open to inclemency of every kind, and the homeless are mobile subjects: display-places, if you will.

Naturally, examples of spaces dedicated to both gathering and transit can also be found outside of cinema. Eight years before the release of the film with which we began this study, *Timecode,* the stage of U2's *Zoo TV Tour* was decked out with four mega-screens along with 36 monitors continually crisscrossed by images, some of which were gathered from local television channels. The music came forth in parallel, open to possible intersections with the images. The audience of fans, gathered to see their favorite band, found itself in front of a largely unpredictable event. However, if cinema does not have exclusive rights to the model, it continues to function as an emblem of it. It is therefore fitting to conclude these pages with three very successful titles that have left their mark on the first decade of the twenty-first century: *The Matrix* trilogy (Wachowsky and Wachowsky, 1999; 2003a, b); *Minority Report* (Spielberg, 2002); and *Inception* (Nolan, 2010). It is not surprising that all these films represent attempts at intercepting images, understanding them in relation to a situation, and defining to whom they are addressed. I am thinking specifically of the scenes in *The Matrix* in which the resisters control the environment through a monitor that turns out to be merely the product of an illusion; of the moment in *Minority Report* in which John Anderton summons up images of the future on an interactive screen in order to understand what is taking place around him, but also in order to stage a sort of spectacle for his companions; and of Cobb's continuous attempts in *Inception* at aggregating projections and memories in order to sketch out possibilities. These films do a fine job of demonstrating what it now means for transitory spectators to localize transitory images. Indeed, the films themselves are in transit, ready to transfer onto television or computer screens, to become video games and to create a social imaginary. They are emblems of what it now means to see in our contemporary era of display. In this sense, they are portraits of the current media condition, and portraits of what cinema, in this context, can still say and teach.

Translation by Daniel Leisawitz

Notes

1. "That which is used to cover, to shield something or someone from external agents, inclement weather, harmful elements, or to hide from view" (Battaglia, 1994).
2. "At once I thought of making this lovely lady a screen to hide the truth" (Alighieri, 1973, para. 5).
3. "A contrivance for warding off the heat of a fire or a draught of air" *Oxford English Dictionary* (OED).
4. "A frame covered with paper or cloth, or a disk or plate of thin wood, cardboard, etc. (often decorated with painting or embroidery) with a handle by which a person may hold it between his face and the fire; a hand-screen. Also applied to a merely ornamental article of similar form and material" (OED).
5. "A contrivance...for affording an upright surface for the display of objects for exhibition" (OED). In the same period the term "screen-cell" also arose to describe "a part of a gaol where a prisoner may be kept under constant observation" (OED).
6. This reference is to the title of Siegfried Kracauer's volume *Theory of Film: The Redemption of Physical Reality* (Kracauer, 1960).
7. In early theories the metaphor of the frame returns in the writings of Victor Oscar Freeburg, linked to his constant attention to pictorial composition. For example, he observes that one of the conditions of cinema is that "it must practically always fill a rectangular frame of unvarying shape" (Freeburg, 1918, p. 39). Elsewhere (Freeburg 1923) he explores various types of composition and their effects on the spectator.
8. Nevertheless, the two media possess quite different characteristics: cinema is a medium of expression, while television is a medium of transmission. The

chapter 'La Televisione' in *La Radio* takes up and expands 'Vedere Lontano' (Arnheim, 1935); 'A Forecast of Television' (Arnheim, 1957) is also a rewriting, more than a translation, of 'Vedere Lontano.' The sentence quoted above appears only in *La Radio*. On Italian writings by Arnheim, see D'Aloia (2009). For more on Arnheim and television, see Galili (2011).

9. See Beatriz Colomina's essay (Chapter 2) in this collection. During the same World's Fair, Francis Thompson made a great impression by projecting the film *To Be Alive* on three screens.
10. Anne Friedberg reminds us that in 1985 some 20% of American households had a VCR; by 1997 this had reached 88% (Friedberg, 2000). The Sony Betamax was introduced in 1975 (Cabral, 2000, p. 318) and the VHS was marketed by JVC in 1976 (ibid., p. 317). Atari's Pong console, the first to enjoy significant success, was designed in 1966 and introduced in 1972 (Computer History Museum, 2006), while the consecration of the videogame console occurred in 1977 with the Atari 2600 (ibid., 2006).
11. The desktop computer began to grow in popularity at the end of the 1970s and beginning of the 1980s: the Apple II debuted in 1977 (Computer History Museum, 2006), the IBM PC in 1981 (ibid., 2006), the Commodore 64 in 1982 (ibid., 2006) and the Macintosh Portable in 1989 (Edwards, 2009), while the ThinkPad 700 came out in 1992 (Mueller, 2004, p. 33).
12. The Minitel was introduced in France in 1982 (Mancini, 2002, p. 101).
13. The DVD dates back to 1995 (Toshiba, 1995).
14. The first commercially automated cellular network (1G: first generation) was launched in Japan by NTT in 1979 (Klemens, 2010, pp. 65–66), the GSM, which represents the second generation (2G) of cellphones, came online in 1991 (Pagtzis, 2011), and 3G began operation in 2001 (BBC News, 2001).
15. Noteworthy among the early palm devices are the Tandy Zoomer (1992) and the Apple Newton Message Pad (1993) (Evans, 2011).
16. Among the early tablets was the GRiDPad, released by GRiDPad System Corporation in 1989 (Evans, 2011). The Amazon Kindle was first introduced to the market by Amazon.com's subsidiary Lab126 in November 2007 (ibid.) Apple released the first iPad in April 2010 (ibid.)
17. Sometimes they imply a mechanical gaze. Drones in war zones gather images that a machine examines to highlight any discrepancies with prior surveillance of a given area – and it is only after this first "gaze" that an analyst is summoned to intervene, in order to give (or not give) the order for an attack on a possible enemy.
18. Dudley Andrew reaches the same conclusion regarding the computer screen: "Monitor and display seem more apt terms than screen to designate the visual experience that computers deliver" (Andrew, 2009, p. 915).
19. On the opposition of the dimensions of push and pull, both in new media and in the wider culture, see Lull (2006).
20. The idea that the screen constitutes a moment in which circulation slackens speed is well illustrated by David Joselit's concept of the "slow down trajective" (Joselit, 2007).
21. Flusser opens his book with a genealogical reconstruction of the various phases of the history of images. The process he describes is one of increasing abstraction with respect to the concreteness of immediate experience: during the first moment (first rung), "natural man" (*Naturmensch*) lives a concrete

and purely sensorial experience, like that of other animals. Then man dedicates himself to the creation of functional, tridimensional artifacts. In a third phase, "traditional" images appear – paintings, drawings, sculptures – which structure the relation between man and the world in magical-imaginative terms. The fourth moment is one in which writing appears and, therefore, conceptual thought. The fifth phase is the one we now find ourselves in, in which abstraction has led to a loss of the "representability" of concrete phenomena (Flusser, 2010, pp. 5–10). For another "history of the image," which is set up according to a schema not distant from Flusser's, see Debray (1992).

22. "Envision should refer to the capacity to step from the particles universe back into the concrete" (Flusser, 2010, p. 34). And moreover, via technical images, "are we able to turn back to concrete experience, recognition, value and action and away from the world of abstraction from which these things have vanished" (ibid., p. 38).
23. On different aspects of contingency in the present cinema, see Harbord (2007, pp. 123–127).
24. See, for example, Feldmann (1956). Boris Groys suggests that the immobility of the spectators risks functioning as a parody of the "active life," which films seem to celebrate (Groys, 2008, pp. 71–72).

Bibliography

Alighieri, Dante (1973) *Vita Nuova*, Mark Musa (trans.) (Bloomington: Indiana University Press).

Altman, Charles (1976) "Psychoanalysis and Cinema: The Imaginary Discourse", *Quarterly Review of Film Studies*, 2, 257–272.

Andrew, Dudley (2009) "The Core and the Flow of Film Studies", *Critical Inquiry*, 35 (Summer), 879–915.

Arnheim, Rudolf (1935) "Vedere Lontano", *Intercine*, 2 (February), 71–82.

Arnheim, Rudolf (1937) *La Radio Cerca la Sua Forma* (Milan: Hoepli).

Arnheim, Rudolf (1957) *Film as Art* (Berkeley, LA and London: University of California Press).

Bakhtin, Mikhail (1981) "Discourse in the Novel", in Holquist, Michael (ed.) *The Dialogic Imagination: Four Essays* (Austin: University of Texas Press).

Balázs, Béla (2010) *Béla Balázs: Early Film Theory: Visible Man and The Spirit of Film*, Carter, Erica (ed.), Rodney Livingstone (trans.) (New York: Berghahn Books).

Battaglia, Salvatore (1994) *Grande Dizionario della Lingua Italiana*, Vol. 17 (Turin: Utet).

Bazin, André (1967) *What is Cinema?* (Berkeley: University of California Press).

BBC News (2001) "First 3G Launched in Japan" (1 October) http://news.bbc.co.uk/1/hi/business/1572372.stm, date accessed 13 April 2012.

Cabral, Luís M. B. (2000) *Introduction to Industrial Organization* (Cambridge: MIT Press).

Canudo, Ricciotto (1908) "Trionfo del Cinematografo", *Il Nuovo Giornale*, (25 December), 3.

Canudo, Ricciotto (1988) "The Birth of a Sixth Art", in Abel, Richard (ed.) *French Film Theory and Criticism* (Princeton: Princeton University Press).

Chelsea Girls (1966) directed and produced by Andy Warhol.

Computer History Museum (2006) Timeline of Computer History: Graphics & Games, http://www.computerhistory.org/timeline/?category=gg, date accessed 25 April 2012.

D'Aloia, Adriano (2009) *I Baffi di Charlot* (Torino: Kaplan).

Debray, Régis (1992) *Vie et Mort de l'Image: Une Histoire du Regard en Occident* (Paris: Gallimard).

Edwards, Benj (2009) The (Misunderstood) Mac Portable Turns 20, http://www.pcworld.com/article/172420/the_misunderstood_mac_portable_turns_20.html, date accessed 25 April 2012.

Eisenstein, Sergei (1931a) "The Dynamic Square", *Close Up*, March–June, 3–16.

Eisenstein, Sergei (1931b) "The Principles of Film Form", *Close Up*, September, 167–181.

Eisenstein, Sergei (1987) *Nonindifferent Nature* (Cambridge: Cambridge University Press).

Elsaesser, Thomas and Hagener, Malte (2010) *Film Theory: An Introduction through the Senses* (New York: Routledge).

Epstein, Jean (1984) "Magnification", in Abel, Richard (ed.) *French Film Theory and Criticism*, Vol. 1, 1907–1939 (Princeton: Princeton University Press).

Evans, Dean (2011) 10 Memorable Milestones in Tablet History, *TechRadar* (31 January), http://www.techradar.com/news/mobile-computing/10-memorable-milestones-in-tablet-history-924916, date accessed 13 April 2012.

Feldmann, Erich (1956) "Considérations sur la Situation du Spectateur au Cinéma", *Revue Internationale de Filmologie*, 26, 83–98.

Flusser, Vilém (2010) *Into the Universe of Technical Images*, Nancy Ann Roth (trans.) (Minneapolis: University of Minnesota Press).

Foucault, Michel (1979) *Discipline and Punish: The Birth of the Prison* (New York: Vintage).

Freeburg, Victor Oscar (1918) *The Art of Photoplay Making* (New York: Macmillan).

Freeburg, Victor Oscar (1923) *Pictorial Beauty on the Screen* (New York: Macmillan).

Friedberg, Anne (2000) "The End of Cinema: Multimedia and Technological Change", in Gledhill, Christine and Williams, Linda (eds.) *Reinventing Film Studies* (London: Arnold).

Galili, Doron (2011) "Television from Afar: Arnheim's Understanding of Media", in Higgins, Scott (ed.) *Arnheim for Film and Media Studies* (London: Routledge).

Gerbi, Antonello (1926) "Iniziazione alle Delizie del Cinema", *Il Convegno*, 7(11–12), 836–848.

Groys, Boris (2008) *Art Power* (Cambridge: MIT Press).

Hagener, Malte (2009) "The Aesthetics of Displays: From the Window on the World to the Logic of the Screen", in Quaresima, Leonardo, Sangalli, Laura Ester and Zocca, Fedrico (eds.) *Cinema e Fumetto/Cinema and Comics* (Udine: Forma).

Harbord, Janet (2007) *The Evolution of Film* (Cambridge: Polity Press).

Huhtamo, Erkki (2004) "Elements of Screenology: Toward an Archaeology of the Screen", *ICONICS: International Studies of the Modern Image*, 7, 31–82.

Inception (2010) Directed by Christopher Nolan, produced by Christopher Nolan and Emma Thomas.

Joselit, David (2007) *Feedback: Television Against Democracy* (Cambridge: MIT Press).

Klemens, Guy (2010) *The Cellphone: The History and Technology of the Gadget that Changed the World* (Jefferson: McFarland).
Kracauer, Sigfried (1930) *Die Angestellten: Aus dem Neuesten Deutschland* (Frankfurt: Societäts-Verlag).
Kracauer, Sigfried (1960) *Theory of Film: The Redemption of Physical Reality* (New York: Oxford University Press).
Kracauer, Sigfried (1998) *The Salaried Masses: Duty and Distraction in Weimar Germany*, Quintin Hoare (trans.) (London: Verso).
Lasswell, Harold (1948) "The Structure and Function of Communication in Society", in Bryson, Lyman (ed.) *The Communication of Ideas* (New York: Institute for Religious and Social Studies).
Lull, James (2006) "The Push and Pull of Global Culture", in Curran, James and Morley, David (eds.) *Media and Cultural Theory* (London: Routledge).
Lyotard, Jean-François Lyotard (1984) *The Postmodern Condition* (Minneapolis: University of Minnesota Press).
Mancini, Anna (2002) *Ancient Egyptian Wisdom for the Internet: Ancient Egyptian Justice and Ancient Roman Law Applied to the Internet* (Lanham: University Press of America).
Manovich, Lev (2000) *The Language of New Media* (Cambridge: MIT Press).
McLuhan, Marshall (2001) *Understanding Media: The Extension of Man* (London: Routledge, 2001).
Minority Report (2002) Directed by Steven Spielberg, produced by Molen, Gerald R., Curtis, Bonnie, Parkes, Walter F., de Bont, Jan and Doven, Michael.
Mueller, Scott (2004) *Upgrading and Repairing Laptops* (Indianapolis: Que).
Pagtzis, Theodoros (2011) GSM: A Bit of History, http://www.cs.ucl.ac.uk/staff/t.pagtzis/, date accessed 13 April 2012.
Panteo, Tullio (1908) "Il Cinematografo", *La Scena Illustrata*, 19(1) (October), 5.
Papini, Giovanni (1907) "La Filosofia del Cinematografo", *La Stampa* (18 May), 1–2.
Sobchack, Vivian (1992) *Address of the Eye* (Princeton: Princeton University Press).
Spigel, Lynn (2010) "Designing the Smart House: Posthuman Domesticity and Conspicuous Production", in Berry, Chris, Kim, Soyoung and Spigel, Lynn (eds.) *Electronic Elsewheres* (Minneapolis: Minnesota University Press).
The Matrix (1999) Directed by Andy Wachowski and Larry Wachowski, produced by Joel Silver.
The Matrix Reloaded (2003a) Directed by Andy Wachowski and Larry Wachowski, produced by Joel Silver.
The Matrix Revolutions (2003b) Directed by Andy Wachowski and Larry Wachowski, produced by Joel Silver.
Timecode (2000) Directed by Mike Figgis, produced by Mike Figgis and Annie Stewart.
To Be Alive! (1965) Directed by Alexander Hammid and Francis Thompson, produced by Francis Thompson.
Toshiba (1995) DVD Format Unification, http://www.toshiba.co.jp/about/press/1995_12/ pr0802.htm, date accessed 13 April 2012.
Voci, Paola (2010) *China on Video: Smaller-Screen Realities* (London: Routledge).
Williams, Raymond (1974) *Television: Technology and Cultural Form* (New York: Schocken Books).

2
Multi-screen Architecture

Beatriz Colomina

We are surrounded today, everywhere, all the time, by arrays of multiple, simultaneous images – in the streets, airports, shopping centers and gyms, and also on our computers and TV sets. The idea of a single image commanding our attention has faded away. It seems as if we need to be distracted in order to concentrate, as if we – all of us living in this new kind of space, the space of information – could be diagnosed *en masse* with attention deficit disorder. The state of distraction in the metropolis, described so eloquently by Walter Benjamin early in the twentieth century, seems to have been replaced by a new form of distraction, which is to say, a new form of attention. Rather than wander cinematically through the city, we now look in one direction and see many juxtaposed moving images, more than we can possibly synthesize or reduce to a single impression. We sit in front of our computers on our ergonomically perfected chairs, staring with a fixed gaze at many simultaneously "open" windows through which different kinds of information stream toward us. We hardly even notice it. It seems natural, as if we were simply breathing in the information.

How would one go about writing a history of this form of perception? Should one go back to the organization of the TV studio, with its wall of monitors from which the director chooses the camera angle that will be presented to the viewer; or should one go to Cape Canaveral and look at its mission-control room; or should one even go back to World War II, when so-called situation rooms were envisioned with multiple projections bringing information from all over the world and presenting it side by side for instant analysis by political leaders and military commanders?

But it is not simply the military or war technology that has defined this new form of perception. Designers, architects and artists were involved from the beginning, playing a crucial role in the evolution of the multi-screen and multi-media techniques of information presentation. Whilst artists' use of these techniques tends to be associated with the happenings and expanded cinema of the 1960s, architects were involved much earlier and in very different contexts, such as military operations and governmental propaganda campaigns.

Take the 1959 American National Exhibition in Moscow, where the government enlisted some of the country's most sophisticated designers. Site of the famous Kitchen Debate between Richard Nixon and Nikita Khrushchev, the exhibition was a Cold War operation in which the Eameses' multi-screen technique turned out to be a powerful weapon.

To reconstruct a little bit of the atmosphere, the USA and the USSR agreed in 1958 to exchange national exhibits on "science, technology and culture." The Soviet exhibition opened in the New York Coliseum at Columbus Circle in New York City in June 1959, and the US exhibition opened in Sokolniki Park in Moscow in July of the same year. Vice President Nixon, in Moscow to open the exhibition, engaged in a heated debate with Khrushchev over the virtues of the American way of life. The exchange became known as the Kitchen Debate because it took place – in an event that appeared impromptu but was actually staged by the Americans – in the kitchen of a suburban house split in half to allow easy viewing. The Russians called the house the "Splitnik," a pun on *Sputnik*, the name of the satellite the Soviets had put into orbit two years before.

What was remarkable about this debate was the focus. As historian Elaine Tyler-May notes, instead of discussing "missiles, bombs, or even modes of government... [the two leaders] argued over the relative merits of American and Soviet washing machines, televisions, and electric ranges" (May, 1994, p. 16; see Marling, 1994). For Nixon, US superiority rested on the ideal of the suburban home, complete with modern appliances and distinct gender roles. He proclaimed that this "model" suburban home represented nothing less than American freedom:

> To us, diversity, the right to choose, is the most important thing... We don't have one decision made at the top by one government official... We have many different manufacturers and many different kinds of washing machines so that the housewife has a choice.
>
> (May, 1994, p. 17)[1]

The exhibition captivated the national and international media. Newspapers, illustrated magazines and TV networks reported on the event.

Symptomatically, *Life* magazine put the wives instead of the politicians on its cover. Pat Nixon appears as the prototype of the American woman depicted in advertisements of the 1950s: slim, well groomed, fashionable and happy. In contrast, the Soviet ladies appear stocky and dowdy and, whilst two of them, Mrs Khrushchev and Mrs Mikoyan, look proudly toward the camera, the third, Mrs Kozlov, in what Roland Barthes may have seen as the *punctum* of this photograph, cannot keep her eyes off Pat Nixon's dress (*Life*, 1959, cover).

Envy. That is what the exhibition seems to have been designed to produce (despite vigorous denials by Nixon in his debate with Khrushchev: "We do not claim to astonish the Soviet people"[2]) – yet not envy of scientific, military or industrial achievements but envy of washing machines, dishwashers, color TVs, suburban houses, lawnmowers, supermarkets stocked full of groceries, Cadillac convertibles, makeup colors, lipstick, spike-heeled shoes, hi-fi sets, cake mixes, TV dinners, Pepsi-Cola and so on. "What is this," the newspaper *Izvestia* asked itself in its news report, "a national exhibit of a great country or a branch department store? Where is American science, American industry, and particularly their factory techniques?" (Otten, 1959, p. 16). And a Russian teacher is quoted by the *Wall Street Journal*: "You have lots of dolls, furniture, dishes, but where are your technical exhibits?" (ibid.). Even American newspapers described the main pavilion of the exhibition as a "lush bargain basement" but one that, owing to the dust from a concrete floor that had crumbled 48 hours after the opening, already looked as if it "had barely survived a fire sale" (Frankel, 1959a, p. 12).

It was for this context that the Eameses produced their film *Glimpses of the USA*, projecting it onto seven 20 by 30 foot screens suspended within a vast (250 feet in diameter) golden geodesic dome designed by Buckminster Fuller. More than 2200 still and moving images (some from Billy Wilder's *Some Like It Hot*) presented "a typical work day" in the life of the USA in nine minutes and "a typical weekend day" in three minutes (Neuhart *et al.*, 1989, pp. 238–241; see also Lipstadt, 1997, pp. 160–166). Pulled from many different sources, including photo archives (such as Magnum Photos, photo researchers and the magazines *Fortune*, *Holiday*, *Life*, *Look*, *Saturday Evening Post*, *Sports Illustrated*, *Sunset*, and *Time*), individual photographers (e.g. Ferenc Berko, Julius Shulman, Ezra Stoller, Ernst Braun, George Zimbel and Charles Eames himself), and friends and associates of the Eameses (e.g. Eliot Noyes, George Nelson, Alexander Girard, Eero Saarinen, Billy Wilder, Don Albinson and Robert Staples),[3] the images were combined into seven separate film reels and projected simultaneously through seven interlocked projectors.

The Eameses did not simply install their film in Fuller's space: they were involved in the organization of the entire exhibition from the beginning. Jack Masey of the United States Information Agency (USIA) and George Nelson, who had been commissioned by the USIA to design the exhibition, brought them onto the team. According to Nelson, it was in an evening meeting in the Eames House in Los Angeles, culminating three days of discussions, where "all the basic decisions for the fair were made. Present were Nelson, Ray and Charles (the latter occasionally swooping past on a swing hung from the ceiling), the movie director Billy Wilder, and Masey" (Abercrombie, 1995, p. 163). According to Nelson, by the end of the evening a basic scheme had emerged:

- a dome (by Bucky Fuller);
- a glass pavilion (by Welton Beckett) "as a kind of bazaar stuffed full of things, [the] idea being that consumer products represented one of the areas in which we were most effective, as well as one in which the Russians... were more interested;"
- an introductory film by the Eameses, since the team felt that the "80,000 square feet of exhibition space was not enough to communicate more than a small fraction of what we wanted to say" (ibid., p. 164).

In addition, the USIA had already contracted for the inclusion of Disney's *Circarama,* a 360-degree motion picture that offered a 20-minute tour of US cities and tourist attractions, and which played to about 1000 Russians an hour (Frankel, 1959b, p. 8)[4]; an architecture exhibit curated by Peter Blake; a fashion show curated by Eleanor Lambert; a packaging exhibition by the Museum of Modern Art's associate curator of design, Mildred Constantine; and Edward Steichen's famous photographic exhibit, *The Family of Man* (Abercrombie, 1995, p. 167). The exhibition also included a full-scale ranch-style suburban house, put up by a Long Island builder and furnished by Macy's. It was in the kitchen of this US$14,000, six-room house filled with appliances that the Kitchen Debate began, with an argument over automatic washers.

The multi-screen performance turned out to be one of the most popular exhibits at the fair (second only to the cars and color TVs).[5] *Time* magazine called it the exposition's "smash hit,"[6] the *Wall Street Journal* described it as the "real bomb shell" and American officials believed it was "the real pile-driver of the fair."[7] Groups of 5000 people were brought into the dome every 45 minutes, 16 times a day

(Frankel, 1959a). Close to 3 million people saw the show, and the floor had to be resurfaced three or four times during the six-week exhibition (Kirkham, 1995, p. 324).[8]

The Eameses were not just popular entertainers in an official exhibition, and *Glimpses* was not just a series of images inside a dome. The huge array of suspended screens defined a space within a space. The Eameses were self-consciously architects of a new kind of space. The film breaks with the fixed perspectival view of the world. In fact, we find ourselves in a space that can be apprehended only with the high technology of telescopes, zoom lenses, airplanes, night-vision cameras, and so on and where there is no privileged point of view. It is not simply that many of the individual images that make up *Glimpses* have been taken with these instruments. More important, the relationship between the images re-enacts the operation of the technologies.

The film starts with images from outer space on all of the screens – stars across the sky, seven constellations, seven star clusters and nebulae – then moves through aerial views of the city at night, from higher up to closer in, until city lights from the air fill the screens. The early morning comes with aerial views of landscapes from different parts of the country: deserts, mountains, hills, seas, farms, suburban developments and urban neighborhoods. When the camera eyes finally descend to the ground, we see close-ups of newspapers and milk bottles at doors – but still no people, only traces of their existence on earth.

Not by chance, the first signs of human life are centered on the house and domestic space. From the stars at night and the aerial views, the cameras zoom to the most intimate scenes: "people having breakfast at home, men leaving for work, kissing their wives, kissing the baby, being given lunchboxes, getting into cars, waving good-bye, children leaving for school, being given lunchboxes, saying good-bye to the dog, piling into station wagons and cars, getting into school buses, baby crying."[9] As with the Eameses' later and much better-known film *Powers of Ten* (1968),[10] which, incidentally, reused images of the night sky from *Glimpses*,[11] the film moves from outer space to the close-up details of everyday life. As the working script of the film indicates, the close-ups are of "last sips of coffee" of men before leaving for work, "children washing hands before dinner," "housewives on the phone with clerks (supermarket food shelves in b.g.)"[12] and so on. In *Powers of Ten*, the movement is set in reverse, beginning in the domestic space of a picnic spread with a man asleep beside a woman in a park in Chicago and moving out into the atmosphere and then back down inside the body through the skin of the man's wrist to microscopic cells and to the atomic level. Even if *Powers of Ten*, initially produced for the Commission on College Physics, was a more scientific, more advanced film in which space was measured in seconds, the logic of the two films (*Glimpses* and *Powers of Ten*) was the same. Intimate domesticity was suspended within an entirely new spatial system – a system that was the product of esoteric scientific-military research but that had entered the everyday public imagination with the launching of *Sputnik* in 1957. Fantasies that had long circulated in science fiction had become reality. This shift from research and fantasy to tangible fact made new forms of communicating to a mass audience possible.[13] The Eameses' innovative technique did not simply present the audience with a new way of seeing things. Rather, it gave form to a new mode of perception that was already in everybody's mind.

Glimpses breaks with the linear narrative of film to bring snippets of information, an ever-changing mosaic image of American life. And yet the message of the film is linear and eerily consistent with the official message represented by the Kitchen Debate. From the stars in the sky at the beginning of the film – which the narrative insists are the same in the USSR as they are in the USA – to the people kissing their good-nights and the forget-me-not flowers in the last image, the film emphasizes universal emotions,[14] whilst at the same time unambiguously reinforcing the material abundance of one country. From the parking lots of factories, which the narrative describes as filled with the cars of workers, to the aerial views of suburban houses with a blue swimming pool in each yard, to the close-ups of shopping carts and supermarket shelves full of goodies, and housewives cooking dinner in kitchens equipped with every imaginable appliance, the message of the film is clear: we are the same as you, but, on the material level, we have more.

Glimpses, like the "Splitnik" house, displaced the USA–USSR debate from the arms-and-space race to the battle of the appliances. And yet the overall effect of the film is that of an extraordinarily powerful viewing technology, a hyperviewing mechanism that is hard to imagine outside the very space program that the exhibition was trying to downplay. In fact, this extreme mode of viewing goes beyond the old fantasy of the eye in the sky. If *Glimpses* simulates the operation of satellite surveillance, it exposes more than the details of life in the streets: it penetrates the most intimate spaces and reveals every secret. Domestic life itself becomes the target, the source of pride or insecurity. The Americans, made insecure by the thought of a Russian eye looking down on them, countered by exposing more than that eye could ever see (or at least pretending to, since "a day in the life of the USA" became an image of the good life without ghettos, poverty, domestic violence or depression).

Glimpses simply intensified an existing mode of perception. In fact, it synthesized several already existing modes that were manifest in TV, space programs and military operations. As is typical of all of the Eameses' work, it was the simplicity and clarity of this synthesis that made it immediately accessible to all.[15]

I

What kind of genealogy can one make of the Eameses' development of this astonishingly successful technique?

It was not the first time they had deployed multi-screens. In fact, the Eameses were involved in one of the first multi-media presentations on record, if not the first. Again it was George Nelson who set up the commission. In 1952 he had been asked to prepare a study for the Department of Fine Arts at the University of Georgia in Athens, and he brought along Ray and Charles Eames and Alexander Girard. Instead of writing a report, they decided to collaborate on a "show for a typical class" of 55 minutes. Nelson referred to it as "Art X," whilst the Eameses called it "A Rough Sketch for a Sample Lesson for a Hypothetical Course." The subject of the lesson was "communications,"[16] and the stated goals included "the breaking down of barriers between fields of learning...making people a little more intuitive...[and] increasing communication between people and things" (Neuhart *et al.*, 1989, p. 177). The performance included a live narrator, multiple images (both still and moving), sound (in the form of music and narration) and even "a collection of bottled synthetic odors that were to be fed into the auditorium during the show through the air-conditioning ducts" (Nelson (1954) cited in Abercrombie, 1995, p. 145). Charles Eames later said, "We used a lot of sound, sometimes carried to a very high volume so you would actually feel the vibrations" (Gingerich, 1977, p. 331). The idea was to produce an intense sensory environment so as to "heighten awareness." The effect was so convincing that apparently some people even believed they smelled things (e.g. the smell of oil in the machinery) when no smell had been introduced, only a suggestion in an image or a sound (ibid.)

It was a major production. Nelson described the team arriving in Athens "burdened with only slightly less equipment than Ringling Brothers. This included a movie projector, three slide projectors, three screens, three or four tape recorders, cans of films, boxes of slides, and reels of magnetic tape."[17] The reference to the circus was not accidental. Speaking with a reporter for *Vogue*, Charles later argued that " 'Sample Lesson' was a blast on all senses, a super-saturated three-ring circus. Simultaneously the students were assaulted by three sets of slides, two tape recorders, a motion picture with sound, and peripheral panels for further distraction" (Talmey, 1959, p. 144).

The circus was one of the Eameses' lifetime fascinations (Colomina, 1997, p. 128) – so much so that in the 1940s, when they were out of work and money, they were about to audition for one. They would have been clowns, but ultimately a contract to make plywood furniture allowed them to continue as designers. And from the mid-1940s on, they took hundreds and hundreds of photographs of the circus. They used these in many contexts, including *Circus* (their 180-slide, three-screen slide show accompanied by a sound track featuring circus music and other sounds recorded at the circus), presented as part of the Charles Eliot Norton Lectures at Harvard University that Charles delivered in 1970, and the film *Clown Face* (1971), a training film about "the precise and classical art of applying makeup" made for Bill Ballentine, director of the Clown College of Ringling Brothers Barnum & Bailey Circus. The Eameses had been friends with the Ballentines since the late 1940s, when the former had photographed the circus's behind-the-scenes activities during an engagement in Los Angeles (Ballentine, 1982; Neuhart *et al.*, 1989, p. 373). Charles was on the board of the Ringling Brothers College and often referred to the circus as an example of what design and art should be, not self-expression but precise discipline:

> Everything in the circus is pushing the possible beyond the limit – bears do not really ride on bicycles, people do not really execute three and a half turn somersaults in the air from a board to a ball, and until recently no one dressed the way fliers do... Yet within this apparent freewheeling license, we find a discipline which is almost unbelievable... The circus may look like the epitome of pleasure, but the person flying on a high wire, or executing a balancing act, or being shot from a cannon must take his pleasure very, very seriously. In the same vein, the scientist, in his laboratory, is pushing the possible beyond the limit and he too must take his pleasure very seriously.
>
> (Eames, 1974, pp. 17–18)

The circus, as an event that offered a multiplicity of simultaneous experiences that could not be taken in entirely by the viewer, was the Eameses' model for their design of multi-media exhibitions and the fast-cutting technique of their films and slide shows, where the objective was always to communicate the maximum amount of information in a way that was both pleasurable and effective (Neuhart *et al.*, 1989, p. 91).

But the technological model for multi-screen, multi-media presentations may have been provided by the war-situation room, which was designed in those same years to bring information in simultaneously from numerous sources around the world so that the president and military commanders could make critical decisions. It is not without irony, in that sense, that the Eameses read the organization of the circus as a form of crisis control. In a circus, Charles said, "there is a strict hierarchy of events, and an elimination of choice under stress, so that one event can automatically follow another... There is a recognized mission for everyone involved. In a crisis there can be no question as to what needs to be done."[18] A number of the Eameses' friends were involved in the secret military project of the war rooms, including Buckminster Fuller, Eero Saarinen and Henry Dreyfuss, whose unrealized design involved a wall of parallel projected images of different kinds of information (Katz, 1996, pp. 3–21).[19] It is not clear that the Eameses knew anything about the project during the war years, but it is very likely, given their friendship with Fuller, Saarinen and Dreyfuss, that they would have found out after the war. In 1970, in the context of his second Norton Lecture, Charles referred to the war room as a model for city management:

> In the management of a city, linear discourse certainly can't cope. We imagine a City Room or a World Health Room (rather like a War Room) where all the information from satellite monitors and other sources could be monitored; [Fuller's World Game is an example.] ... The city problem involves conflicting interest and points of view. So the place where information is correlated also has to be a place where each group can try out plans for its own changing needs.[20]

The overall subject of the Norton Lectures was announced as "Problems Relating to Visual Communication and the Visual Environment," and a consistent theme was the "necessity to devise visual models for matters of practical concern where linear description isn't enough." Kepes' *Language of Vision* was a constant reference point for the Eameses. The "language of vision" was seen as a "real threat to the discontinuity" (between the arts, between university departments, between art and everyday life, and so on) that the Eameses were always fighting.[21]

Architecture ("a most non-discontinuous art") was seen as both the ultimate model for discontinuity and the discipline where the new technologies should be implemented.

A number of wartime research projects, including work on communications, ballistics and experimental computers, had quickly developed after the war into a fully fledged theory of information flow, most famously with the publication of Claude Shannon's *Mathematical Theory of Communication* in 1949, which formalized the idea of an information channel from sender to recipient whose efficiency could be measured in terms of speed and noise. This sense of information flow organized the "Sample Lesson" performance. The Eameses said they "were trying to cram into a short time, a class hour, the most background material possible" (Gingerich, 1977, p. 332). As part of the project, they produced *A Communication Primer*, a film that presented the theory of information, explaining Shannon's famous diagram of the passage of information, and was subsequently developed in an effort to present current ideas in communication theory to architects and planners, and to encourage them to use these ideas in their work. The basic idea was to integrate architecture and information flow. If the great heroes of the Renaissance were, for the Eameses, "people concerned with ways of modeling/imaging... not with self-expression or bravura... Brunelleschi, but not Michelangelo,"[22] the great architects of our time would be the ones concerned with the new forms of communication, particularly computers:

> It appeared to us that the real current problems for architects now – the problems that a Brunelleschi, say, would gravitate to – are problems of *organization of information*. For city planning, for regional planning, the first need is clear, accessible models of current states-of-affairs, drawn from a data base that only a computer can handle for you.[23]

The logic of information flow was further developed in the Eameses' 1955 film *House: After Five Years of Living*. This was made entirely from thousands of color slides that the Eameses took of their home over the first five years of its life (Colomina, 1997), shown in quick succession (a technique called "fast cutting," for which the Eameses won an Emmy Award in 1960[24]) and accompanied by music composed by Elmer Bernstein. As Michael Braune writes,

> The interesting point about this method of film making is not only that it is relatively simple to produce and that rather more

> information can be conveyed than when there is movement on the screen, but that it corresponds surprisingly closely with the way in which the brain normally records the images it receives. I would assume that it also corresponds rather closely with the way Eames's own thought processes tend to work. I think it symptomatic, for instance, that he is extremely interested in computers... and that one of the essential characteristics of computers is their need to separate information into components before being able to assemble them into a large number of different wholes.
>
> (Braune, 1966, p. 452)

This technique was developed even further in *Glimpses*, which is organized around a strict logic of information transmission. The role of the designer is to orchestrate a particular flow of information. The central principle is one of compression. At the end of the design meeting at the Eames House in preparation for the American exhibition in Moscow, the idea of the film emerged precisely "as a way of compressing into a small volume the tremendous quantity of information" they wanted to present, which would have been impossible to do in the 80,000 square feet of the exhibition (see Abercrombie, 1995, pp. 163–164). The space of the multi-screen film, like the space of the computer, compresses physical space. Each screen shows a different scene, but all seven at each moment are on the same general subject – housing, transportation, jazz and so forth. As the *New York Times* describes it, "Perhaps fifty clover-leaf highway intersections are shown in just a few seconds. So are dozens of housing projects, bridges, skyscrapers scenes, supermarkets, universities, museums, theatres, churches, farms, laboratories and much more" (Frankel, 1959b, p. 8).

According to the Eameses, repetition was employed for credibility:

> If, for example, we were to show a freeway interchange, somebody would look at it and say, "We have one at Smolensk and one at Minsk; we have two, they have one" – that kind of thing. So we conceived the idea of having the imagery come on in multiple forms, as in the *Rough Sketch for a Sample Lesson."*
>
> (Gingerich, 1977, pp. 332–333)

But the issue was much more than one of efficiency of communication or the polemical need to have multiple examples. The idea was, as with the "Sample Lesson," to produce sensory overload. As the Eameses had suggested to *Vogue*, "Sample Lesson" tried to provide many forms of "distraction" instead of asking students to concentrate on a singular message. The audience drifted through a multi-media space that exceeded their capacity to absorb it. The Eames-Nelson team thought that the most important thing to communicate to undergraduates was a sense of what the Eameses would later call "connections" among seemingly unrelated phenomena. Arguing that awareness of these relationships was achieved by "high-speed techniques," Nelson and the Eameses produced an excessive input from different directions that had to be synthesized by the audience. Likewise, Charles said of *Glimpses*:

> We wanted to have a credible number of images, but not so many that they couldn't be scanned in the time allotted. At the same time, the number of images had to be large enough so that people wouldn't be exactly sure how many they have seen. We arrived at the number seven. With four images, you always knew there were four, but by the time you got up to eight images you weren't quite sure. They were very big images – the width across four of them was half the length of a football field.
>
> (ibid., p. 333)

One journalist described it as "information overload – an avalanche of related data that comes at a viewer too fast for him to cull and reject it... a twelve-minute blitz." The viewer is overwhelmed. More than anything, the Eameses wanted an emotional response, produced as much by the excess of images as by their content:

> At the Moscow World's Fair in 1959 – when we used seven screens over an area that was over half the length of a football field – that was just a desperate attempt to make a credible statement to a group of people in Moscow when words had almost ceased to have meaning. We were telling the story straight, and we wanted to do it in 12 minutes, with images; but we found that we couldn't really give credibility to it in a linear way. However when we could put 50 images on the screen for a certain subject in a matter of 10 seconds, we got a kind of breadth which we felt we couldn't get any other way.[25]

The multi-screen technique went through one more significant development at the 1964 World's Fair in New York. In the IBM Ovoid Theater, designed by the Saarinen office, visitors boarded the "people wall" and were greeted by a "host" dressed in coattails who slowly dropped down from the IBM ovoid; the seated 500-person audience was then lifted up hydraulically from the ground level into the dark interior of the egg, where they were surrounded by 14 screens on which the Eameses projected the film *Think* (Hamilton, 1964, pp. 37–41). To enter the theater was no longer to cross the threshold, to pass through the ceremonial space of the entrance, as in a traditional public building. To enter here was to be lifted in front of a multiplicity of screens. The screens wrapped the audience in a way reminiscent of Herbert Bayer's 1930 "diagram of the field of vision," produced as a sketch for the installation of an architecture and furniture exhibition (Cohen, 1994, p. 292; Staniszewski, 1998, pp. 25–28). The eye could not escape the screens, and each screen was bordered by other screens. Unlike the screens in Moscow, those in the IBM building were of different sizes and shapes. But once again, the eye had to jump from image to image and could never fully catch up with all of them and their diverse contents. Fragments are presented to be momentarily linked together before the connections between them are replaced with others. The film is organized by the same logic of compression, its speed intended to be the speed of the mind.

A "host" welcomed the audience to "the IBM Information Machine":

> a machine designed to help me give you a lot of information in a very short time... [It] brings you information in much the same way as your mind gets it – in fragments and glimpses – sometimes relating to the same idea or incident. Like making toast in the morning.[26]

Already in 1959, the design team (Nelson, the Eameses, *et al.*) had used exactly the same term – "information machine" – to describe the role of Fuller's dome in Moscow, taking it from the title of a 1957 film that the Eameses had prepared for the 1958 Brussels World's Fair. In addition to the multi-screens, the dome housed a huge RAMAC 305 computer, an "electronic brain" that offered written replies to 3500 questions about life in the USA ('U.S. Gives Soviet Glittering Show', 1959, p. 2). The architecture was conceived from the very start as a combination of structure, multi-screen film and computer. Each technology created an architecture in which inside/outside and entering/leaving meant something entirely different, and yet they all coexisted. All were housed by the same physical structure, Fuller's dome, but each defined a different kind of space to be explored in different ways. From the "Sample Lesson" in 1953 to IBM in 1964, the Eameses treated architecture as a multi-channel information machine – and, equally, multi-media installations as a kind of architecture.

II

All of the Eameses' designs can be understood as multi-screen performances: they provide a framework in which objects can be placed and replaced. Even the parts of their furniture can be rearranged. Spaces are defined as arrays of information, collected and constantly changed by their users.

This is the space of the media. The space of a newspaper or an illustrated magazine is a grid in which information is arranged and rearranged as it comes in: a space the reader navigates in their own way, at a glance, or by fully entering a particular story. The reader, viewer or consumer constructs the space, participating actively in the design. It is a space where continuities are made through "cutting." The same is true of the space of newsreels and TV. The logic of the Eameses' multi-screens is simply the logic of the mass media.

It is not by chance that Charles Eames was always nostalgic for his time as a set designer for MGM in the early 1940s, continually arranging and rearranging existing props at short notice (Colomina, 1997, p. 129). All Eames architecture can be understood as set design. The Eameses even presented themselves like Hollywood figures, as if in a movie or an advertisement, always so happy, with the ever-changing array of objects as their backdrop.

This logic of architecture as a set for staging the good life was central to the design of the Moscow exhibition. Even the famous kitchen, for example, was cut in half not only to allow viewing by visitors but, most important, to turn it into a photo op for the Kitchen Debate. Photographers and journalists knew already the night before that they had to be there, choosing their angle. Architecture was reorganized to produce a certain image. Charles had already spoken, in 1950, of our time as the era of communication. He was acutely aware that the new media were displacing the old role of architecture. And yet everything for the Eameses, in this world of communication that they were embracing so happily, was architecture: "The chairs are architecture, the films – they have a structure, just as the front page of a newspaper has a structure. The chairs are literally like architecture in miniature... architecture you can get your hands on" (Gingerich, 1977, p. 327). In the notes for a letter to Italian architect Vittorio Gregotti accompanying a copy of *Powers of Ten*, they write:

> In the past fifty years the world has gradually been finding out something that architects have always known, that is, that *everything* is

> architecture. The problems of environment have become more and more interrelated. This is a sketch for a film that shows something of how large – and small – our environment is.[27]

In every sense, Eames architecture is all about the space of information. Perhaps we can talk no longer about "space" but, rather, about "structure" or, more precisely, about time. Structure, for the Eameses, was organization in time. The details that were central to Mies van der Rohe's architecture were replaced by "connections." As Charles says in a film about a storage system he and Ray had designed, "The details are not details. They make the product. The connections, the connections, the connections" (Eames, quoted in Caplan, 1976, p. 15). But, as Ralph Caplan points out, the connections in their work were not only between such "disparate materials as wood and steel" or between "seemingly alien disciplines" like physics and the circus but also between ideas. Their technique of information overload, used in films and multimedia presentations as well as in their trademark "information wall" in exhibitions, was used not to "overtax the viewer's brain" but precisely to offer a "broad menu of options" and to create an "impulse to make connections" (ibid., p. 43).

For the Eameses, structure was not linear. They often reflected on the impossibility of linear discourse. The structure of their exhibitions has been compared to that of a scholarly paper, loaded with footnotes, where "the highest level of participation consists in getting fascinated by the pieces and connecting them for oneself" (ibid., p. 45). Seemingly static structures like the frames of their buildings or of their plywood cabinets were but frameworks for positioning ever-changing objects. And the frame itself was, anyway, meant to be changed all the time. These changes, this fluctuating movement, could never be pinned down.

Mies van der Rohe's exhibition of his work at the Museum of Modern Art in 1947 was significant, according to the Eameses, not because of the individual objects on display but because of the organizational system that the architect had devised to present them (Colomina, 1997, p. 146), which communicated, in their view, the idea of Mies's architecture better than any single model, drawing or photograph could. When Charles published his photographs of the exhibition in *Arts & Architecture*, he wrote: "The significant thing seems to be the way in which he [Mies] has taken documents of his architecture and furniture and used them as elements in creating a space that says, 'this is what its all about.' "[28] (Eames, 1947, p. 27). The multi-screen presentations, the exhibition technique and the Eameses' films are likewise significant not because of the individual factoids they offer or even the story they tell but because of the way the factoids are used as elements in creating a space that says: "This is what the space of information is all about."

Like all architects, the Eameses controlled the space they produced. The most important factor was to regulate the flow of information. They prepared extremely detailed technical instructions for the running of even their simplest three-screen slide show.[29] Performances were carefully planned to appear as effortless as a circus act. Timing and the elimination of "noise" were the major considerations. Their office produced masses of documents, even drawings showing the rise and fall of intensity through the course of a film, literally defining the space they wanted to produce or, more precisely, the existing space of the media that they wanted to intensify. With *Glimpses*, the Eameses retained complete control over their work by turning up in Moscow only 48 hours before the opening, as Peter Blake recalls it, "dressed like a boy scout and a girl scout," clutching the reels of the film.[30] A photograph shows the smiling couple descending from the plane, reels in Charles' hands, posing for the camera. As he later put it,

> Theoretically, it was a statement made by our State Department, and yet we did it entirely here and it was never seen by anyone from our government until they saw it in Moscow... If you ask for criticism, you get it. If you don't, there is a chance everyone will be too busy to worry about it.
>
> (Gingerich, 1977, p. 333)

The experience for the audience in Moscow was almost overwhelming. Journalists speak of too many images, too much information, too fast. For the MTV and Internet generation watching the film today, it would not be fast enough, and yet we do not seem to have come that far either. The logic of the Internet was already spelled out in the Eameses' multi-screen projects. Coming out of the war mentality, the Eameses' innovations in the world of communication, their exhibitions, films, and multi-screen performances transformed the status of architecture. Their highly controlled flows of simultaneous images provided a space, an enclosure – the kind of space we now occupy continuously without thinking.

Notes

1. For transcripts of the debate, see "The Two Worlds: A Day-Long Debate", 1959, pp. 1–3; "When Nixon Took on Khrushchev" in "Setting Russia Straight on Facts about U.S.", 1959, pp. 36–39, 70–72; "Encounter", 1959, pp. 15–19; and "Better to See Once", 1959, pp. 12–14.
2. Khrushchev: "You Americans expect that the Soviet people will be amazed. It is not so. We have all these things in our new apartments." Nixon: "We do not claim to astonish the Soviet people" ("Setting Russia Straight on Facts about U.S.", 1959, pp. 36–37).
3. Box 202, *The Work of Charles and Ray Eames*, Manuscript Division, Library of Congress, Washington, DC.
4. *Circarama* had already been shown at the 1958 World's Fair in Brussels.
5. "The seven-screen quickie is intended as a general introduction to the fair. According to the votes of Russians, however, it is the most popular exhibit after the automobiles and the color television" (Frankel, 1959b, p. 8).
6. "Watching the thousands of colorful glimpses of the U.S. and its people, the Russians were entranced, and the slides are the smash hit of the fair" ("The U.S. in Moscow: Russia Comes to the Fair", 1959, p. 14).
7. "And Mr. Khrushchev watched unsmilingly as the real bomb-shell exploded – a huge exhibit of typical American scenes flashed on seven huge ceiling screens. Each screen shows a different scene but all seven at each moment are on the same general subject – housing, transportation, jazz and so forth. U.S. officials believe this is the real pile-driver of the fair, and the premier's phlegmatic attitude – not even smiling when seven huge Marilyn Monroes dashed on the screen or when Mr. Nixon pointed out golfing scenes – showed his unhappiness with the display" (Otten, 1959, p. 16).
8. From an interview with Wilder by Kirkham in 1993.
9. Charles and Ray Eames, *Glimpses of the USA*, working script, box 202, *The Work of Charles and Ray Eames*, Manuscript Division, Library of Congress, Washington, DC.
10. *Powers of Ten* was based on a 1957 book by Kees Boeke, *Cosmic View: The Universe in Forty Jumps*. The film was produced for the Commission on College Physics. An updated and more developed version was produced in 1977. In the second version the starting point is still a picnic scene but it takes place in a park bordering Lake Michigan in Chicago (see Neuhart *et al.*, 1989, pp. 336–337, 440–441).
11. See handwritten notes on the manuscript of the first version of *Powers of Ten*. Box 207, *The Work of Charles and Ray Eames*, Manuscript Division, Library of Congress, Washington, DC. The film is still referred to as *Cosmic View*.
12. *Glimpses*, working script.
13. In 1970, in the context of Charles Eames's third Charles Eliot Norton Lecture at Harvard University, where he once again insisted on the need to incorporate media into the classroom, he still spoke of changing forms of communications with reference to *Sputnik*: "In post-Sputnik panic, a great demand for taping science lectures; when they were shown on television,

distribution cost ended up as 100:1 of production cost; no way to run a railroad." Box 217, folder 10, *The Work of Charles and Ray Eames*, Manuscript Division, Library of Congress, Washington, DC.

14. Apparently even the forget-me-nots were understood in precisely the intended way, as symbols of friendship and loyalty. According to the Eameses, the audience could be heard saying "*nezabutki*," "forget-me-not," as the flowers appeared on the screen as the last image of the film (Neuhart *et al.*, 1989, p. 241).
15. For example, *Powers of Ten* was a "sketch film" to be presented at an "assembly of one thousand of America's top physicists," but the Eameses decided that it should "appeal to a ten-year-old as well as a physicist" (Schrader, 1970, p. 10).
16. "Grist for Atlanta paper version," manuscript, box 217, folder 15, *The Work of Charles and Ray Eames*, Manuscript Division, Library of Congress, Washington, DC.
17. Nelson, "Georgia Experiment."
18. Charles Eames, "Language of Vision," 17–18. See also the typescript of the actual lecture in box 217, folder 12, *The Work of Charles and Ray Eames*, Manuscript Division, Library of Congress, Washington, DC.
19. I am grateful to Dennis Doordan for pointing out this article to me.
20. Partial transcript of Norton Lectures, box 217, folder 10, *The Work of Charles and Ray Eames*, Manuscript Division, Library of Congress, Washington, DC. Square brackets appear in the original.
21. See, for example, Charles Eames, "On Reducing Discontinuity" (talk given at the American Academy of Arts and Sciences, 1976), manuscript, box 217, folder 17, *The Work of Charles and Ray Eames*, Manuscript Division, Library of Congress, Washington, DC: "My wife and I had made a commitment to disregard the sacred enclosure around a special set of phenomena called art; in our view preoccupation with respecting that boundary leads to an unfortunate and unwarranted limitation on the aesthetic experience."
22. Notes for second Norton Lecture, box 217, folder 10, *The Work of Charles and Ray Eames*, Manuscript Division, Library of Congress, Washington, DC. Eames is referring here to "Professor Lawrence Hill's Renaissance/".
23. " 'Communications Primer' was a recommendation to architects to recognize the need for more complex information…for new kinds of *models* of information." Eames, "Grist for Atlanta."
24. Charles and Ray Eames won an Emmy Award for graphics for their rapid cutting experiments on *The Fabulous Fifties*, a TV program broadcast on January 22, 1960, on the CBS network. It included six film segments made by the Eames Office (Schrader, 1970, p. 3).
25. Digby Diehl, "West Q&A: Charles Eames," transcript, box 24, folder 4–5, *The Work of Charles and Ray Eames*, Manuscript Division, Library of Congress, Washington, DC. Published as "Q&A: Charles Eames," *Los Angeles Times WEST Magazine*, October 8, 1972, reprinted in Digby Diehl (1974) *Supertalk* (New York: Doubleday).
26. Script of the IBM film *View from the People Wall* for the Ovoid Theater, New York World's Fair, 1964, *The Work of Charles and Ray Eames*, Manuscript Division, Library of Congress, Washington, DC.

27. "Powers of Ten – Gregotti," handwritten notes, box 217, folder 11, *The Work of Charles and Ray Eames*, Manuscript Division, Library of Congress, Washington, DC.
28. Charles Eames, "Mies van der Rohe" (photographs by Charles Eames taken at the Museum of Modern Art exhibition), *Arts & Architecture*, December 1947, 27.
29. "To Show a 3-Screen Slide Show," manuscript detailing the necessary preparations for an "Eames 3 screen 6 projectors slide show" with "sound" and "picture operation procedure," illustrated with multiple drawings, 14 pp., box 211, folder 10, *The Work of Charles and Ray Eames*, Manuscript Division, Library of Congress, Washington, DC.
30. Peter Blake, in *An Eames Celebration: The Several Worlds of Charles and Ray Eames*, WNET Television, New York, February 3, 1975 (quoted in Kirkham, 1995, p. 320).

Bibliography

Abercrombie, Stanley (1995) *George Nelson: The Design of Modern Design* (Cambridge, MA: MIT Press).

Albrecht, Donald (1997) *The Work of Charles and Ray Eames* (New York: Abrams).

Ballentine, Bill (1982) *Clown Alley* (Boston: Little, Brown).

"Better to See Once" (1959) *Time*, 3 August, 12–14.

Braune, Michael (1966) "The Wit of Technology", *Architectural Design*, September, 449–457.

Caplan, Ralph (1976) "Making Connections: The Work of Charles and Ray Eames", in *Connections: The Work of Charles and Ray Eames* (Los Angeles: University of California).

Cohen, Arthur A. (1994) *Herbert Bayer: The Complete Work* (Cambridge: MIT Press).

Colomina, Beatriz (1997) "Reflections on the Eames House", in Albrecht, Donald (ed.) *The Work of Charles and Ray Eames* (New York: Abrams).

Diehl, Digby (1972) "West Q&A: Charles Eames" [transcript], *The Work of Charles and Ray Eames*, box 24, folder 4–5. Manuscript Division, Library of Congress, Washington, DC.

Eames, Charles (1947) "Mies van der Rohe", *Arts & Architecture*, December, 27.

Eames, Charles (1974) "Language of Vision: The Nuts and Bolts", *Bulletin of the American Academy of Arts and Sciences*, October, 17–18.

Eames, Charles and Eames, Ray (1949–1988) *The Work of Charles and Ray Eames*, boxes 202, 207, 211, 217. Manuscript Division, Library of Congress, Washington, DC.

"Encounter" (1959) *Newsweek*, 3 August, 15–19.

Frankel, Max (1959a) "Dust from Floor Plagues U.S. Fair", *New York Times*, July 28.

Frankel, Max (1959b) "Image of America at Issue in Soviet", *New York Times*, 23 August, 8.

Gingerich, Owen (1977) "A Conversation with Charles Eames", *American Scholar*, 46, no. 3 (Summer), 326–337.

Hamilton, Mina (1964) "Films at the Fair II", *Industrial Design*, May, 37–41.

Katz, Barry (1996) "The Arts of War: "Visual Presentation" and National Intelligence", *Design Issues*, 12(2) (Summer), 3–21.

Kirkham, Pat (1995) *Charles and Ray Eames: Designers of the Twentieth Century* (Cambridge: MIT Press).
Life (1959), Cover, 10 August.
Lipstadt, Hélène (1997) "Natural Overlap: Charles and Ray Eames and the Federal Government", in Albrecht, Donald (ed.) *The Work of Charles and Ray Eames: A Legacy of Invention* (New York: Abrams).
Marling, Karal Ann (1994) *As Seen on TV: The Visual Culture of Everyday Life in the 1950s* (Cambridge: Harvard University Press).
May, Elaine Tyler (1994) *Homeward Bound: American Families in the Cold War Era* (New York: Basic Books).
Nelson, George (1954) "The Georgia Experiment: An Industrial Approach to Problems of Education", Manuscript (October).
Neuhart, John, Neuhart, Marilyn and Eames, Ray (1989) *Eames Design: The Work of the Office of Charles and Ray Eames* (New York: Harry N. Abrams).
Otten, Alan L. (1959) "Russians Eagerly Tour U.S. Exhibit Despite Cool Official Attitude", *Wall Street Journal*, 28 July, 16.
Schrader, Paul (1970) "Poetry of Ideas: The Films of Charles Eames", *Film Quarterly*, 23(3) (Spring), 2–19.
"Setting Russia Straight on Facts about U.S." (1959) *U.S. News and World Report*, 3 August, 36–39, 70–72.
Staniszewski, Mary Anne (1998) *The Power of Display: A History of Exhibition Installations at the Museum of Modern Art* (Cambridge: MIT Press).
Talmey, Allene (1959) "Eames", *Vogue*, 15 August, 144.
"The Two Worlds: A Day-Long Debate" (1959) *New York Times*, 15 July, 1–3.
"The U.S. in Moscow: Russia Comes to the Fair" (1959) *Time*, 3 August, 14.
"U.S. Gives Soviet Glittering Show" (1959) *New York Times*, 25 July, 2.
"When Nixon Took on Khrushchev" (1959) *U.S. News and World Report*, 3 August.

3
Mapping Orbit: Toward a Vertical Public Space

Lisa Parks

Buckminster Fuller's Dymaxion Map (Figure 3.1) first surfaced as a sketch in 1927 entitled "One-Town World." A decade and a half later, in 1943, *Life* magazine published a refined version of it called the "Air Ocean World map." By 1954 the Dymaxion Air Ocean World map had become the full expression of what Fuller referred to as "Spaceship Earth" (Marks, 1960, p. 50). As it circulated, one of Fuller's biographers explains, "many geographic facts, not usually observed, became dramatically apparent" (ibid., p. 50). The final version of the map represents the planet as an island in one ocean without any visible distortion of the relative shapes and sizes of the land areas and without splitting any continents. It is relevant to the mapping of orbit for several reasons. First, it exemplifies an experimental and conceptual approach to the mapping of earth that challenges methods and assumptions of traditional cartography, which tend to reinforce elements that divide societies, obscuring the relational patterns emerging from processes of globalization. Second, it foregrounds principles of contiguity and integration by presenting the earth, air and oceans as continuous domains, and in so doing implies that change in one inevitably affects conditions in another. Third, it became a template for the demonstration and analysis of the unequal distribution and use of world energy resources, and thus articulated broader global political, economic and environmental concerns (ibid., pp. 50–53). Finally, the map changed the ways in which the public thought about the world as well as the ways in which geographers thought about mapping it.

Earlier versions of this paper were presented at the Mapping Maps conference at the University of Siegen and the Mobility and Fantasy in Visual Culture conference at Bahçeşehir Üniversitesi in Istanbul. I am grateful to the participants for their questions and feedback.

Figure 3.1 Buckminster Fuller's Dymaxion map
Source: Reprinted under the Wikimedia commons license; http://en.wikipedia.org/wiki/Dymaxion_map

This essay builds upon the conceptual impulses of the Dymaxion map to explore the mapping of orbital space. Surprisingly, there is very little work in the field of geography[1] on this topic and many of the orbital maps that do exist are proprietary, which means that they are often costly, and public access to them is limited. This is ironic given that public taxpayers have paid billions of dollars over the past 50 years to subsidize the development and installation of thousands of satellites in orbit. Orbit is now home to a satellite meta-infrastructure that enables telecommunication, direct broadcasting, remote sensing and global positioning around the planet. Satellites are used to relay radio, TV, telephony and Internet signals, to monitor the earth's surface for weather reports, natural resource development and military campaigns, and to support navigation on land, in the air and at sea. While many people have encountered satellite TV, remote-sensing imagery or GPS navigation, strikingly few understand how orbital space is structured to make such practices possible. Whether citizens are viewing TV news reports, drawing cash from an ATM machine, driving through city streets or using Google Earth, they are participating in a world historical process that is shaped by satellite technologies. Since so many signals, transactions, images and events either take shape within or pass through orbital space, it is in the public interest to know how this space is organized, who controls it and how it has been contested.

To address these issues, this essay explores how orbit has been imagined and visualized in a series of maps gathered from various sources on the Internet. I use the word "map" broadly to include diagrams, models, interfaces and illustrations. By invoking the mapping of orbit I am referring both to cartography's precise systems of measurement and to other non-scientific imaginings, simulations and approximations of orbital space. Such visualizations play a key role in making orbital space intelligible to citizen-viewers and enabling them to understand it as a dynamic domain of global significance. The mapping of orbit involves specifying the locations of orbital paths, satellites and earth stations that make up this global infrastructure, rendering movements and activities that occur between earth and orbit, recognizing the disparate political interests of orbital players, such as military agencies, telecommunication firms and non-profit organizations, attending to problems of scale and speed, and acknowledging satellites and orbital events as part of world history. Mapping orbit involves trying to be detailed and precise about a place that is inaccessible and imperceptible to most people.

While industrialized nation-states have dominated orbit for decades,[2] developing countries have challenged this hegemony on multiple occasions. The first section of this essay provides a contextual discussion that explores the legal definition of outer (and orbital) space as a space of equal access and mutual benefits, and highlights historical moments when orbit became a contested domain. Drawing on international treaties and critical scholarship, I suggest that orbit should be thought of as a "vertical public space" that extends from the earth's surface to the outer limits of orbit, a space that has historically been struggled over by multiple competing interests. In a world dominated by global capitalism and militarism, a vertical space cannot remain "public" without a struggle to define and maintain it as such. In the second section of the essay, I suggest that the mapping and visualization of orbit are vital to the process of claiming it as public. Since physical occupations of orbit are impossible for most, struggles over this domain must take place within the symbolic economy. To draw attention to this contested terrain, I critically examine a series of orbital maps and develop four categories of orbital mapping:

- otherworldly perspectives;
- satellite-centric views;
- orbital projections;
- conceptual maps.

Using examples, I demonstrate the kind of knowledges and critical questions that such visualizations can generate, while also pointing to their limitations. Just as the Dymaxion map challenged citizen-viewers to think differently about the relations between continents or between the lands, air and oceans, orbital maps can encourage them to become more acutely aware of the material relations and historical processes that extend into, unfold within and structure this extraterritorial domain. By putting orbital space into discourse, the orbital map also brings opportunities to (re)claim this vertical field as a public domain.

Contesting orbit

The etymology of "orbit" has a long history that is linked to vision and movement. In Old French (circa 1314), "orbit" referred to the "eye socket" (Oxford Dictionaries, 2004). In classical Latin it had been used to signify a "wheel-track" or the "path of a celestial object" (ibid.) By the late seventeenth century, astronomical use of "orbit" became common, especially in efforts to describe the course of the moon or sun. More recently, orbit has been used figuratively to refer to "a fixed course or path" or to a "sphere of activity, influence, or application within which a person or thing normally moves or operates" (ibid.) Not until the twentieth century, in the early days of the space age, did the verb "to orbit" come into use within the English language. By 1946, "to orbit" meant "to travel round (especially a celestial object)" and came to be associated with particular patterns of movement around the earth or other planets (ibid.)

In contemporary times, the word is commonly used to describe the band of space surrounding the earth trafficked by satellites. This area, which extends from the earth's surface to approximately 60,000 km above it, is organized into different orbital domains or paths, including the geostationary orbit (GEO), medium earth orbit (MEO), low earth orbit (LEO) and super-synchronous or parking orbit. Each is typically used for different satellite applications: GEO is used for telecommunication and broadcasting, MEO is used for global positioning and LEO is used for remote sensing. While paths in LEO and MEO are relatively unregulated, to send a satellite into GEO a country must file a multi-stage proposal with the International Telecommunications Union (ITU). Once the proposal is approved, the applicant receives orbital slot and frequency assignments. Orbit is thus a composite resource made up of a physical location (orbital slot and path) and access to the electromagnetic spectrum (frequency assignment).

The concept of orbit is so tightly tethered to scientific innovation, national security and corporate expansion that it is scarcely invoked in relation to public interests or public space. Like many terrestrial spaces, however, orbit is a highly valued and hotly contested domain. In 1983, after more than 20 years of satellite deployments, legal scholar Siegfried Wiessner called upon the international community to "build the public order of the geostationary orbit," proclaiming, "technology and human ingenuity have made the band of space around the planet a natural resource of advanced global civilization. They have not devised an equally advanced public order for its regulation" (Wiessner, 1983, pp. 235, 273). He went on to define orbit as a *res publica internationalis* (a site of "international public affairs") and proposed a new regulatory regime based on a "congruence of interests and the experience of mutual benefits" (ibid., p. 274). Significantly, Wiessner's vision of orbit as a kind of global commons set out to challenge the orbital hegemony of the USA and the USSR, but it also promulgated a liberal pluralist ideology, assuming there were readily identifiable mutual benefits and shared interests in orbit among nations around the world. Such a view ultimately failed to acknowledge the structural inequities among different nations as well as their different dispositions toward orbital space.

Nevertheless, Wiessner's case for a public order of the GEO relied upon earlier legal precedents and political challenges. In 1967 the United Nations' Treaty on Principles Governing the Activities of States in the Exploration and Use of Outer Space, including the Moon and Other Celestial Bodies was signed in the USA, the UK and the USSR. The "Outer Space Treaty," as it is known, established a legal framework for activities in orbit, on the moon and beyond, and it remains the primary regulatory structure for outer space, having been ratified by 98 United Nations members and signed by 27 others as of 2006 (United Nations Office for Outer Space Affairs, 2011). First signed on January 27, 1967, the treaty mandated that the exploration and use of outer space, including orbital space, "shall be carried out for the benefit and in the interests of all countries, irrespective of their degree of economic or scientific development, and shall be the province of all mankind" (US Department of State, 1967). It insisted that outer space should not be "subject to national appropriation by claim of sovereignty, by means of use or occupation, or by any other means" (ibid.) And it instructed signatories "not to place in orbit around the earth any objects carrying nuclear weapons or any other kinds of weapons of mass destruction" (ibid.) In short, the treaty espoused principles of international equality, peace and collaboration, and recognized the right of all countries to access and use outer space (and orbital space), regardless of the level of their financial and scientific resources.

In his essay "The Invention of Air Space, Outer Space, and Cyberspace," James Hay suggests that extraterritorial domains have historically been "invented" within juridical and political discourses precisely so that they could be regulated and used to articulate the ideals of liberal democracies. In relation to the Outer Space Treaty, Hay observes, "'Outer space' became a new historical, geographic, and theatrical/performative *stage* for shaping a discourse about rights and responsibilities, war and peace, security and risk – and thus for redefining the objectives of government and of national sovereignty on a global scale" (Hay, 2012). As the first field of outer space exploration, orbit became an important dimension of this new "stage" as Western governments used it to showcase the new frontiers of entrepreneurial freedoms along with the sprawling reach of national security. As more satellites were launched, more questions and concerns emerged about how and whether governance and sovereignty could operate in this vertical field.

Despite the Outer Space Treaty's high ideals, only a handful of nation-states had the resources to develop and launch satellites during the 1960s (the USA, the USSR, the UK, Canada, France and Germany). As a result, the organization tasked with the assignment of GEO orbit slots, the ITU, decided to grant orbital slots on a "first come first served" basis, which some felt flagrantly violated the equal access principles of the Outer Space Treaty. Developing countries responded to what they perceived as the ITU's favoritism toward wealthy industrialized states in different ways. Recognizing that orbit had become a valuable resource, in 1976 several equatorial states, led by Colombia, asserted sovereignty over the GEO superjacent to their terrestrial borders (Declaration of the First Meeting of Equatorial Countries, 1974). In a vivid demonstration of bottom-up power, Colombia, Brazil, Republic of the Congo, Ecuador, Indonesia, Kenya, Uganda and Zaire (now Democratic Republic of the Congo) declared their sovereignty through the vertical field that extended from their national lands on earth up through the orbital space above them, issuing a bold challenge to countries that already occupied orbital slots. The Bogotá Declaration, as it is known, also mandated that any future satellites to be placed in orbital slots above these equatorial countries would require the country's consent.

Unable to occupy orbit themselves, the signatories of the Bogotá Declaration waged their battle over orbit within the symbolic economy. Declaring their sovereignty in orbit became a way of reminding the world that orbit had been defined as a "non-sovereign" domain "open to all countries," and yet was being rapidly colonized by wealthy world superpowers. As Christy Collis explains,

> While Bogotá did not succeed in transforming the GEO into the property of equatorial states, it did firmly situate developing states on the agenda of GEO spatial considerations: that developing states should have equitable access was now largely accepted; that transforming the GEO into Earth-bound sovereign territory was the way to accomplish this was refused.
>
> (Collis, 2012)

The Bogotá Declaration demonstrated that developing countries recognized the value of orbit and sought to benefit from it. By the end of 1986, however, almost half of all geostationary satellites were controlled by the USA alone (Delzeit and Beal, 1996). Given the startling inequality in the possession of orbital slots, the ITU established an *a priori* policy whereby every country would be allowed at least one orbital position, and countries could submit applications to control slots even if they did not yet have funding to build and launch a satellite to occupy it (ibid.)[3] During the 1990s, the Kingdom of Tonga in the Pacific set out to capitalize upon these conditions. Rather than declare its sovereignty in the orbital space overhead, it planned to acquire valuable GEO slots in the Asia/Pacific region. By late 1990 the country had partnered with retired American entrepreneur Matt C. Nilson (who had previously worked for Comsat and Intelsat) to form a company called Tongasat, and had acquired 16 unused orbital slots over the Pacific region that could be used to link North America and Asia (Andrews, 1990b). Since Tonga lacked funds to build and launch its own satellites, it planned to lease these slots to other satellite operators for $2 million per year or to the highest bidder (ibid.; see also Andrews, 1990a). Tonga's maneuver to become an orbital landlord with "paper satellites" became highly controversial (Price, 2002, p. 151). Intelsat argued that these prime orbital slots with a footprint of 3.5 billion people should be allotted to established satellite operators that are prepared to serve populations throughout the Asia/Pacific region (Mendosa, 1994).[4] In the end, several countries, including the USA, complained to the ITU about Tonga's legal filings and the island nation was left with only seven slots. Plagued by internal business disputes, Tongasat never had funding to build its own satellite, but in 2002 it purchased the used Comstar 1D satellite from Comsat, renamed it ESIAFI-1 (or "Star Trail") and operated it for approximately three years at 70 degrees east over the Indian Ocean (Tongasat, 2002).

As the Bogotá Declaration and the case of Tongasat reveal, orbital space has historically been a contested domain. In both instances, developing countries asserted control over orbital space by relying on the equal access principles of the Outer Space Treaty, while challenging other aspects of the treaty (e.g. non-sovereignty) in the process. Rather than actually occupying orbital slots, these countries claimed them symbolically through a formal declaration and ITU legal filings. Battles staged in a symbolic economy are all the more crucial when they cannot occur in a physical location. To be able to make such claims, the equatorial states and Tongasat had to imagine a vertical field of power relations, while recognizing that the value of and access to orbital space are determined by hegemonic forces on earth. As Barney Warf aptly puts it, "while satellites float thousands of kilometres overhead, the determinants of access and use are firmly grounded in terrestrial politics" (Warf, 2007, p. 394).

In a world defined by various hierarchizations, the subordinated are all too familiar with vertical metaphors and operations of power. If orbit is yet another domain for such relations to take shape, then it can also become a site for exposing and contesting them. The Bogotá Declaration and Tongasat case are important because they are historical moments in which the meanings of orbit converged with the political imaginary of the subordinated. These events altered the geopolitical stage of outer space by challenging orbital hegemony. The capacity to imagine how power operates through this vertical field is key to future challenges to this dominant order. One way to encourage such imaginings is through the mapping of orbital space. Maps can enable citizen-viewers to feel some material connection to a location or process that is remote, both physically and intellectually. Being able to visualize the new sovereignty boundaries asserted by the equatorial states in the Bogotá Declaration, or the stretch of GEO Tongasat sought to control, could renew and extend the discursive terrain upon which these struggles played out and trigger further public interest and involvement in orbital contestations.

Verticality and visuality

If mapping is part of the process of inventing a space and rendering it intelligible within discourse, then the mapping of orbit is crucial to its inscription within public consciousness. Mapping – the act of laying out the elements, contours or dimensions of a space – is a familiar technique of representation and positioning. The map invites the citizen-viewer to situate, orient or imagine herself in relation to the space represented. In the process, a relation of knowledge is produced as the citizen-viewer uses the map's visual information to draw inferences about and make sense of an abstract terrain. Viewing a map can be a pragmatic exercise, but it can also generate affective responses, triggering such feelings as intimacy, curiosity, fear, contempt and possession. Since public access to orbital maps is limited (especially compared with world maps), it is difficult to ascertain how they might be engaged with affectively. Suffice it to say, the mapping of orbit has the potential to inscribe orbital space and practices within the political imaginary – to bring this domain down to earth and into a field of discursive relations.

Orbital maps use the visual languages of cartography, graphic design, data visualization and, in some rare cases, photography to generate two-dimensional representations of a vast domain that encircles the earth and extends up to 60,000 km away from its surface. While orbital maps rely on familiar conventions of world cartography, they also confront new problems of directionality, speed and scale in their attempts to represent phenomena and fields far beyond the earth's surface. Orbital maps reduce the depth and eliminate the motion that characterize this vertical space so that it can be read as a flat, framed surface. Despite their limitations, without such maps it would be difficult to develop a material sense of orbital space – to be able to imagine it as a site of occupation, structure and value.

When thinking about the mapping of orbit from a critical perspective, a series of questions arise: How has orbital space been mapped and visualized both historically and in contemporary times? Who has mapped orbit? To what end? How is the spectator positioned in relation to these representations? What aspects of these maps, visualizations or models shape public consciousness of and literacies about the organization and uses of orbital space? What challenges do satellites and orbital space present to knowledge systems that are organized around visual observation? How can orbit be mapped in more creative and provocative ways? To begin to address these questions I critically examine a selection of orbital maps and delineate four categories of orbital mapping:

- otherworldly perspectives;
- satellite-centric views;
- orbital projections;
- conceptual maps.

In the process of developing these categories, I highlight the kind of knowledges that can be gleaned from orbital maps that have been produced by professional cartographers, NASA scientists, graphic designers and artists. While some maps discussed fit neatly into one category, others are relevant across several. My intention is to provide an overview of the different ways in which orbital space has been mapped and to suggest that acts of reading and engaging with orbital maps can become an important dimension of struggling over vertical public space.

Otherworldly perspectives

Like many historical world maps, some orbital maps are envisioned from an otherworldly perspective. These views typically feature the earth in a galactic context surrounded by empty dark space. Orbital paths are conveyed by thin lines that encircle the earth or by icons representing satellites. The implied spectator is situated deeper in outer space, as if part of another world, and possesses a panoramic view of the earth and the space surrounding it. This perspective has been discussed by a number of scholars. Denis Cosgrove, for instance, characterizes it as an "Apollonian gaze" that "pulls diverse life on earth into a vision of unity...a divine mastering view from a single perspective" (Cosgrove, 2001, p. xi). He continues "that view is at once empowering and visionary, implying ascent from the terrestrial sphere into the zones of planets and stars..." (ibid.) Jody Berland describes this view of the "planetary body" (especially the Earth shot photos by Apollo astronauts) as a "metonym for global technocratic power," suggesting: "In fusing together monumental technological, commercial, and military resources, the panoptic lens arouses ecological awakening and cybernetic management, and the militarized technological sublime is reharmonized as a planetary icon" (Berland, 2009, pp. 257, 256). Finally, this otherworldly perspective could be imagined as a cosmic-level reverse shot, a literal or figurative position of interest in, concern about or response to earthly extensions into outer space, one from which earth is "read back" to us from a *different* place.[5]

In any case, this otherworldly perspective has persisted for centuries and many contemporary orbital maps continue to rely upon this same visual template. Analytical Graphics, Inc. (AGI), a company that designs many orbital maps, produced one that employs this view to illustrate the GEO orbit as a 360-degree ring around the earth with orbital slots indicated from 0–180 degrees east to 0–180 degrees west (see Figure 3.2). Small spheres encircle the earth to indicate the positions of satellites and the spheres are color-coded according to which parts of the radio spectrum they use.[6] The map also illustrates the practice of co-location – the stacking of multiple satellites at the same orbital address – and thus facilitates awareness of differential orbital property values. Certain

Figure 3.2 The GEO belt, Analytical Graphics, Inc. This is a map of satellites in the GEO
Source: Reprinted under the fair use doctrine; http://www.hobbyspace.com/AAdmin/Images/LivingSpace/stk/geo_belt_1024.jpg

orbital slots are more valuable because they are positioned above densely populated regions or markets. For instance, seven satellites owned by Luxembourg-based company SES Astra (Astra 1A, 1B, 1C, 1D, 1F, 1G and 1H) are co-located at 19.2 degrees east. SES Astra claims that it can carry 800 TV channels to 105 million homes in Europe from this orbital address (SES, 2011). A similarly lucrative orbital slot lies above North America at 101 degrees west, where seven satellites are co-located, including several owned by USA satellite TV giant DirecTV. Co-location allows satellite operators to extract maximum value from an orbital slot. This map (Figure 3.3) enables viewers to distinguish slots in the GEO, learn the names of the satellites that occupy them, recognize different parts of the spectrum they use and identify the most valuable orbital addresses. The map privileges an orderly and controlled view of the GEO that makes all satellite operations appear similar and seamless. Such a view effaces the dynamism and temporality of this domain, the complex and high-speed signal transactions that occur onboard each of these satellites as their transponders relay transmissions around the planet.

Another example of an orbital map with an otherworldly perspective comes from NASA's Orbital Debris program office. This visualizes

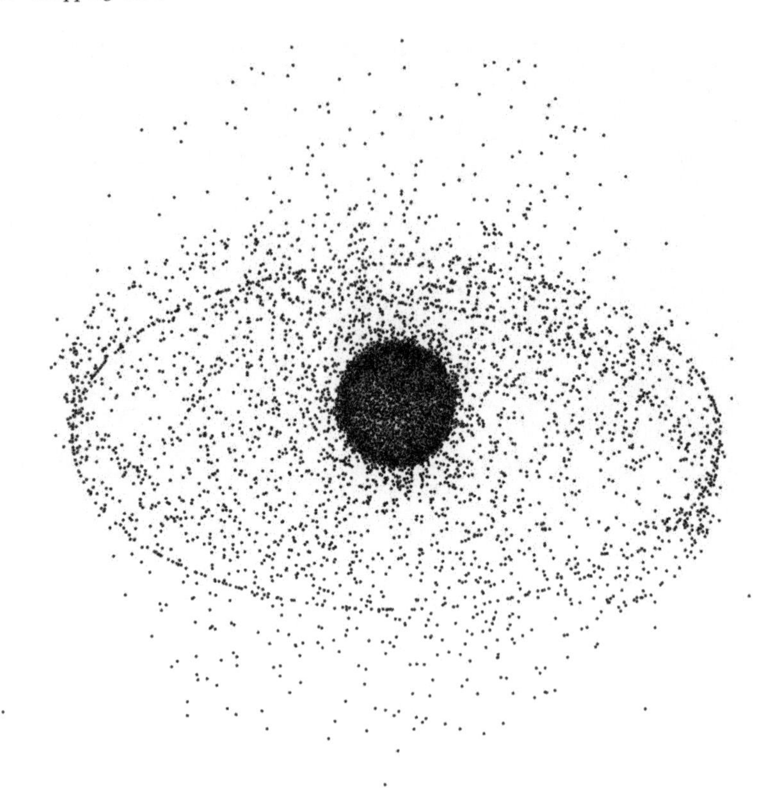

Figure 3.3 Orbiting objects in the LEO and the GEO, NASA. In this map, black dots represent orbiting objects concentrated in the LEO (nearly obscuring the earth's surface in the illustration) and the GEO (revealed by the ring of satellites along the outer edges)
Source: Reprinted courtesy of NASA Orbital Debris Program; http://earthobservatory.nasa.gov/Features/OrbitsCatalog/page3.php

data collected by the US Space Surveillance System, which tracks all objects in orbit larger than 10 cm in diameter (Figure 3.3). Each black dot represents a functioning satellite, an inactive satellite or a piece of debris. Approximately 95% of the black dots represent debris. The map showcases the thick accumulation of human-made materials floating in LEO, GEO, MEO and super-synchronous orbits. Since only 5% of the objects represented are functioning satellites, the map also reveals that orbital space has become a graveyard filled with dead satellites and dysfunctional parts.[7] In doing so, it draws viewers' attention to the problem of orbital pollution and raises questions about the effects of these materials upon the earth's environment.

Satellite-centric views

The next series of maps provide greater specificity about satellites in orbit and identify them by name. In some cases they are accompanied by a discussion of the function of the satellite or an event related to it. In other cases they offer detailed views of particular stretches of orbital space to highlight the satellites located there. One NASA visualization called "Eyes on the Earth" (Figure 3.4, also presented from an other-worldly perspective) features 14 remote-sensing satellites in LEO with unique pictograms representing each one. The illustration encourages the viewer to learn the names of satellites that generate remote-sensing imagery of the earth, discover their different shapes and sizes, and recognize their low earth orbit which positions them to scan and sense the earth's surface. While these particular remote-sensing satellites are

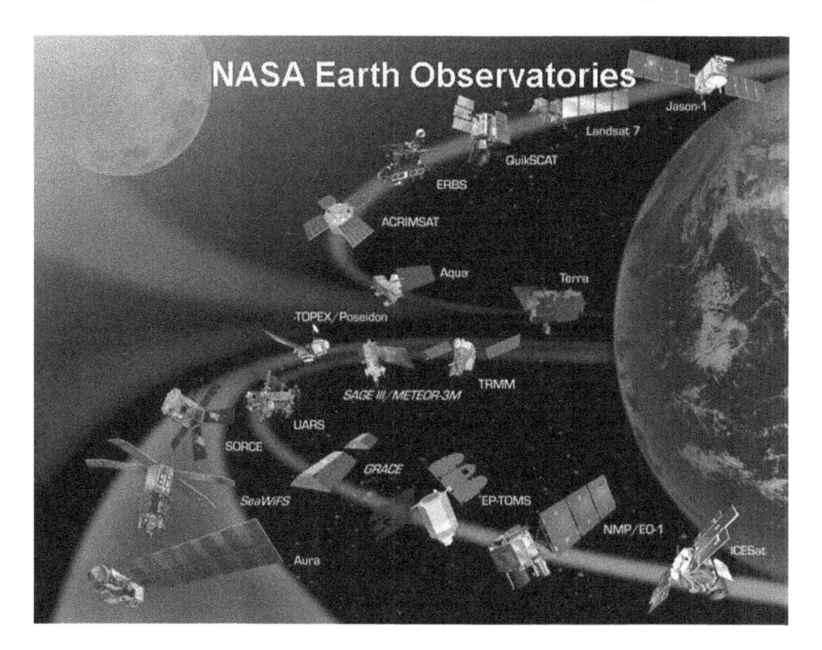

Figure 3.4 Eyes on the Earth, NASA. This diagram features 14 remote-sensing satellites by name

Source: Reprinted courtesy of NASA; http://www.nasa.gov/externalflash/eyes/

publicly known, it is important to remember that there are hundreds of secret or classified satellites in LEO used for military reconnaissance and warfare. Though taxpaying publics have funded these secret satellites, maps of their orbital paths are not available. A small group of amateur satellite trackers has, however, managed to photograph some of these secret satellites in an effort to circulate knowledge about them (Paglen, 2009, pp. 97–125).

Another satellite-centric map shows communication satellites located in the GEO above North America.[8] Representing the orbital arc from 72 degrees west to 129 degrees west, the map identifies 22 satellites by name and orbital address. Such maps can be used as a reference by uplink operators and broadcasters when shopping for inexpensive transponder time in the same orbital vicinity. Satellite-centric maps often feature a regionalized stretch of orbital space since it is difficult to represent the entire domain in a single frame. A related visualization is a rare long exposure (8.5 hours) photograph of another arc of the GEO taken from the Kitt Peak Observatory in Arizona (Figure 3.5). Here the lines represent star trails and the bright tiny dots mark the positions of geostationary satellites. The photo shows 38 satellites in the geostationary arc from 95 to 131 degrees west, which comprises nearly 10% of satellites in the GEO. The image's abstraction and remoteness reveal that even the world's most powerful observatories strain to see orbiting satellites from a photorealist perspective. Yet this satellite-centric map was generated by capturing and storing light reflected off of the satellites' surfaces and thus it provides an indexical record of satellites in this stretch of the GEO.

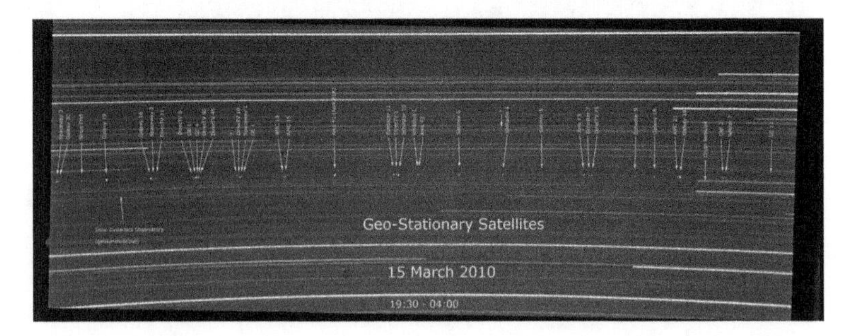

Figure 3.5 Geostationary satellites, William Livingstone. This long-exposure 2010 photograph taken from the Kitt Peak Observatory reveals 38 satellites in the GEO

Source: Reprinted courtesy of Dr William Livingstone.

Orbital projections

While otherworldly and satellite-centric views illustrate orbital paths, identify satellites and reveal material accumulations around the earth, others project orbital activities onto world maps. In orbital projections, lines, icons and shading are overlaid on world maps to convey a satellite's orbit or the boundary of its coverage zone or "footprint." If cartography can be understood as a process of projection in which the cartographer envisions and designs a world on paper (or on screen) from an overhead imaginary perspective, then the orbital projection further elaborates this process. The orbital projection is a "layering of projections": graphics signifying orbital slots, paths and objects that are physically located in the opposite direction are inscribed on the world map. The orbital projection confronts problems of directionality and scale. It asks the viewer to look at a world map and imagine activity happening in the opposite direction – in the vertical field above and around the earth. Since most humans have no physical referent for orbital space, they can only engage with such maps on an abstract level. As Rudolf Arnheim suggests in *The Power of the Center*, "the spatial involvement of the viewer diminishes when the scale of the map ceases to resemble the kind of landscape a traveler can actually encompass with his eyes but presents whole continents" (Arnheim, 1982, p. 20). He associates such representations of the vertical dimension with "the realm of visual contemplation" and aligns those of the horizontal with "the realm of activity" (ibid., pp. 12–13). The orbital projection has the potential to fuse these realms.

An example of orbital projection can be seen in a commemorative map of astronaut John Glenn's orbit of the earth on February 20, 1962.[9] The map overlays the trajectory of Glenn's Mercury-Atlas 6 mission upon a world map using a curved line to indicate its orbital path. The map also uses circles to specify the locations of tracking stations that monitored the spacecraft as it passed overhead. By projecting Glenn's orbit onto a world map, this visualization brings orbital activity into the register of world history, grafting faraway processes we cannot see onto a familiar surface. At the same time, however, the map is a quintessential expression of American nationalism. It commemorates Glenn's orbit by showcasing the capacities to move through, track and map this new domain, and it places the USA smack at its center.

A more recent example of orbital projection can be found on the Heavens Above website, which is a portal to information about all publicly known satellites currently in orbit, whether operational or retired

(Heavens Above, 2011). Drawing on data from United States Strategic Command (which tracks more than 13,000 objects in space), the Heavens Above interface displays the current location of any given satellite or object by projecting it onto a scene of the earth and providing a list of data about the satellite, including its orbit, inclination, perigee (the point at which the satellite is closest to the earth), apogee (the point at which the satellite is furthest from the earth) and revolutions per day. Given its interactive design, the interface offers a more tactile visual experience, allowing the user to press the keypad and manipulate the mouse to see and access elements of orbital space. As the website offers users the opportunity to "touch" the Heavens Above, it also provides useful information to civilians around the world who, for one reason or another, are tracking satellites.

Analytical Graphics Inc. has used the same data to generate a layer (kmz file) for Google Earth. This superimposes icons that represent orbiting satellites onto views of the earth and enables the user to see all objects tracked in real time (Figure 3.6). Like the Heaven's Above website, when the user clicks on a satellite icon, information about the satellite and its orbital trajectory appear (Amato, 2008). The mapping of orbit in Google Earth, however, seems to test the platform's capacities because the layer attempts to visualize so much data that the interface becomes congested with a dense fog of satellite icons as the user zooms

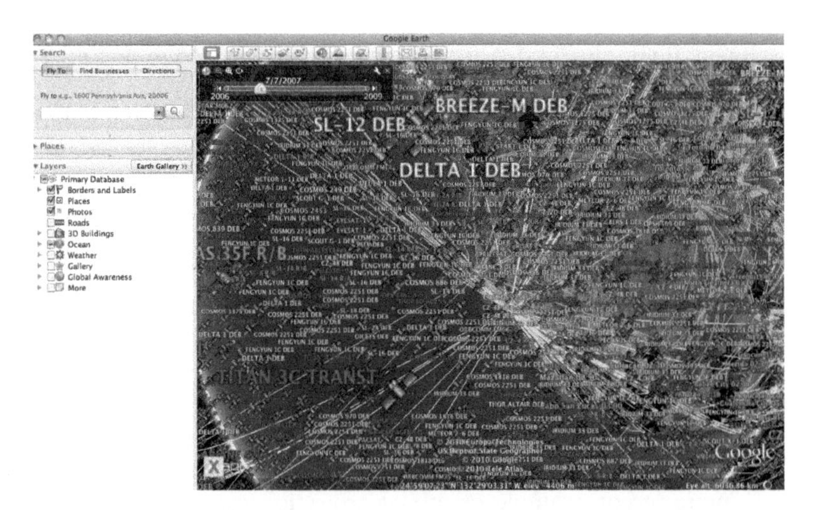

Figure 3.6 Screen capture of AGI satellite layer, Google Earth. This Google Earth interface features a congested field of satellite icons when the AGI satellite layer is activated

Source: Reprinted under the fair use doctrine.

in. Furthermore, while the orbital data are public, when accessed and viewed in Google Earth they become part of a privatized mediascape since Google claims it owns the right to present and view the earth and orbit in this way (Vaidhyanathan, 2011; Parks, 2012). What is unique about the Google Earth projection is that it exemplifies a kind of "satellitization of the interface" in that icons representing orbiting satellites are superimposed onto composited scenes of the earth that have been generated by satellite and aerial imagery. In principle, the user should be able to use the Google Earth layer to locate the very satellite(s) that gathered the image-data upon which the satellite icon is projected. Thus, more than an interactive gateway to orbit, the Google Earth interface functions as a kind of rearview or overview mirror, revealing the satellites that produced the very scenes that enable the world to be seen and navigated in this way.

Another important kind of orbital projection is the footprint map. Here, lines or shading are used to reveal the geographic boundaries in which a signal from a given satellite can be received. These maps also visualize the different beams (directed, partial coverage patterns) available on the same satellite. Footprint maps are distributed by the companies that own and operate communication satellites. In a sense, they function as cartographic billboards in that they illustrate a satellite's footprint(s) as part of the process of marketing transponder space to potential customers. At the same time they reveal the ways in which satellites transform world territories into vast transnational marketplaces and zones of media reception. On Lyngsat's website, for instance, a footprint map of the Astra 1H satellite at 19.2 degrees east can be found (along with those of many other satellites).[10] It shows the area across Europe in which Astra 1H's signal can be received, and it is color-coded so as to indicate that those on the perimeter of the footprint need a larger dish to receive a signal, with blue indicating a dish diameter of 65–85 cm, yellow indicating 55–65 cm and pink indicating 50–60 cm. The world is now crisscrossed by such footprints. There are in fact more satellite footprints than there are boundaries of sovereign nation-states. Orbital projections thus not only demonstrate the satellitization of the interface, they also expose the satellitization of the earth's surface.

Conceptual maps

Conceptual maps of orbit are experimental visualizations, often made by artists, to provoke reflection about the organization, uses and possibilities of satellite technologies and orbital domains. Emphasizing the conceptual dimensions of art practice, Jacques Rancière suggests that artists "do not wish to instruct the spectator... They simply wish to produce a form of consciousness, an intensity of feeling, an energy for action" (Rancière, 2011, p. 14). Similar in spirit to Fuller's Dymaxion map, conceptual maps attempt to provoke critical reflection about the organization and use of orbit, in this case by offering alternative visions for future uses of orbital space, exposing unequal occupations and control of orbital slots and paths, and emphasizing the dynamic relations between world history and orbital activity. In this way, conceptual maps are vital to the project of defining orbit as a vertical public space.

Figure 3.7 is an orbital visualization known as the Stanford Torus. Designed by a group of engineers and physicists during a 1975 NASA Summer Seminar at Stanford University, this conceptual map, illustrated by Rick Guidice, envisions orbit as a site of human habitation. As former head of NASA, James Fletcher, said of this project in 1976: "the participants in this effort have provided us with a vision that will engage our imagination and stretch our minds" (Fletcher, 1976). The design consists of a 1.8 km in diameter torus, or donut-shaped ring,

Figure 3.7 Stanford Torus cutaway view, Rick Guidice. This NASA illustration of the Stanford Torus (1975) envisions a public occupation of orbital space
Source: Reprinted courtesy of NASA; http://settlement.arc.nasa.gov/70sArt/AC75-1086-1f.jpeg

which would serve as a habitat for 10,000–140,000 people (Johnson and Holbrow, 1977). The torus would contain a residential area with a population density similar to a suburb surrounded by a "natural" environment. While this vision of orbit as a site of human colonization may be read as a bit audacious, it has the potential to challenge viewers to think about vertical public space in a new way, as it uses the place of orbit to rethink fundamental issues such as housing, economics, governance and the environment. In short, it asks us to imagine what an orbiting public might look like.

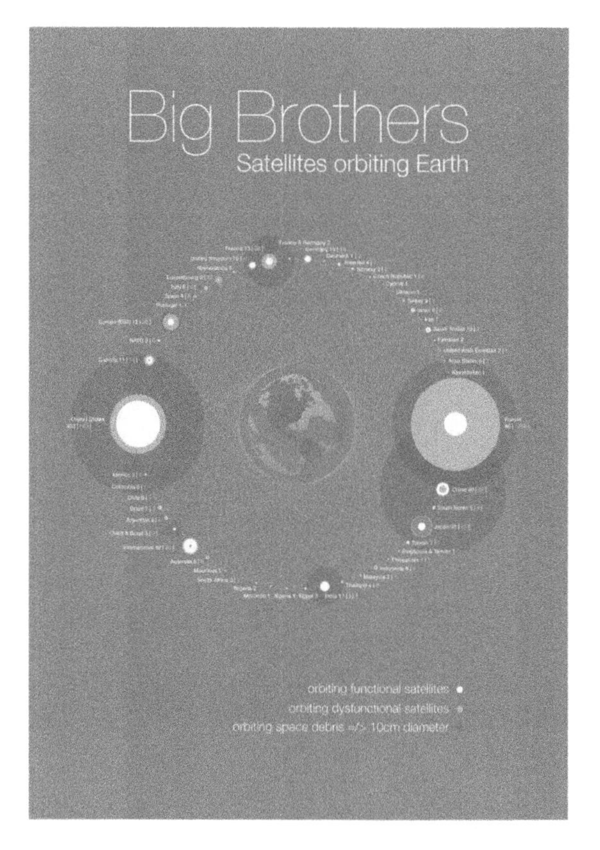

Figure 3.8 "Big Brothers: Satellites Orbiting Earth," Michael Paukner. "Big Brothers" is a conceptual map that visualizes ownership of satellites and orbital debris by nation-state

Source: Reprinted courtesy of Michael Paukner; http://www.flickr.com/photos/michaelpaukner/4314987544/

A more recent conceptual map (Figure 3.8) by Austrian graphic designer Michael Paukner entitled "Big Brothers: Satellites Orbiting Earth" conveys important structural information about orbit. Using graphics and data visualization, this map color codes concentrations of satellite ownership by country with white representing functional satellites, gray dysfunctional satellites, and black pieces of debris larger than 10 cm in diameter.[11] The "Big Brothers" map not only demonstrates the dominant role of the USA, the USSR and China in the orbital economy but also illustrates that more than 50 countries now operate satellites in orbit, which means that approximately 145 do not. While the USA owns the most functioning satellites, the USSR owns the most dysfunctional ones, and together China, the USA and the USSR are responsible for the most orbital debris.

Figure 3.9 "Postwar Footprints," Lisa Parks and Marcus Schaefer. This map reveals the changing satellite mediascape after the war in the former Yugoslavia
Source: Reprinted courtesy of Lisa Parks and Marcus Schaefer.

"Postwar Footprints" (Figure 3.9) is a conceptual map that attempts to demonstrate how world historical events can affect the orbital economy. Part of a media art installation that I created to explore the changing mediascape of the former Yugoslavia, it reveals the expansion of satellite broadcasting in the region after the war in the 1990s. Before the breakup of Yugoslavia there was one national broadcaster using one satellite to transmit signals throughout Europe. After the war there were 5 public and 15 commercial broadcasters, using 15 satellites to beam their signals around the world (Parks, 2005b, pp. 306–347). The "Postwar Footprints" map reveals the names and locations of these satellites and their footprints as well as all the satellite operators and new broadcasters in Bosnia-Herzegovina, Croatia, Montenegro, Serbia and Slovenia. It demonstrates that satellite operators were financial beneficiaries of the postwar restructuring of the mediascape in the former Yugoslavia. Using composited footprints, the map also reveals how new national broadcasters used satellites to shadow diasporic or displaced populations that left the region for Western Europe, North America or Australia during or after the war. It offers a visual record of changes in orbital activity that transpired after the war in and breakup of Yugoslavia.

The final conceptual map I will discuss comes from UK-based artist Joanna Griffin. It was created during a 2009 workshop she led for school children in Bangalore, India, focused on India's Chandrayaan lunar probe. During the event Griffin used a variety of experimental techniques to teach Indian students about satellites and orbital space. One of them involved having the children draw the GEO on the ground with chalk and then use rocks and paper to illustrate the positions and names of various satellites (Figure 3.10). Cleverly combining childhood curiosity, tactile work with hands and experimental education, Griffin and the workshop participants created a collective, multi-sensory and ground-up mapping of orbital space, which they then photographed so that it could be circulated as a counterpoint to more official and scientific accounts of this vertical field. Committed to finding ways of bringing space investments and technologies into the everyday lives of people around the planet, Griffin suggests that understanding outer space requires "an inclusive public of scientists and non-scientists, unintimidated by [space] technology or institutions and with the magnanimity to explore their frictions and differences" (Griffin, 2010, p. 10; see also Griffin, 2012).

Griffin's observation resonates with my own approach to the gathering and discussion of orbital maps. As a media scholar, my efforts to collect and think through these maps are guided by critical projects and

Figure 3.10 GEO with chalk, rocks and paper, photograph by Joanna Griffin. This image represents the results of a collaborative satellite literacy workshop led by artist Joanna Griffin in Bangalore, 2009
Source: Reprinted courtesy of Joanna Griffin.

pedagogical aspirations, and by an interest in building satellite literacy for non-scientists and in mitigating the complexity and intimidation associated with orbital matters. Most of the maps discussed in this essay were found online, whether on corporate websites, on an artist's Flickr page or in NASA archives. I have used many of them to illustrate public lectures about satellite technologies, to provoke students, colleagues, and citizens to consider orbit as a material domain – as an extension of socio-historical and political economic conditions on earth. While one might think that publicly accessible orbital maps would abound in the age of the Internet, there are still relatively few that are freely available. Interactive interfaces such as Google Earth may allow citizen-users to investigate orbital space in unprecedented ways, but its digital domains are quite visually regimented and often privatized, and its capacity to generate provocative or conceptual orbital maps is rather limited.

Although the orbital maps I have discussed were produced by different institutions or individuals and were made for different purposes, they provide an overall sense of the kinds of knowledges, literacies and imaginings that such maps can help to generate. Whether drawing attention to distinct orbital paths, processes of co-location, the names of satellites, the locations of satellite footprints or patterns of satellite ownership, orbital maps help to make this distant yet dynamic domain intelligible, providing a materialist sense of the organization of orbit and the objects that occupy it. Examining orbital maps equips citizen-viewers with the kinds of knowledge needed to raise further questions about the privatization, militarization and occupation of vertical public space. It also suggests the need for more orbital maps that can help to specify the material relations that make up the vertical field.

Conclusion

Mapping orbit involves understanding the historical ways in which this domain has been contested. It means imagining a vertical public space in relation to visual discourses of cartography, data visualization, graphic design and photography. It also requires new categories and concepts that recognize the dynamic and contiguous relations between earth and orbit, as well as the unique scale and complexity of this domain. Mapping orbit serves several critical agendas. First, it mobilizes "the public" into a new field and direction. Since most people will never go into orbit, the map can become a public gathering ground for the discussion of historical and future uses of this vertical commons to become a discursive platform through which contestations over orbital space can emerge and take shape. Such contestations can only happen, however, if orbit is understood as a site of public value, opportunity and relevance. It was in part the recognition that there were no publicly owned satellites that inspired the non-governmental organization A Human Right to launch the "Buy this Satellite!" project. Its organizers used crowdsourcing to raise more than US$64,000 in an effort to purchase the TerreStar 1 communications satellite, whose owner, Terrestar Corporation, filed for bankruptcy in 2009. The organization aspired to move Terrestar 1 into a new orbital slot that would allow the satellite to provide free Internet access to millions of people in developing countries (buythissatellite.org, 2011). This ambitious plan, which echoes the open access principles of the Outer Space Treaty, approaches orbit as a domain worth fighting for, even if it means navigating the high-cost game of orbital real estate.

Second, the mapping of orbit cultivates a structure of feeling I refer to as "invisible adjacency", which involves the capacity to recognize the presence and significance of a material field, object and/or body without directly sensing it. It is a kind of abstract awareness or consciousness built upon obscure observations and inferential knowledge.

In the case of orbit, invisible adjacency involves the capacity to imagine and take interest in a field of operations and highly powerful machines that are adjacent to the earth without being able to directly sense them or the space they inhabit. Both the Bogotá Declaration and the Tongasat case were predicated upon such a capacity. The orbital map activates this structure of feeling by displaying an iconic version of a field that most observers will never directly see, travel to or sense. Thus, as it "reveals" orbital space, the orbital map exposes what Kaja Silverman refers to as "the threshold of the visible world" (Silverman, 1995). Invisible adjacency suggests the possibility of a critical paradigm, political imaginary or knowledge system that traffics between the visible and the invisible. It can be thought about in relation to a variety of imperceptible phenomena at macro and micro scales, ranging from massive satellite infrastructures to tiny DNA sequences. Orbit thus becomes a space for thinking through the politicization of the imperceptible and for understanding how phenomena come into discursive relations.

Finally, mapping orbit creates a demand for more and better orbital maps. In the age of the satellite, citizen-viewers need to be able to imagine the public sphere as up, out and around, not just on the ground. The complex vectors of earth–orbit relations create new cartographic challenges and require new critical commitments. As I have tried to suggest, the mapping of orbit encompasses many practices and forms. It involves thinking about verticality and visuality in different ways, whether through traditional world maps, projections, tactile interactivity with interfaces, or chalk, rocks and paper. More conceptual maps are needed to encourage critical reflection on the material relations that constitute orbit. If Buckminster Fuller were to re-make the Dymaxion map today, what would it look like? It might feature the trajectories of global signal traffic or a world inscribed by satellite footprints. The point is that the map represents a potential to communicate about a variety of orbital matters, whether the locations of satellite launch pads, the sites of satellite-related natural resource extractions, or the involvement of non-Western or indigenous publics in the orbital economy. By inscribing this invisible, adjacent domain into the symbolic economy, the orbital map enables people to recognize orbit as an extension of material conditions of life on earth and challenges the world's publics to act accordingly.

Notes

1. With the exception of critical works such as MacDonald (2007) and Warf (2007).

2. See Schiller's discussion of media imperialism as it relates to satellites (Schiller, 1992).
3. This policy was designed to accommodate the "special needs of developing countries" as required by Article 33(2) of the ITU Convention.
4. An edited version of this article appeared as "Turf Battles in Outer Space", *International Cable*, December 1994, 18–24.
5. For further discussion of imaginings of "other views" of earth, see Parks (2005a, Chapter 5).
6. Pink use c-band, green use ku-band, yellow with a strip use ka-band, black use MSS (mobile satellite services) and white use UHF-band or are hybrid.
7. For an interesting discussion of space debris more generally, see Gorman (2009).
8. See "TV Uplink: Satellite Newsgathering," Diversified Communications, Inc., http://www.tvuplink.net/sngnf.html, date accessed August 19, 2011.
9. See map for sale, available at http://www.georgeglazer.com/archives/maps/archive-pictorial/glennorbit.html, date accessed April 25, 2012.
10. The Astra 1H footprint map can be found at the Lynsat website, http://www.lyngsat-maps.com/maps/astra1h.html, date accessed April 24, 2012.
11. This map draws upon data from the Union of Concerned Scientists satellite database (2011), and *The Satellite Encyclopedia* (TBS Internet, 2003).

Bibliography

Amato, Matt (2008) "Every Satellite Tracked in Real Time", *Slashdot* (5 September), http://science.slashdot.org/story/08/09/05/1231228/Every-Satellite-Tracked-In-Realtime-Via-Google-Earth, date accessed 5 January 2011.

Analytical Graphics, Inc. (ca. 2005) The GEO Belt, http://www.hobbyspace.com/AAdmin/ Images/LivingSpace/stk/geo_belt_1024.jpg, date accessed 31 May 2012.

Andrews, Edmund L. (1990a) "Tiny Tonga Seeks Satellite Empire in Space", *New York Times* (28 August), http://www.nytimes.com/1990/08/28/business/tiny-tonga-seeks-satellite-empire-in-space.html, date accessed 15 August 2011.

Andrews, Edmund L. (1990b) "Tonga's Plan for Satellites Set Back by Global Agency", *New York Times* (1 December), http://www.nytimes.com/1990/12/01/business/tonga-s-plan-for-satellites-set-back-by-global-agency.html?src=pm, date accessed 15 August 2011.

Arnheim, Rudolf (1982) *The Power of the Center: A Study of Composition in the Visual Arts* (Berkeley: University of California Press).

Berland, Jody (2009) *North of Empire: Essays on the Cultural Technologies of Space* (Durham: Duke University Press).

buythissatellite.org (2011) "Buy This Satellite: Bringing Internet Access to the People Who Need It Most", http://buythissatellite.org/, date accessed 12 September 2011.

Collis, Christy (2012) "The Geostationary Orbit: A Critical Legal Geography of Space's Most Valuable Real Estate", in Parks, Lisa and Schwoch, James (eds.) *Down to Earth: Satellite Technologies, Industries and Cultures* (New Brunswick: Rutgers University Press).

Cosgrove, Denis (2001) *Apollo's Eye: A Cartographic Genealogy of the Earth in the Western Imagination* (Baltimore: Johns Hopkins University Press).

Declaration of the First Meeting of Equatorial Countries (1974), http://www.jaxa.jp/library/ space_law/chapter_2/2-2-1-2_e.html, date accessed 15 August 2011.
Delzeit, Albert N. and Robert, F. Beal. (1996) "The Vulnerability of the Pacific Rim Spectrum Under International Space Law", *New York International Law Review* (Winter 1996), http://www.vanuatu.usp.ac.fj/sol_adobe_documents/usp%20only/Pacific%20law/Delzeit.htm, date accessed 15 August 2011.
Dymaxion Map (2009) *Wikipedia*, http://en.wikipedia.org/wiki/Dymaxion_map, date accessed 7 May 2012.
Fletcher, James C. (1976) "Foreword of 'Space Settlements: A Design Study'", http://www.nas.nasa.gov/Services/Education/SpaceSettlement/75Summer Study/Foreword1.html, date accessed 11 September 2011.
Google Earth (2011) Screen Capture of AGI Satellite Layer (image in author's possession).
Gorman, Alice (2009) "The Archaeology of Space Exploration", in Parker, Martin and Bell, David (eds.) *Space Travel and Culture: From Apollo to Space Tourism* (Malden: Wiley-Blackwell).
Griffin, Joanna (2009) Geostationary Orbit with Chalk, Rocks and Paper (image courtesy of author).
Griffin, Joanna (2010) "Finding Meaning" (unpublished).
Griffin, Joanna (2012) "Moon Vehicle: Reflections from an Artist-Led Children's Workshop on the Chandrayaan-1 Spacecraft's Mission to the Moon", *Leonardo*, 45(3), 219–224.
Guidice, Rick (1977) Stanford Torus Cutaway View in Richard, D. Johnson and Holbrow, Charles (eds.) *Space Settlements: A Design Study* (Washington: NASA), http://settlement.arc.nasa.gov/70sArt/AC75-1086-1f.jpeg, date accessed 3 June 2012.
Hay, James (2012) "The Invention of Air Space, Outer Space and Cyberspace", in Parks, Lisa and Schwoch, James (eds.) *Down to Earth: Satellite Technologies, Industries and Cultures* (New Brunswick: Rutgers University Press).
Heavens Above (2011) "Heavens Above", http://www.heavens-above.com/, date accessed 12 September 2011.
Johnson, Richard D. and Holbrow, Charles (eds.) (1977) *Space Settlements: A Design Study* (Washington: NASA), http://www.nas.nasa.gov/Services/Education/SpaceSettlement/ 75SummerStudy/Table_of_Contents1.html, date accessed 9 September 2011.
Livingstone, William (2010) Geo-Stationary Satellites (image courtesy of author).
MacDonald, Fraser (2007) "Anti-Astropolitik: Outer Space and the Orbit of Geography", *Progress in Human Geography*, 31(5), 592–615.
Marks, Robert W. (1960) *The Dymaxion World of Buckminster Fuller* (New York, Reinhold Publishing Corporation).
Mendosa, David Mendosa (1994) "Tongasat's Flawed Genius", http://www.mendosa.com/ tongasat.html, date accessed 15 August 2011.
NASA (2011) Eyes on the Earth, http://www.nasa.gov/externalflash/eyes/, date accessed 7 May 2012.
NASA Orbital Debris Program Office (undated) Orbiting Objects in Low Earth Orbit and Geostationary Orbit, http://earthobservatory.nasa.gov/Features/OrbitsCatalog/page3.php, date accessed 31 May 2012.

Oxford Dictionaries (2004) *Oxford English Dictionary*, 3rd edn, September 2004, http://www.oed.com.proxy.library.ucsb.edu:2048/view/Entry/132247, date accessed 26 August 2011.

Paglen, Trevor (2009) *Blank Spots on the Map: The Dark Geography of the Pentagon's Secret World* (New York: Dutton).

Parks, Lisa (2005a) *Cultures in Orbit: Satellites and the Televisual* (Durham and London: Duke University Press).

Parks, Lisa (2005b) "Postwar Footprints: Satellite and Wireless Stories in Slovenia and Croatia", in Franke, Anselm (ed.) *B-Zone: Becoming Europe and Beyond* (Barcelona: ACTAR).

Parks, Lisa (2012) "Zeroing in: Overhead Imagery, Infrastructure Ruins, and Datalands in Afghanistan and Iraq" in Mirzoeff, Nicholas (ed.) *The Visual Culture Reader*, 3rd edn (London: Routledge).

Parks, Lisa and Schaefer, Marcus (2005) Postwar Footprints (image courtesy of authors).

Paukner, Michael (2010) Big Brothers: Satellites Orbiting Earth, http://www.flickr.com/photos/michaelpaukner/4314987544/, date accessed 12 September 2011.

Price, Monroe (2002) "Satellites as Trade Routes in the Sky", in Joseph, M. Chan and Bryce, T. McIntyre (eds.) *In Search of Boundaries: Communication, Nation States and Cultural Identities* (Westport: Ablex Publishing).

Rancière, Jacques (2011) *The Emancipated Spectator* (London: Verso).

Schiller, Herbert (1992) *Mass Communications and American Empire* (Boulder: Westview Press).

SES (2011) "Video Neighborhoods: 19.2 E", http://www.ses-astra.com/business/en/satellite-fleet/19-2E/index.php, date accessed 20 August 2011.

Silverman, Kaja (1995) *The Threshold of the Visible World* (London: Routledge).

TBS Internet (2003) The Satellite Encyclopedia, http://www.tbs-satellite.com/tse/online/ thema_origine.html, date accessed 12 September 2011.

Tongasat (2002) Tongasat Announces Acquisition of ESIAFI-1 Satellite, http://www.tongasat.com/news/article1_Esiafi.htm, date accessed 7 September 2011.

Union of Concerned Scientists (2011), Nuclear Weapons and Global Security, http://www.ucsusa.org/nuclear_weapons_and_global_security/space_weapons/technical_issues/ucs-satellite-database.html, date accessed 12 September 2011.

United Nations Office for Outer Space Affairs (2011) Space Law: Frequently Asked Questions, http://www.oosa.unvienna.org/oosa/FAQ/splawfaq.html#Q4, date accessed 8 September 2011.

US Department of State (1967) Treaty on Principles Governing the Activities of States in the Exploration and Use of Outer Space, including the Moon and other Extraterrestrial Bodies, http://www.state.gov/www/global/arms/treaties/space1.html, date accessed 18 August 2011.

Vaidhyanathan, Siva (2011) *The Googlization of Everything (And Why We Should Worry)* (Berkeley: University of California Press).

Warf, Barney (2007) "Geopolitics of the Satellite Industry", *Tijdschrift voor Economische en Sociale Geografie*, 98(3), 385–397.

Wiessner, Siegfried (1983) "The Public Order of the Geostationary Orbit: Blueprints for the Future", *Yale Journal of World Public Order*, 9, 217–274.

4 Cairo Diary: Space-Wars, Public Visibility and the Transformation of Public Space in Post-revolutionary Egypt

Mona Abaza

I have to admit that I have rarely encountered such reserve in putting pen to paper as I have since January 2011. During recent months I have kept on writing scattered notes every now and then. Whenever I was finished with a short article, another dramatic event, massacre or killing occurred. This led me to stop writing at once. The overwhelming events affected me by triggering a deep resistance to writing, let alone publishing, as if the written word could have been a direct betrayal of the lived experience (Figure 4.1).

Volatility, insecurity and often fear provoked by not knowing when violence would erupt are what accompany anyone going to Tahrir Square today. For a year now, different opposing publics and political movements have been competing over the legitimacy of the epicenter of the events – the Salafis, the Muslim Brothers, thugs (*balṭaği*) paid by internal security to sexually harass female protesters and intimidate them, as well as the internal security forces and the military police acting against the revolutionaries. All these forces are fighting to conquer the space of Tahrir, to such an extent that Tahrir Square has created its own independent life. Also evident are the marginalized and poorer classes, who flooded into the square soon after the revolution. Today, Tahrir attracts the survivors of the informal economy: the ambulant salesmen of the consumer gadgets and the paraphernalia of the revolution (flags, badges, T-shirts, toys, tags, accessories and so on); the vendors of maize, sweet potatoes, local desserts, tea and coffee; the Chinese peddlers of mobile phones and other gadgets; and the street children who were

Figure 4.1 Mural depicting the martyrs of the Ultras Ahli football team on Mohammed Mahmud Street
Source: All photographs by Mona Abaza

always in the square from the start of the revolution and sided with both the revolutionaries and the paid thugs. Many were unfortunately victims of the violence. All this adds to the image of the square as a space that resembles a bazaar or popular market. It also reminds us of the popular saints' days that are always accompanied by festivities in those markets.

Evidently, Cairo has been witnessing tumultuous and fascinating moments and struggles over the conquest of public spaces. The *sanīyya* – the center, the circle or the roundabout in the middle of Tahrir Square – continued throughout 2011 to epitomize the physical and symbolic seizure of power for both the revolutionaries and the military. But the struggles have extended far beyond the *sanīyya* to not only include other public squares (like 'Abdiin and Sulayman Pasha when Tahrir was either becoming too dangerous or had been re-conquered by the army, which evicted the protestors), but also incorporate protest graffiti on the walls. The idea has been to spread the spirit of Tahrir to all of the squares of Egypt. It is those struggles over public space that this diary records.

Segregating walls, zoning

Whether the revolution has succeeded or not – many believe that it is best to define it as incomplete – Tahrir Square did trigger a powerful process for advocacy of freedom and democracy by reshaping street politics. The effective power of public spaces has been discovered as a useful means of putting pressure on the military junta. The square became the space *per se* for contestation, for grieving and for public performance, painting and filming. Tahrir triggered a new visual culture. It became the spot to film and to be filmed, as well as being a space in which to see others and to be seen.

This new public culture is reformulating a novel understanding of public spaces as spaces of contestation, of communication of artistic expression or public interaction, and as spaces of the "spectacle," as my colleague Samia Mehrez has argued in *Global Dialogue* (Mehrez, 2012, pp. 4–5). The offline world here has been interacting with the world of the online, which has been given a free hand via the growing significance of *YouTube* postings of photography and documentary films that are then screened or exhibited in public spaces. *YouTube* posting has allowed large audiences of *Facebook* members to follow the events on Tahrir by the minute. This is certainly transforming the visual landscape and people's behavior in public spaces. Yet, this public culture is emerging as part of a reshaping of the city, which is in a precarious moment under military rule.

This reshaping could be characterized by two parallel phenomena. On the one hand, the city is witnessing localized war zones that are followed by the erection of barriers, barricades and controlled areas. The Supreme Council of the Armed Forces (SCAF) seems to think it can solve the problem of confrontations with the protesters by erecting isolating walls, and spreading internationally sanctioned lethal gas and teargas, which not only render mobility impossible but also make daily life in the downtown area surrounding Tahrir Square simply unbearable for its residents. The walling of entire areas also paralyzes the economic life of the small shopkeepers, coffee shops, taxi drivers and the large downtown informal economy. That is why it is often the residents who demand the removal of these barricades erected after violent clashes (*Egypt Independent*, 2012) (Figure 4.2).

The walling, as a buffer zone between protesters and the police, was first implemented in November 2011 in Mohammed Mahmud Street. This was when more than 40 protesters were killed by the police after the Central Security Forces used extreme violence to push them away

Figure 4.2 Walling, isolating, segregating ...

from Tahrir Square. What inflamed people's anger was the violence used against the martyrs' families who were squatting in the square. More walls were later erected in December 2011 after the protests in front of the Cabinet Building because of the contested appointment of Minister Ganzouri by the SCAF, which led to even more violent clashes and the burning of l'Institut d'Égypte. This incident led to many more deaths. The security forces then constructed another wall, completely blocking Sheikh Rehan Street, parallel with Mohammed Mahmud Street. Also another wall, blocking Kasr al-'Ainy Street, was erected, and so on. By February 2012, the number of walls around the area of Mohammed Mahmud, Noubar and Mansur Sheikh Rehan streets had reached eight, not to count the wired zones in front of the Ministry of Interior, and the blocking tanks and large green police vehicles (Trew *et al.*, 2012).

The military has learnt its lesson from the frozen moment of the 18 days of January 2011, which paralyzed the entire city and thus was effective in the downfall of the regime. Now they are countering the revolutionaries by "zoning" and squeezing the protesters to segregate them in limited spaces of war. This is also a tactic to blame the revolutionaries for paralyzing downtown, while "normalizing" the rest of the circulation, and the business and bank sectors of the city.

Erecting and destroying walls (in February 2012 the protesters managed to tear down the Mohammed Mahmud wall that had been erected in December 2011) has become a powerful symbol of oppression as well as of resistance. Zoning goes together with dividing the city into two spaces: the normalized versus the war zone. It is also one way of making citizens acquainted with violence and rendering it a banality, which one has to cope with on a daily basis. And certainly walling the city brings immediately to mind the analogy with the occupied territories in Israel and the segregation of populations experienced there.

The urge to document, archive and film the revolution

The revolution triggered a strong wish to document, classify and record every moment experienced in Tahrir. Amongst other initiatives, a group of historians headed by Khaled Fahmy from the American University in Cairo (AUC) called themselves the Committee to Document the 25 January Revolution. It is their intention to make documents available to everyone, which has not been the case so far. The AUC has created another archive that is collecting the testimonies of the revolution (Shenker, 2011).

2011 was a heyday for documentary films, such as the recently released *Tahrir 2011: The Good, The Bad and the Politician* (Al Tahrir 2011: Al Tayib wa al Sharis wa al Siyassi, 2011) by Amr Salama, Ayten Amin and Tamer Ezzat, and *In Tahrir Square: 18 Days of Egypt's Unfinished Revolution* by Jon Alpert and Matthew O'Neill (2011). *Reporting...a Revolution* (Al Thawra...Khabar, 2011) is a documentary about seven reporters from *al-Masry al-Yawm* newspaper who covered the revolution. Recording the event by filming, photographing and collecting the activists' stories is timely. For example, *Al Jazeera English* has already produced several documentaries on the testimonies of the revolution.

Tahrir continues to be the greatest inspiration for photography. AUC Press has already published three photography books and a calendar in less than six months following the revolution. Also, numerous exhibitions took place at various cultural centers, private art galleries, universities and state institutions, in addition to the courageous and inspiring work of many activists, bloggers, photo journalists or simply amateurs who displayed the most eye-catching photos of Tahrir via *Facebook* and blogs.

This reveals two points. First, the status of photography is undergoing a fascinating positive evolution in Egypt, after long decades of marginalization, suspicion and association with either "spying" or debasing

Figure 4.3 Photography in Tahrir

the "locals" by making them into curiosity objects. Photography was rather devalued as a practice mostly restricted to the privileged Western exotic gaze. Tahrir made it possible for the Egyptian masses to appropriate photography and democratize it, paradoxically with the very tools of mass culture. The square became the "spot" for taking photos and for being photographed and filmed. It became the Mecca for ordinary people to take a pride in being photographed with mobile phones, which are affordable today for even the poorest classes (Figure 4.3).

The sit-ins, the marches and the demonstrations have attracted ever-increasing coverage by local and foreign photographers and journalists from newspapers such as *Ahram Online, al-Masry al-Yawm* and *al-Shurouk*. Some of these people lost their lives or their eyes during the Mohammed Mahmud and Mansur street events of November 2011. More recently, photographer Salma Said, an activist from the group *Mosireen* ("We Are Persevering/Insisting"), a group which promotes the idea of "film activism," was peppered with over a hundred birdshot pellets to the face, stomach and legs when she stood against the police on February 5, 2011 (Shukrallah, 2012).

Also, the numerous exhibitions that have taken place during the past few months open up questions for the future about how photographic displays – as collective, collaborative works with multiple and yet merging narratives and paths – might be displayed in novel ways in public spaces and street installations. Particularly fascinating was the collective exhibition by 14 photographers at Gezira Art Center entitled People – The Red Line on November 16, 2011, which documented the revolution, not only in the square and its surroundings but also through its impact on the daily life of the poor. Some photos were shot one year before the revolution in demonstrations, strikes and churches after the killings of Copts. They are premonitions of what unfolded in January 2011 (Khallaf, 2011).

Public screenings and performances

Collective street paintings have become more common than ever before. This has triggered new ways of looking at public installations, such as the one-minute time-lapse online video produced by Pierre Kattar of the Young Artists Coalition's Tal'aat Harb Mural (Kattar, 2011).

El Fan Medan ("Art/Square" or "Art is the Square") is an endeavor undertaken by the Independent Cultural Coalition that advertises itself as "A cultural coalition in the squares and the streets of Egypt" (Magdy, 2011). The foundation has been very active in promoting public performances and exhibiting artworks in public squares all over Egypt. For example, after the November 2011 clashes in Tahrir, painter Mohammed Abla managed to exhibit a series of paintings entitled *Wolves,* which was a direct attack on the violence perpetrated by the military and security forces. It was a forceful act. In his painting we see the memorable dragging of the female protester along the ground by the police, so that her clothes were stripped to reveal her blue bra. Mohammed Abla was only able to exhibit his paintings for one day at 'Abdiin Square on the first Saturday of January 2012. He then exhibited it briefly in Tahrir (Figure 4.4).

YouTube videos gained such prominence not only through *Facebook* but also elsewhere on the Internet and via iPhones. Hundreds, if not thousands, of inspiring and imaginative *YouTube* songs, short comments, jokes, cartoons and artworks defending the revolution have been circulated. A wonderful collective work appeared on *YouTube* produced by numerous actors who narrated in a lyrical style the moments of the revolution in their clip entitled *Baladna bil Masry; "Operette Hikayat al-Thawra."* (Operette the Story of the Revolution) *Taxi Band Magnoon* is

Figure 4.4 Mohamed Abla's painting, *Wolves*, January 28, 2012
Source: Photography courtesy of Mohamed Abla.

an anti-authoritarian, sardonic song about madness and sanity (why is it madness if one wants to transform the country?) (Taxi Band Magnoon, 2010).

The idea of creating a Tahrir cinema was born, followed by instituting "an archive of material and footage ... to be stored in a public place," as explained by an article in *Ahram Online* (Abdel, 2011). All of these public performances coincided with the remarkable popularity of the TEDex Cairo Talks, which were conceived to encourage visionary perspectives and inspiring story telling (TEDx Cairo, 2012). They are yet another form of public performance. Amongst the most inspiring speakers was Google executive Wael Ghonim, who set up a *Facebook* page memorializing a victim of government violence (Ghonim, 2012). Also powerful was Bassem Youssef, another sardonic, brilliant *YouTube* contributor who documented the Tahrir days in his peculiar highly ironic style, reaching out to thousands of viewers from a tiny room, which he divided into his studio and a space for hanging up the family washing (Youssef, 2012). Beautiful and ironic Monatov is a young female *YouTube* video maker, who exposed the lies and madness of the media in the first days of the revolution in her videos *Aqwa Aflām al-Mawsim* ("The Most

Powerful/or Pervasive Films of the Season") and *GaddafiLeaks*, in which she produced a biting parody of Gaddafi (Monatov, 2011a, b).

All of these examples have a common denominator: they are inventing new public spaces, which are merging with the virtual imaginary. These are public spaces that are produced through collective performances and actions. By displaying in public the grievances, demands, performances and knowledge for "public archives," as a form of knowledge for which "nobody needs permits anymore," as filmmaker Omar Robert Hamilton stated (Abdel, 2011), these practices converge toward new ways of imagining and practicing democratic advocacy. These novel practices are associated with public visibility and imagery through collective performances in which humor is sovereign. They remain most dreaded and uncontrollable for authoritarianism, since history tells us that humor has always been authoritarianism's nemesis.

Ḥakaawi al-taḥrir ("Tahrir Monologues") is one of the most moving performances. A group of some 18 young women and men narrate their own experiences during the 18 days of Tahrir in January 2011. On stage, each actor recalls the minute details, the fear and angst, and the attacks and retreats that they experienced during the deadliest days of brutality and violence. The idea came from Sundus Shabayek, a young journalist in her early 20s whose message is that this revolution was not just about reporting but about being involved in making the revolution. The group has been performing in various parts of Egypt, including in bookshops and theaters.

Kazeboon ("Liars Campaign, or the Generals are Liars Campaign") is another significant endeavor launched by a group of activists to propose a counter-narrative to the SCAF and to expose the violence by screening footage of the army's torturing and killing. The availability of the videos through *YouTube* allowed them to be shown all over Egypt. *Kazeboon* was screened in ordinary neighborhoods as well as middle-class suburbs. The organizers often encountered opposition from the police and paid thugs, who attacked them and stopped the screenings (Rashwan, 2012). Especially interesting is that people's reactions to the *Kazeboon* films were filmed and included in some of the *YouTube* videos that were screened elsewhere. Some screenings triggered violent reactions and a state of bewilderment because the videos are a direct attack on the army. The counter-revolution has been feeding on the sentiment that the army is the only remaining institution that holds the country together, so to attack it would mean to destroy the country. However, it is clear that such performances did trigger pro-revolution sentiments as well as anger and clashes with the campaigners.

Kazeboon was also aired by the al-Tahrir pro-revolution TV channel, led by talk show presenter Dina Abdel Rahman. As a result, her program was axed without her even being notified, an incident protested against by the Arab Network for Human Rights Information (2012).

Graffiti

Graffiti has undergone a fascinating boom in Cairo and Alexandria since the ousting of Mubarak. Newspaper articles, exhibitions, talk shows and installations have all focused on clandestine street art and artists. Multiple publications will surely soon emerge offering compilations of the differing graffiti styles that are overwhelming the city of Cairo (Figure 4.5).

Be it the pro-revolution installations and art exhibitions that took place in Europe, or the fantastic sardonic graffiti which blossomed in the city and whose success one can follow on the *Facebook* page "Revolution Graffiti" (2012), I am glad to say that none of these subcultures can simply be suppressed by military orders, or the vehement endeavor of neurotically repainting the walls every second day. Graffiti is perceived as an underworld clandestine art; it is a forbidden act for those wanting

Figure 4.5 Photographing each other in front of graffiti

to establish public order and cleanliness and defend official culture. Yet, it is one of the most fascinating means of disseminating dissenting ideas and innovative images while maintaining anonymity, because it is often drawn without any signature. Who would have believed that the monumental administration building, the colossal Mugama', could have been turned into the ideal space for expressing creativity and dissent? Who could have imagined colorful and ironic anti-government satirical paintings on Mugama's walls? Who would have believed that we can speak today of a specific "Mugama' Graffiti" that has caught the attention of many, including the downtown visionary Pierre Sioufi, who is known for his courage in sheltering hundreds in his flat to view Tahrir during the revolution (Cohen, 2011) (Figure 4.6).

Graffiti is also a major theme handled with great intelligence and sensitivity in the recent film by Ahmed Abdalla, *Microphone* (2010), which has already won several awards. English slogans interplay with Arabic language, placards, public drawings, public demands, joke after joke, painting one's body and face as a site for protest, making one's body an iconic site, and continuous occupation – all these reveal how public space and with it public expression is taking a new turn.

The "blue bra" of the unknown female protester has turned into an iconic symbol since December 2011. In Tahrir, a veiled female protester

Figure 4.6 On the walls of Mugama'

was stripped of her black cloak and kicked in her belly by a soldier's boot. Millions watched the humiliating act of her being dragged along the ground, exposing her blue bra. Since then the city's murals and barricades have been filled with hundreds of blue bras. Ironically, the blue bra has turned into a symbol of national contestation against the SCAF ever since some Salafi shaikhs and pro-Mubarak talk show speakers used the blue bra to smear her as a prostitute who deserved to be beaten up and stripped naked in public. These counter-revolutionaries evidently ignored the simple fact of the violation of human rights, not to mention that none of those shaikhs ever thought about the fact that it was a public humiliation that targeted specifically women. In fact, what they implied was that any woman in the street ought to be assaulted because she chose to be in the street and a woman's place is, self-evidently, in the home. These horrifying statements were then turned against them, to become the butt of jokes and biting comments. This led in December 2011 to one of the most significant women's demonstrations against the SCAF policies, policies that have only led to the systematic escalation of sexual harassment, rape, gender humiliation and violent attacks on protesters. The blue bra then abounded in so many works of graffiti and became a major theme for several artists (Figure 4.7).

Figure 4.7 Blue bra graffiti

If one were to compare the many murals around the city, one would realize that Egyptian cities are today witnessing a rich variety of highly sardonic and imaginative styles for conveying political dissent. Recently, graffiti artist Keizer has attracted much attention from the press for his powerful images combining direct and witty slogans. What grabbed me most is a statement in Arabic: "If you are not part of the solution, you are part of the problem." His recent sardonic portraits of former pro-Mubarak Minister of Antiquities Zahi Hawass were accompanied by statements such as "traitor to the Pharaohs." As for the famous actor 'Adel Imam, who expressed anti- revolutionary sentiments in January 2011, Keizer drew a portrait of him, followed by the comment, "Rāḥet 'Alyak ya Zaim," ("You have missed the bandwagon, leader"). The former Minister of Interior Habib al-'Adly's portrait is accompanied by a rhyming sentence: " 'Adl al-Nahārdah ya 'Adly" ("Justice today 'Adly"), playing on the words 'Adl (justice) and 'Adly (derived from the word for justice). His jokes are short and to the point.

The Sad Panda is another piece of graffiti found all over the city. It became famous with the following slogan: "al-mushīr mikhallīni hazīn akthar" ("the general makes me even sadder"). Another rising star is Ganzeer, who was arrested with two other artists in May 2011. The arrests made him even better known for his daring drawing of a huge tank standing in front of a cyclist carrying a large tray of bread over his head. Ganzeer was detained mainly because he posted a sticker of the "Mask of Freedom", which must have infuriated the SCAF (Ganzeer, 2011, 2012; see figure 8) (Figure 4.8).

But this was not the end. On May 20–21, 2011, Ganzeer launched a successful campaign that he called "The Mad Graffiti Week," which was picked up and resulted in hundreds of anonymous graffiti that filled the city (El Hebeishy, 2011).

Mohammed Mahmud Street

Mohammed Mahmud Street is one of the main streets leading to Tahrir Square, which includes one of the main entrances to the old campus of the AUC. This street will remain a memorable space for the revolution because it witnessed a series of the most dramatic and violent moments during last November, December and February. It has been renamed by the revolutionaries as *shāri' 'uyun al-ḥurriyyah* ("the street of the eyes of freedom") after so many protesters lost their eyes to the officer and sniper who targeted the protesters with such precision (Figure 4.9).

NEW
Mask of Freedom
Salut from the Supreme Council of the Armed Forces to the loving sons of the nation.
Now available for an unlimited period of time.

Figure 4.8 Ganzeer's mask of freedom, from http://ganzeer.blogspot.com/

The street also witnessed the erection of an isolated cement block wall in December 2011 that cuts it down the middle, and then the destruction of this same wall in February 2012 by the revolutionaries and the residents. More importantly, though, throughout 2011, the wall of the old campus of the AUC witnessed fantastic mutations on a weekly basis. These transformations were epitomized by a war about painting the walls – a war between the graffiti painters and the military forces, who repeatedly whitewashed the walls in a hopeless attempt to eliminate the mocking slogans and drawings. If the SCAF still has the upper hand in running the country, on the symbolic level it has lost the respect of the street. The evidence is graffiti, which has been relentlessly ridiculing and insulting the establishment on these murals. Apart from mockery, the theme of commemorating the martyrs is the most moving aspect of these artworks (Figure 4.10).

Figure 4.9 Graffiti on "the street of the eyes of freedom," December 15, 2011

Figure 4.10 Mohamed Mahmud Street, freshly whitewashed, January 24, 2012

The November and December events on Mohammed Mahmud Street and in its surroundings led to significant looting of the headquarters of the AUC and the wounding of several of its helpless security guards. Afterwards, the wall was built even higher and meticulously painted and repaired for the festivities after the first anniversary of the January 25 revolution. No sooner than January 26, 2012 dawned than the wall was once again beautifully repainted with fantastic mocking murals (Figure 4.11).

Not a single day passed without whitewashed walls being refilled with fantastic anti-SCAF drawings and simple insults. When the protesters were gassed, graffiti appeared with protestors in masks; when snipers targeted their eyes, numerous one-eyed victims were painted; after the massacre at the football match in Port Said, the martyrs of the Ultra Ahli football team were painted as angels resting in heaven, or being carried in a sarcophagus in an ancient Egyptian-style death ceremony. Mohammed Mahmud Street seems to be turning into a temple, or rather a "memorial space," visited repeatedly to be photographed, just before the graffiti is whitewashed away again. It is also becoming a space for posing to be photographed against its fantastic murals. On February 24,

Figure 4.11 Freshly whitewashed, fresh graffiti, January 26, 2012

Figure 4.12 Gas mask graffiti after the gassings, December 15, 2011

2012, the walls of the street were whitewashed for at least the tenth time. Only the Ultras' mural of the martyrs and the Pharaoh paintings located near the entrance of the AUC gate were left intact, but, as usual, no one knows for how long this will be the case (Figures 4.12–4.14).

The marches

From the very first day of the revolution, the marches were crucial in mobilizing people to reach Tahrir. On the first anniversary of the revolution, millions poured into Tahrir to convey the message that they are willing to challenge the junta. An amazing number of marches, reaching 25 that came from all the corners of the city, overwhelmed the square.

To mark the January 25, 2012 march, a map was distributed via *Facebook* explaining the departure points and itineraries of all the marches throughout Cairo and how these would reach Tahrir Square. *Al-Ahram Online* also provided a map with all of the marches, the meeting points and the itineraries.

These marches have remarkably increased during the past three months, in particular after the October Maspero massacre of Coptic

Figure 4.13 Graffiti memorializing the Ultras in an ancient Egyptian-style death ceremony

Figure 4.14 Mural at the AUC: Tahrir Square, by Alaam Awad

protesters. They reveal a sophisticated level of organization and great effectiveness in attracting people by calling upon those standing on the balconies to come down to the street. Many protesters carry striking written messages and symbols. The march of January 25 departing from Mustafa Mahmud Mosque in Mohandessin Quarter was even more impressive after several other marches from other neighborhoods merged with it. The march was synchronized with loud speakers, compelling slogans and large drums. A significant number of the demonstrators had extremely impressive masks of the faces of famous martyrs, like Khaled Said (who was killed by officers in Alexandria and was a symbol that triggered the January revolution), Sheikh Emad (a learned Azharite religious scholar who was killed in the events on Mohamed Mahmud Street), and Mina Daniel (killed in the Maspero massacre), as well as the "V for Vendetta" mask that was previously attacked by the Muslim Brotherhood newspaper for instigating chaos and anarchy. The Muslim Brotherhood newspaper's campaign against the "V for Vendetta" had misspelled the "V" as "B" and called the mask "Bendetta." To the Muslim Brotherhood's misfortune, the revolutionaries did not spare them from a torrent of jokes about their ignorance.

Figure 4.15 Filming the march, February 2012

The next march on Friday February 3 was even better organized. It was a morning march in commemoration of the 74 victims of the Ultras football team murdered in the stadium at Port Said while the police stood idly by. It was guarded by a long cordon of men from the front, and the back was protected by cars and another long cordon of men holding hands who were doing their best to ensure that the march would not be infiltrated by thugs who would then systematically attack the demonstrators. Slogans, placards and blown-up photos of the children who died in the incident led the march. Graffiti artists accompanied it and drew on the ground and the walls. Most interesting, a film crew on top of a van recorded the event (Figure 4.15).

By way of a conclusion

The point of no return is being felt more than ever in the transformation of the psychological mindset of Egyptians, thanks to the mesmerizing power of having succeeded in the insurrection against tyranny. And if there is visible evidence of this transformation, it is, I think, most pervasive in the cultural sphere. It is expressed in the blossoming and daring youth subcultures and artistic expressions, which Tahrir magically released. These have opened new visionary paths and dreams that will be difficult to suppress. The rap musicians; the *zār* singers experienced during the last days of the revolution; Rami Essam; the producers of "song of the revolution" spread via *YouTube* and then appropriated by national TV channels; the newly created numerous music bands; the sardonic slogans; the rhymes and fantastic improvised poetry; the drawings, writings and placards that mesmerized the entire world – fortunately, none of these subcultures can simply be suppressed by military orders or by repainting walls.

A major achievement of the revolution has been that it allowed the re-invention and valorization of public spaces, through not only the act of protesting but also a new dimension for self-expression and communication in the public sphere.

However, the revolution's final victory remains undecided. The obvious violations of human rights demonstrate that the forces of the counter-revolution will remain pervasive for some time. Their violence is clearly against not only the revolutionaries but also the public performances, new emerging youth subcultures and peaceful artistic expression. The public sphere still remains a precarious domain that can be very quickly suppressed as long as the junta continues to have the final say over civil society.

Bibliography

Abdel, Deena (2011) "Revolutionary Cinema in Tahrir Square", *Ahram Online*, July 14, http://english.ahram.org.eg/NewsContent/5/35/16357/Arts--Culture/Stage--Street/Revolutionary-cinema-in-Tahrir-Square-.aspx, date accessed 15 April 2012.

Arabic Network for Human Rights Information (2012) "Egypt: Journalist's TV Show Taken Off the Air", http://www.anhri.net/en/?p=6700, date accessed 15 April 2012.

Cohen, Roger (2011) "Guru of the Revolution", *New York Times*, 17 February, http://www.nytimes.com/2011/02/18/opinion/18iht-edcohen18.html, date accessed 15 April 2012.

Egypt Independent (2012) "Abdeen Residents Demand Removal of Downtown Street Barricades", 24 February, http://www.egyptindependent.com/node/671371, date accessed 15 April 2012.

El Hebeishy, Mohamed (2011) "Mad Graffiti Weekend Storms the Egyptian Capital", *Ahram Online*, 23 May, http://english.ahram.org.eg/NewsContent/5/25/12720/Arts--Culture/Visual-Art/Mad-Graffiti-Weekend-storms-the-Egyptian-capital.aspx, date accessed 15 April 2012.

Ganzeer (2011) "Things I've Learned From the Mask of Freedom", *Rolling Bulb*, 7 June, http://rollingbulb.com/post/6290244614/things-ive-learned-from-the-mask-of-freedom, date accessed 15 April 2012.

Ganzeer (2012) Blog Ganzeer, http://ganzeer.blogspot.co.uk/, date accessed 5 May 2012.

Ghonim, Wael (2012) Inside the Egyptian Revolution, http://www.tedxcairo.com/index.php?show=Talks&id=10, date accessed 15 April 2012.

In Tahrir Square: 18 Days of Egypt's Unfinished Revolution (2011) directed by Jon Alpert and Matthew O'Neill, produced by Jon Alpert, Matthew O'Neill and Jacqueline Soohen.

Kattar, Pierre (2011) "Talaat Harb Mural Time-Lapse", http://vimeo.com/26681551, date accessed 15 April 2012.

Khallaf, Rania (2011) "The Reddish Line", *Al-Ahram Weekly On-Line*, 1074, 1–7 December, http://weekly.ahram.org.eg/2011/1074/entertain.htm, date accessed 16 April 2012.

Magdy, Zainab (2011) "El Fan Medan: Egypt Takes to the Streets for Culture and Fun", *Cairo 360*, 5 May, http://www.cairo360.com/article/artsandculture/1899/el-fan-medan-egypt-takes-to-the-streets-for-culture-and-fun/, date accessed 7 May 2012.

Mehrez, Samia (2012) " 'Watching' Tahrir", *Global Dialogue*, 2(3), 4–5.

Microphone (2010) directed by Ahmad Abdalla, produced by Mohamed Hefzy and Khaled Abol Naga.

Monatov (2011a) GaddafiLeaks, http://www.youtube.com/watch?v=pQrlS77WHRs& feature=relmfu, date accessed 18 April 2012.

Monatov (2011b) The Most Powerful/or Pervasive Films of the Season (Aqwa Aflām al-Mawssim), http://www.youtube.com/watch?v=oLLoyOazwiQ, date accessed 18 April 2012.

Rashwan, Nada Hussein (2012) "Egypt's Junta: From 'One hand' to 'Liars', Say Revolutionaries", *Ahram Online*, 30 January, http://english.ahram.org.eg/NewsContent/1/64/33108/Egypt/Politics-/Egypts-junta-From-One-hand-to-Liars,-say-revolutio.aspx, date accessed 15 April 2012.

Reporting...A Revolution (Al Thawra...Khabar) (2012) directed by Bassam Mortada.

Revolution Graffiti (2012) Current Egyptian Revolution Graffiti, http://en-gb.facebook.com/GraffitiEgypt?sk=wall&filter=12, date accessed 6 May 2012.

Shenker, Jack (2011) "The Struggle to Document Egypt's Revolution", *Guardian*, 15 July , http://www.guardian.co.uk/world/2011/jul/15/struggle-to-document-egypt-revolution, date accessed 16 April 2012.

Shukrallah, Salma (2012) "Egypt's Interior Minister Proven a Liar: Overwhelming Evidence Police Fired Birdshot at Protesters", *Al Ahram Online*, 7 February, http://english.ahram.org.eg/News/ 33950.aspx, date accessed 15 April 2012.

Tahrir 2011: The Good, the Bad and the Politician (Al Tahrir 2011: Al Tayib wa al Sharis wa al Siyassi) (2011) directed by Tamer Ezzat, Ahmad Abdalla, Ayten Amin and Amr Salama, produced by Frederic Sichler and Mohamed Hefzy.

Taxi Band Magnoon (2010), http://www.youtube.com/watch?v=Y1o6H7cvWWc, date accessed 15 April 2012.

TEDx Cairo (2012) TEDx Cairo homepage, http://www.tedxcairo.com/index.php, date accessed 15 April 2012.

Trew, Bel, Mohamed Abdalla and Ahmed Feteha (2012) "Walled In: SCAF's Concrete Barricades", *Ahramonline*, 9 February, http://english.ahram.org.eg/NewsContent/1/64/33929/Egypt/Politics-/Walled-in-SCAFs-concrete-barricades-.aspx, date accessed 16 April 2012.

Youssef, Bassem (2012) A "Room" on Youtube!, http://www.tedxcairo.com/index.php? show=Talks&id=33, date accessed 15 April 2012.

5
Shanghai's Public Screen Culture: Local and Coeval

Chris Berry

Moving image screens used to be confined indoors, in the form of either movie theater screens or TV screens. But, over the last decade and more, electronic moving image screens of various sizes and types have moved out to proliferate across the public spaces of the world's cities. From the huge LED screens that cover whole sides of office towers and shopping malls to ATM screens and information screens in the lobbies and entrance halls of stations, banks and other publicly accessible buildings, they have become commonplace. How should we understand these public screens and their role in the public spaces of contemporary urban life? Many scholars who work on public screens are drawn by the novelty of certain screens and their unusual uses, such as the monumental size of certain screens; how some are not attached to but are an integral part of architecture; efforts to use them to stimulate public debate; and art shows using public screens. But, with the significant exception of Anna McCarthy's seminal work on what she terms "ambient television," written before the arrival of the flat screen, the everydayness of public screens has been relatively neglected so far (McCarthy, 2001). Perhaps they are so taken for granted that it is hard to pay attention to them except when they are exceptionally large or something unexpected is seen on them. But how are they actually used in everyday life? And are they used in the same way all over the world, as part of some post-modern homogenization of urban life?

This chapter takes the example of Shanghai to question assumptions about the generic quality of everyday public screen culture and public space today. It focuses on two aspects of everyday local specificity. First, public space is contested space, and screens participate in attempts to regulate and smooth our public behaviors. But their ability to perform this function is dependent on the screens' ability to engage spectators amidst all the visual clutter of contemporary public space. This chapter argues that an important factor enabling this engagement depends on an element of "secular enchantment" bestowed on moving image screens by relocating and remediating the magic of the moving image from the cinema. However, following McCarthy's emphasis on "site specificity," the deployment of that secular enchantment varies according to the function of the public spaces in which the screens are embedded. In other words, in this instance, localness and local deployments of the enchantment of the moving image are less about Shanghai-ness or Chinese-ness than they are about the different social functions of different public spaces. For example, the primary function of screens in transport hubs like the Shanghai South Railway Station is to direct *flows* of people through the space; screens in the Shanghai Science and Technology Museum (SSTM) mediate the visitor's *experience* of the exhibits; and in the Wujiaochang retail hub they not only advertise products and stores but also act as part of a "lightscape" of *enchantment* that helps to attract visitors. In each case, the individual circumstances of the site and those who frequent it create further local specificity.

Second, the chapter looks at the unusual prevalence of moving text-based screens in Shanghai, compared with cities outside Asia. Mostly using red Chinese characters on black LED screens fixed in certain locations, these come in two main forms. There are tickertape-style screens where the words move across horizontally (usually from left to right), which in Chinese are called "walking word" (*zouzi*, 走字) screens. The other type consists of slideshow-style presentations where a loop of different texts (and sometimes images) plays itself out repeatedly. Here, I am looking at something that is quite distinctive about Shanghai, or perhaps about East Asian cities, although the question of regional generalization remains to be researched. I argue that the prevalence of these text-based screens needs to be understood as part of a long but varied local lineage of putting writing into public spaces and, in particular, at the liminal spaces of various kinds of entryways. This in turn implies a conceptual lineage concerning what public space is in China.

Taken together, these two forms of local specificity indicate that everyday public screen culture and public space may be less generic under conditions of post-modern globalization than is often thought. Furthermore, the local usages that can be observed are not a "glocal" adaptation of a Western or metropolitan standard but part of a pattern of coeval development of local uses under conditions of rapid proliferation of new media technologies around the world.

Everydayness and secular enchantment

Everydayness remains largely ignored in the emergent literature on public screens. This can be seen in the collection of essays found in the *Urban Screens Reader*, which is the first significant book in English on this topic (McQuire *et al.*, 2009). Although one essay in the book does place public screens in a lineage of display media going back to the earliest billboards and before (Huhtamo, 2009), at least seven examine the relatively rare use of them for public art (Beiguelman, 2009; Bounegru, 2009; Dekker, 2009; Eppink and Arnold, 2009; Lancel and Maat, 2009; Nevárez, 2009; Schuijren and McQuire, 2009). Other work in the volume focuses on pioneering projects to use large public screens for special events or for public broadcasting in public spaces, in an effort to stimulate civic culture, urban regeneration and participatory citizenship (Arcagni, 2009; Roh and Papastergiadis, 2009; Yue, 2009). Significant examples include the Federation Square screen in Melbourne, Australia (Brennan *et al.*, 2009), and the BBC's Public Space Broadcasting Project, which installed nine big screens in cities around the UK (Gibbons and McQuire, 2009). All of these interventions could be seen as part of the ever-elusive quest for the realization of a modern "public sphere" of rational debate and decision-making (Habermas, 1989).

However, in everyday wanderings through the city, we are unlikely to come across the use of public screens for art events or even broadcasting. On the vast majority of occasions, our encounters with public screens are much more prosaic. In this regard, the deployment of today's vast range of different-sized public screens using different technologies can be seen as an extension of the phenomenon of ambient TV analyzed by Anna McCarthy a decade ago, when such screens were still confined to cathode ray tubes (McCarthy, 2001). This chapter looks at the more often overlooked and taken for granted everyday deployments of moving image screens in public spaces, be they publicly owned or only publicly accessible.[1] In principle, the same screen technology is available for purchase and installation anywhere in the world. Indeed, looking at the transformation of the urban environment under conditions of globalization, digitalization and rapid development, eminent architect and Harvard University professor Rem Koolhaas has claimed that "The Generic City is what is left after large sections of urban life crossed over to cyberspace" (Koolhaas, 1995). No doubt he is onto something, especially with regard to the migration of many activities into cyberspace. But does this really mean that new media usage is making all cities the same? To investigate this question, I have been engaged in a larger project examining everydayness and public screens in Cairo, Shanghai and London – arguably the largest cities in their respective continents. The full comparative findings of that larger project await publication elsewhere. But, as I hope to show in this chapter focused on Shanghai, I found considerable evidence of locally specific uses of moving image screens in public spaces.[2]

The working method in Shanghai and on the larger project involved an initial exploratory phase of walking in each city. Inspired in part by the Situationist *dérive*'s capacity for random wandering and bumping into the unexpected (McDonagh, 1996),[3] three things were rapidly discovered. First, moving image screens are everyday but they are not everywhere. They are not a form of "ubiquitous media." Although huge screens might grab our attention on special occasions, screens are now mixed in with everyday life. They are part of our experience of the bus stop, of buying a certain object and of traversing the world in numerous ordinary ways. Screen technologies may be discretely embedded in the architecture of place (the ATM machine) or loudly advertising a connection to other sites (screens advertising a holiday destination), but fixed moving image screens are also almost entirely absent in large swathes of the city. Overall, almost all deployments of these screens are connected in some way with aspirational culture, be it the aspiration for urban regeneration, the promotion of consumerism or the quest for knowledge and self-improvement. However, under this overall umbrella of aspiration, different public screens have specific sizes, forms and uses in particular places.

Second, particular social use patterns manifest themselves in these varied contexts. These patterns are characterized by a combination of common overall functions with what McCarthy calls "site specificity" (McCarthy, 2001, p. 2). For example, in transport hubs, the use of screens to deliver information and direct flows of passengers dominates. But particular architectures, regulations, economics, cultural expectations and more determine absolutely singular local manifestations of this dominant pattern in particular airports, train stations and bus stations. With this in mind, three of these social use patterns were selected: the direction of flows in transport hubs; the constitution of the visitor experience in museums and other public exhibition sites; and the enchantment of the consumer by lightscapes at retail and leisure sites.

Prosaic and banal though these sites may be, enchantment is a necessary component of the deployment of the screens in all cases, because it is what catches our eye and helps to make the screen stand out from the visual clutter of the contemporary city. This is most self-evident in the case of retail and entertainment sites. But the moving images on information screens – even if they are only the banal changes in destinations and train numbers – catch the eye in stations and airports, however fleetingly. Exhibits that incorporate moving image screens seem to draw the museum visitor more quickly and in larger numbers than others tend to. Even though no story may be told, this enchanting quality is connected to the cinematic lineage of these moving image screens.

Francesco Casetti speaks of the "re-location" of screens from the bounded site of the cinema to their dispersal across urban terrain, noting that in the process, screens themselves undergo transformation (Casetti, 2008). The same logic subtends the movement of McCarthy's "ambient" TV out from domestic space. In the case of today's public screens, the scale of the image is variable, sound is often (although not always) absent, and the screen increasingly acts as platform for a range of rapidly changing materials (news, weather, advertisements and film, to name a few). The process that Bolter and Grusin have called remediation goes some way in providing an understanding of the mixing of media formats and their content, and one of the media that gets remediated with these moving image screens in public places is the cinema (Bolter and Grusin, 1999).

Yet, these moving image screens in public spaces rarely possess the narrative quality associated with feature films, nor do they share the exhibition conditions of darkness and silence that encourage the concentrated gaze found in the movie theater. So what is the "cinematic" quality that they share with earlier forms? Writing in the post-digital era when the ontological distinctiveness of celluloid has disappeared and the definition of cinema is once again up for grabs, Sean Cubitt returns to the Lumière Brothers' famous *Sortie des Usines* ("Leaving the Factory", 1895) to argue for the idea of a quality that he calls *le vif* as the quintessentially cinematic. This is the "magical transformation" that puts things into movement (Cubitt, 2004, pp. 19–21). When cinema first appeared, it inspired amazement. Although it rapidly became quotidian, its special quality as the site of the *le vif* did not disappear entirely. By extension, when moving image advertisements and notices are brought into public spaces, however banal their content and taken for granted the technology is, this magic of *le vif* also insinuates itself.

As Cubitt's term "magical transformation" suggests, there is an element of enchantment in *le vif.* The argument that one of the characteristics, and even requirements, of modernity is "the disenchantment of the world" is associated with Max Weber, who held that the acceptance of science and rationality meant the disappearance of mystery in all its forms ranging from religion to magic (Weber, 1988). There are many differences and disagreements amongst those writing on disenchantment and modernity. For many, disenchantment meant the liberation of humanity. For others, including Weber, disenchantment robbed the world of meaning and was a profoundly alienating experience. Many Marxists shared Weber's negativity about existing modernity, but they believed that disenchantment had not gone far enough. And where Weber was pessimistic about modernity in general, they were hopeful that revolution would dispel remnants of enchantment.

However, what most writers on disenchantment share is the assumption of a fundamental opposition between modernity and enchantment. As Michael Saler points out, it is this position that has changed in the last decade and more. With it has changed the status of the enchanting in everyday life. It is no longer necessarily opposed to modernity either as a remnant from the pre-modern or as a perversion within modernity. For some, this can mean trying to work out a space for religion and the supernatural within modernity, or accounting for "modern religion." For others, it means engaging with what Saler calls "disenchanted enchantment" (Saler, 2006). In public screen environments, this disenchanted or secular enchantment, as it is termed in this project, meets and mingles with the everyday and taken for granted in a variety of forms and uses.

Social function and site singularity

Where does local specificity appear in the varied forms and uses of the enchanting public screens? As indicated above, one primary way is in the combination of different social patterns of use with the singularity of the individual site. This section of the chapter shows how the enchantment of moving image screens is used in different ways in the transport hub, retail and leisure center, and public exhibition space selected in Shanghai, and further illustrates site singularity by brief comparison with the sites worked on in London and Cairo.

The visitor experience in the SSTM

In Michael Saler's account, a primary area where "disenchanted enchantment" is found is the discourse of wonder around science itself. He points out that with science, seemingly magical effects are used to excite audience interest and are then explained in a dialectic of the mysterious and the rational employed to pedagogical ends. Michele Pierson has also investigated this interest in scientific "phantasmagoria" as part of the heritage of today's excitement and interest in cinema's special effects. These effects themselves inspire secular enchantment manifested in magazines and websites devoted in an almost fetishistic manner to effects and their explanation (Pierson, 2002). The secular enchantment of science as both mysterious and rational certainly helps to explain the intensity of engagement observed in the public exhibition site selected in Shanghai, which is the SSTM. Screens in the SSTM play an integral role in generating this wondrous experience of science.

Primary observations on the SSTM and all the sites discussed in this essay took place during a number of visits between 2008 and 2011. The excitement of the SSTM experience is not immediately visible from outside the building. An arc of steel and glass covering 68,000 square meters that opened in 2001 (SSTM, 2011), it is so vast that it has its own dedicated stop on the Shanghai subway system. As you approach the building for the first time, it and the surrounding area seem sparsely populated, and the few human beings in sight are overwhelmed by the grand scale of everything. But, on entering, it is clear that screen technologies play an important role. As well as the admission ticket, visitors can also buy tickets for the museum's own IMAX 3D Theater, IMAX Dome Theater, IWERKS Theater and Space Theater. Nonetheless, the lobby and the surrounding areas appear relatively empty.

In my experience of the museum, it is when you enter one of its 14 exhibition halls that an entirely different impression is created. On busy days in the most popular halls, such as "Light of Wisdom" and "The World of Robots," the cold, empty and echoing atmosphere of the outer spaces is replaced by crowds of excited children shouting as they run noisily from one exhibit to the next. Accompanying family members are scarcely less excited. The exhibits promote a high level of interactivity, both between the visitor and the exhibit and between the visitors themselves. For example, a very popular new exhibit in the "Light of Wisdom" hall (installed, I believe, some time between my visits in October 2009 and March 2010) illustrates the power of concentration. Two visitors each put on a headband, then sit opposite each other and try to move a metal ball toward their opponent by focusing on it intensely. Their concentration, as sensed through the headband, is displayed as a graph on a screen above the exhibit. Friends and relatives cheer them on, their attention alternating back and forth between the "players" and the screen. This integration of screens into exhibits that encourage an embodied experience as visitors ride them, pull levers, climb on them and more is typical of the SSTM's design. Where visitors interact directly with the screens, the point-and-click computer mouse is the most common device.

When I interviewed the Deputy Director of the SSTM's Research and Design Institute, Xin Ge (忻歌), together with research assistant Wu Dan, she told us that if they could make every exhibit interactive, they would. She explained that they had moved away from the old division of exhibits according to science disciplines and moved toward themes, and that they had also consciously learnt from theme parks such as Disneyland in their efforts to create an exciting experience for the visitor. She expressed some concern about whether merely pulling a lever meant that there was intellectual or educational interaction going on inside the visitor, but acknowledged that interactivity was unquestionably very popular with visitors of all ages (Xin, 2009).

If the logic of the visitor experience overdetermines the deployment of screens in public institutions like the SSTM, the enhanced localness of site specificity can be illustrated by a comparison with the London Science Museum, which is the public exhibition site selected for London. Some differences are immediately clear. Interaction between visitors and computer screens in the SSTM is mediated by a computer mouse embedded in the panel for the exhibit, with a moving ball enabling the visitor to move the cursor. In contrast, in the London Science Museum, touch screens dominate. These are almost entirely absent in Shanghai. Relatively few exhibits in London are designed for direct embodied interaction, and auratic objects in glass cases are a major part of the London museum. The latter are far fewer in Shanghai. London's touch screens enable the visitor to access archival "layers" of further information, newsreel footage, interviews and so forth. Again, this is mostly absent in Shanghai.

Among the reasons that could be advanced for these differences is the free admission to the London Science Museum. A visitor can decide to focus on the screen-accessed archive attached to an individual exhibit for as long as they like, secure in the knowledge that it will not cost them more money to return another day and explore the rest of the museum. Zhang Dajin (张大谨) of the SSTM Exhibition Education Section told Wu Dan and me that visitor research indicated that 40% of visitors prioritized fun and entertainment. He speculated that after buying a ticket, they would not want to linger too long at a single exhibit and felt that they needed to experience as much variety as they could rather than focus on information that they might be able to see on Chinese equivalents of *YouTube* when they got home (Zhang, 2010). In addition, the

London Science Museum's touch screens seemed more geared toward an individual visitor than the group-led experience that dominates in the SSTM.

Managing passenger flows in the Shanghai South Railway Station

The transport hub analyzed for this project in Shanghai is the new Shanghai South Railway Station, which opened in 2006. There are two forms of screens in the station, and their primary functions are straightforwardly and systematically associated with the management of passenger flows. One type displays colored Chinese characters on a black background. The predominant color is red, although green and orange are also used.[4] These screens display constantly changing information about train numbers, platforms, departure times, the sites of waiting rooms and so forth. They operate either in slideshow mode or as horizontally moving streams of characters, tickertape-style and information such as "now boarding" (现在检票) flashes on and off.

The second type of screen streams TV programming specially prepared for the All-China Railway Bureau Television Advertising Broadcasting Network (全国火车站电视广告联播网) by a company called Mega Info Media (兆讯传媒公司). This consists of a mix of brief entertainment features (often including travel destinations, such as Hong Kong Disneyland) and commercials. At the bottom of the screen there is a blue bar with white writing moving across it in a tickertape-style stream of news and weather information. Although people occasionally glance at these screens, very few, if any, consistently watch this programming. The installation of these TV screens also implies that they are not designed for such viewing, because the nearby seats are rarely aligned for gazing at the screen. The waiting rooms for first-class passengers are in lounges that are part of a ring that runs around the upper level of the station. Here, the screens are above many of the seats, so that a passenger would have to make a careful choice of seat if they wanted to watch consistently. In the large waiting area for regular passengers in the central part of the upper level, sections are arranged to wait in for each separate train. These run off a central aisle and resemble a departure lounge in an airport. At the far end where passengers go to the platforms are information screens, and at the end near the central aisle are screens showing TV programs. Rows of seats run between them, so that passengers can glance easily at both screens, but would have to twist round in their seats to watch either one consistently.

In these circumstances, it is possible to conclude that the primary function of both types of screen is the management of passenger flow. The primary purpose of the TV screens, along with the seats near them, is not to encourage focused viewing but simply to communicate to passengers that they can wait there. Together, the two types of screen operate a dialectic of directed movement. The first type directs passengers to go somewhere, whereas the second type tells them to wait until they are told by another screen of the first type to go somewhere else (and possibly wait again).

The use of screens to manage passenger flow is, in a sense, local to transport hubs in all the cities examined for the larger project. However, an additional degree of local specificity is produced by the specificity of the particular site. This can be observed readily in a brief comparison of Shanghai South Railway Station with London's St. Pancras International. Shanghai South Railway Station is a round, steel and glass building. As such, it is conspicuously different from older brick and concrete railway stations, such as St. Pancras International. It also departs radically from the usual rectangular configuration of terminus railway stations, featuring an entrance on one side opposite platforms and tracks that go out from the other side. This is the pattern found at St. Pancras International (albeit modified under reconstruction) and also at the main Shanghai Railway Station, opened in 1987. In contrast, Shanghai South Railway Station is more reminiscent of an air terminal, where the planes are often arranged around an oval or circular structure.

The circular form of Shanghai South Railway Station in itself is one sign of how aspiration animates the site, as it aims to re-signify rail travel as modern and even futuristic by borrowing from air travel. Indeed, this is a building that aims to create a sense of wonder. Departing passengers ascend escalators from the dark depths to the wide, open and light-filled space of the station's uppermost level, where they must surely think, "Where are the trains?" (They are in fact hidden below.) If the unconventional and air terminal-like qualities of the building itself inspire wonder, so does the wonder of high-speed rail travel – China has the fastest high-speed rail services in the world and is adding to them rapidly (*China Daily*, 2010). Electronic screens are a prominent feature of the station, too. Perhaps the mystery of screen movement and the excitement of transport movement combine here to create a buzz of excitement – a zone of secular enchantment and aspirations premised on the promise of literal transport rather than the virtual transport of cinema.

St. Pancras International also borrows from air travel by installing "check-in" desks for its Eurostar service to the continent, and it uses the "modern" and "new" technology of the public moving image screen to communicate futuristic aspirations. However, these aspirational elements are installed within an old building that is itself one of the characteristic and valued "signature" features of the station. Therefore, the designers of St. Pancras International have had to negotiate the existing architecture and install screens in a more idiosyncratic pattern than at Shanghai South. There, the highly consistent and clearly distinguished use of the two types of screens seems to respond to another site-specific characteristic: the round shape of the building makes it potentially easy for passengers to get lost. The roof above the upper level departures area at Shanghai South Railway Station is held up by a ring of pillars, each of which is flagged with a number. These numbers help railway employees to direct confused passengers.[5] But the consistent distinction between information screens and TV programming screens along with their repeated deployment in the same types of positions across the symmetrical building is also important in assisting passengers to navigate the space. For example, the placement of the screens in each of the waiting areas running off the central aisle is identical. No matter which of the four escalators a passenger ascends and which of the four entrances they use to access the departures area, they will find identical information screens at each entrance.

Finally on the question of site specificity, maybe the largest difference between St. Pancras International and Shanghai South Railway Station concerns retail opportunities. The railway system in China is a publicly owned institution in which profits and losses are less of a priority than efficient transportation of passengers and freight. There has been nothing like the complex and contentious privatization that has occurred in the UK, nor the private–public partnerships that characterize the transport system there. Whereas St. Pancras International also mimics British airports by forcing passengers to run the gauntlet of numerous shops and restaurants before they reach the platforms, Shanghai South Railway Station arranges its limited array of shops and restaurants so that they do not impede or even distract from flow toward the trains. In Shanghai South Railway Station, the passenger's eye is caught most immediately by screens rather than shops, and one's experience of the open space of the huge departures level across the entire top of the building is mediated by those screens and their systematic deployment. In contrast, inside St. Pancras International, there is no point from which to view the whole departures area, and our apprehension of the spaces of the station is not structured by a systematic and consistent deployment of electronic screens. Instead, screens are embedded in a heterogeneous array of shop and restaurant signs, window displays and so forth. In this way, the interior of St. Pancras in some aspects resembles the enchanting lightscapes that characterize retail and leisure centers, which are the subject of the next section.

The enchantment of consumption at Wujiaochang

The retail and leisure center examined for this project in Shanghai is an intersection in the northern district of Yangpu where five roads meet. Called Wujiaochang (五角场) in Chinese, in English is it usually translated as "Pentagon Plaza."[6] Back in the early 1930s, just before the Japanese occupation, the neighborhood around Wujiaochang was planned to become the new center for the municipal government of Chinese Shanghai outside the foreign concession territories (MacPherson,1990). Today, it is a designated "sub-center" of Shanghai, intended to serve as the retail and leisure center for over 2 million people (Zhong, 2009, p. 113). Most of these are from Yangpu District, home to 1.24 million people (Shanghai Municipal Government, 2011). Although Tongji and Fudan universities are nearby, Yangpu is better known as a low-income former factory district struggling to re-invent itself (Zhang, 2009).

The redevelopment of Wujiaochang and the surrounding blocks is part of that effort. On the southern side of the Pentagon, the Orient Shopping Center (东方商厦) was one of the first new buildings. A hotel is planned for the remaining empty southeast corner next to it, whereas another large commercial building was just being completed during my visit in early 2011 on the southwest corner. A station on the number ten subway line opened in 2010. On the northeast corner is the Wanda Plaza (万达广场), a complex of buildings housing a variety of stores and restaurants, as well as a multiplex cinema. On the northwest corner is the Bailian New Era Mall (百联又一城购物中心), a single building structured around an atrium, and also housing a multiplex cinema.

Screens take many forms at Wujiaochang, from huge ones on the sides of the Orient Shopping Center and the Bailian New Era Mall to advertising screens on pillars along the side of the road, smaller screens above shop doorways with red characters running tickertape-style across them, and TV-style screens on charity donation boxes placed in the entranceways to some of the major department stores. In the Shanghai South Railway Station, moving image screens are almost the only significant light-emitting objects aside from ambient electrical lighting, and the only sources of moving images, making them very eye-catching. This is less true at Wujiaochang, where they are embedded in a huge range of light displays, including the movement produced by neon displays.

In these circumstances, moving image screens at Wujiaochang need to be recognized as part of a larger, heterogeneous and ever-changing three-dimensional lightscape. This includes the lightboxes for advertising posters that we are all familiar with, as well as colored lighting strips on the pillars of the overpass that spans the Wujiaochang intersection, and also seasonal displays of special lighting, such as the red lanterns for National Day I observed in 2009 in the underground plaza where pedestrians descend to cross the intersection. It also includes an impressive variety of neon light displays, ranging from rainbow effects along the side of the building that houses the Orient Shopping Center to a rain of sparkling light that appears to cascade perpetually down one wall of the tallest building in the Wanda Plaza. At night, the white wall of the Bailian New Era Mall is turned into a projection screen, with beams from the top of the Wanda Plaza bathing it with both abstract colored lighting patterns and advertising. Last, but not least, is Wujiaochang's centerpiece – the huge colored "egg."

According to the landscape designer, Zhong Song, this element in the re-design of Wujiaochang was conceived of more futuristically as a UFO-like structure. But the locals brought it down to earth by referring to it more prosaically as the "egg," and the name has stuck. Commissioned to do the design for the sub-center of Wujiaochang in 2003, the main problem Zhong and his colleagues faced was the overpass that bifurcated and dominated the five-road intersection. The awe-inspiring "egg" was their solution (Zhong, 2009, p. 114).[7] It consists of a large steel frame that wraps the overpass. At night, starting at around seven in the evening, the egg comes alive with a light display. Initially a few white lights blink, but soon rainbow-colored patterns are pulsating across it. The huge advertising screens on the Orient Shopping Center and the Bailian New Era Mall shine down from above, and ballroom and line dancers from the neighborhood come out after dinner with their boom boxes to take over the pavement areas outside the Paris Printemps (巴黎春天) department store on the corner of the Wanda Plaza nearest to the egg.

If the management of flows overdetermines the deployment of screens in the Shanghai South Railway Station, at Wujiaochang, secular enchantment as part of the lure of consumerism and its myriad pleasures dominates. Here the age-old magic of light and movement in the still of the night is harnessed to the promise of personal transformation through consumption. Advertisements consistently promise a magical consequence to purchase and consumption – an ecstatic happiness that far exceeds what one could reasonably expect for the price of a can of drink. Amongst all the light displays at Wujiaochang, the biggest screen of them all, on the side of Bailian New Era Mall, is especially bright. Like a beacon in the night beckoning the local inhabitants, it can be seen from kilometers away along the roads leading to Wujiaochang.

The integration of screens with a variety of other enticements under the umbrella of enchantment is common to retail and leisure centers in all of the cities examined for the larger project. But again, site specificity manifests itself in various ways. If one compares Wujiaochang with the City Stars Mall in Cairo, which was widely held to be the most fashionable mall at the time of the research, whereas Wujiaochang is at an intersection and includes a variety of different buildings as well as roadways and pedestrian areas, City Stars consists of three massive linked buildings, all run by the same company. As a result, where screens at Wujiaochang are heterogeneous to a dizzying degree, in City Stars they appear as pairs of flat-screen TV monitors suspended from ceilings throughout and all displaying exactly the same loop of advertisements and announcements about City Stars. Presumably, this unusual orderliness, along with the carefully controlled climate and the immaculate cleanliness, is part of the appeal of City Stars to the exhausted and stressed elite of Cairo.

As for Wujiaochang, in a book about material modernity in Republican China (1911–1949), Frank Dikötter writes that "Department stores were invariably outlined spectacularly from towering cupola and mansard to pavement and basement" with lighting, and of Shanghai's Nanjing Road that "illumination appeared to be part of the magic of electricity" (Dikötter, 2007, pp. 137–138). If visitors to China's cities in the Republican era were impressed by the extravagant light displays, it is also true that Wujiaochang outshines the light displays at London and Cairo's retail and leisure centers, at least in the literal sense. Such considerations lead Dikötter to speculate that "To a country which made an abundant display of lanterns carried on bamboo poles at traditional festivals and important social occasions, profuse electric bulbs must have seemed both propitious and decorous" (ibid., p. 140). This leads to the question of localness not in the form of the different social functions and the singularity of particular sites but in terms of cultural lineage.

Walking words and cultural genealogy

It might be plausible to speculate about a connection between some particular Chinese love of *renao* (热闹, literally "hot noise" or bustling excitement) and the proliferation of screens in the public lightscapes of Shanghai. But there is plenty of evidence that people in other cultures were also excited by the introduction of electric light (Whissel, 2008; see also Schivelbusch, 1995).[8] Overall, although the localness of specific social functions and site singularity may inform the types of secular enchantment as part of public screen cultures argued for in the previous section, it is less clear that the localness of cultural specificity is a prominent feature of that picture.

However, this final section of the chapter does outline a lineage more specific to China. When one compares Cairo, Shanghai and London, it is clear that some uses of public screens are relatively specific to each city. In Shanghai, screens that show text-based materials, most often in entranceways or other liminal spaces, are especially common. The text-based information screens at the Shanghai South Railway Station, discussed in the previous section, are examples of this. And, like the screens at this station, red is the dominant color on such screens throughout the city, followed by green and yellow or orange. The text displays take two dominant forms – either the "walking word" screens with tickertape-style text moving horizontally across them, or a loop of slides, operating like a PowerPoint presentation (Figure 5.1).

Figure 5.1 Tickertape-style "walking word" screen at a store entrance at Wujiaochang. The characters are red and move from left to right. Here they display public service advertising about the Shanghai World Expo
Source: All photographs by Chris Berry.

In my research, I did not notice the prevalence of these text-based public screens at first. This oversight is in itself a demonstration of the power of the everyday to be taken for granted, even when one is consciously attempting to attend to it. But as my explorations took me and research assistant Wu Dan away from the center of Shanghai to the outer suburb of Songjiang, at one end of subway line nine, we found ourselves in an environment where the only "moving image" screens were those on which what moved was in fact text.[9] This impression of text screens as the most widespread and basic form was reinforced later on the same day, when we traveled back toward the city center and explored the neighborhood around the Yaohua Road subway station. At the intersection of lines seven and eight, construction was going ahead full steam for the nearby Shanghai World Expo, which was due to open in a few months. However, this is an ordinary neighborhood without major intersections full of department stores or public facilities like large train stations and museums. Again, the only kind of public screens found were text-based ones (Figure 5.2).

As already noted, liminal spaces are the most frequent locations for these screens. These include the entrances to buildings that the public

Figure 5.2 Slideshow-style text screen at the entrance to a housing compound in Songjiang. Characters are red and orange, bearing a message about security

have access to and the entrances to residential neighborhoods, as well as the entrances to buses. In the Yaohua Road neighborhood, I even found walking word screens above the entrances to a new public toilet, advising which door led to the men's urinal, the men's bathroom and the women's bathrooms. In the case of retail spaces ranging from regular shops to banks and even the post office, walking word screens function to attract customers by detailing the latest offers. However, in the run-up to the Shanghai 2010 World Expo, many promotional messages about the event were also featured, indicating that they carry public service advertising as well as their own commercial promotions. Other screens offer greetings, advice about circumstances in the space one is entering and other information. For example, during my exploration of Songjiang, I came across a screen at the north entrance to the Jinguiyuan (锦桂苑) housing compound on Beicui Road (北翠路). It displayed a slideshow of information and advice, ranging from the daily weather forecast and World Expo slogans to warnings about thieves operating in the area and messages against taking drugs or drunk driving.

China is, of course, the country of the Great Wall.[10] So, perhaps it is not surprising that walls and the demarcation of inside and outside spaces continue to be a major feature of urban space there today. The Chinese word for a city and a wall are the same (*cheng*, 城). As Youqin Huang and Setha M. Low have pointed out in their essay on private housing developments in China,

> gated and walled communities have always existed in Chinese cities. The traditional Chinese house...was built in an enclosed form.... Most housing built in the socialist era was in the form of 'work-unit compounds' (*danwei dayuan*, 单位大院), which were often walled, gated and guarded.
>
> (Huang and Low, 2008, p. 183)

In a culture that seems to place great significance on the demarcation of inside and outside, the patterns of text screen placement at entranceways and their usage seem to reinforce those existing cultural patterns.

Indeed, the use of words on entryways is by no means new. As is widely known, at lunar New Year, it is customary to stick good luck couplets written on paper on either side of the doorway to your home. This habit is believed to date back more than 1000 years, although it was only in the fourteenth century that the use of red paper by ordinary citizens became a standardized and formalized practice (Hsieh and Chou, 1981, p. 125). At liminal points in public spaces in villages and towns, decorated archways known as *paifang* (牌坊) or *pailou* (牌楼) were frequently found stretching across streets and at the entrances to compounds of various kinds, and some still survive. Their central panels often carry inscriptions. Mostly these are simply the name of the building ahead or of the gate itself. But others are moral homilies praising filial piety, charity and other socially endorsed ideological values, in particular on memorial archways dedicated to exemplary people (Han, 2008).[11]

More recently, after the founding of the People's Republic of China, a "blackboard newspaper" (*heiban bao*, 黑板报) culture developed. This medium has been seen as an effective way to generate and circulate local news and to reach ordinary people who might not buy or attend to newspapers. Guidebooks on how to produce effective news blackboards have been published since the 1950s, often profusely illustrated (Zhou, 1952; Zhou and Bo, 2002).[12] As the illustrations in these publications indicate, at the entrances to work units or housing areas during the Maoist era, blackboards often greeted visitors, workers and residents with news about production output and upcoming meetings, or information about public health and political campaigns.

Today, these blackboards are often replaced with text screens with slideshow-style displays. But the originals can still be found, although these days their content is less overtly political. At the time of my explorations, many carried chalk illustrations of the World Expo "*haibao*" (海宝) mascot. At the entranceway to a traditional Shanghai *lilong* (里弄) housing compound in the Yangpu District (where Wujiaochang is also located), I found one such illustration accompanied by a notice advising residents there might be outsiders in the area during the World Expo and to try to help them with directions – but not to pretend to know the way if unsure (Figure 5.3).[13]

This long historical lineage of marking liminal points in (and into and out of) public spaces with writing may help to account for the rapid uptake of text screens across Shanghai (and China generally) in recent years, although I was also told that a significant drop in price was another factor. In this sense, perhaps one can see these distinctively local Shanghai public screens as a kind of remediation, in Bolter and Grusin's sense, of earlier media forms (Bolter and Grusin, 1999). However, it is important to point out that they are not simply a case of old wine in new bottles. Rather, these remediations are better understood as a genealogy, in Foucault's sense that emphasizes contingency and disjuncture

Figure 5.3 Blackboard in Yangpu

rather than linear historical development (Foucault, 1977). The shift to blackboard newspapers is not just a technological change that allows for updating, but also part of the abandonment of the Confucian ideology that characterizes the messages found on *pailou* in favor of revolutionary ideology.

The content displayed on today's electronic text screens partakes of the changes in Chinese urban culture that have accompanied the last 20 years of marketization. This is straightforwardly apparent in the presence of commercial advertising, which would have been extremely limited during the heyday of Maoism. But it is also evident in the text screens at the entrances to residential neighborhoods. First, according to what I was told by the gatekeepers (*menwei*, 门卫) I spoke to, these screens are often not installed and monitored by the lowest level of the party-state apparatus, the residents' committee, as would have been the case with the old blackboard culture. Instead, it is often the property owners' committee that is in charge of them. These bodies are composed of those residents who have bought the leases on their flats in what are increasingly commercial residential compounds. Therefore, installing an electronic screen is part of the aspirational culture of upgrading and improving one's property. It is no longer solely part of the pedagogical culture that monopolized public culture in the past, although such practices continue to inform many of the messages they carry, as indicated above. Finally, I was also told that these screens are often paid for by advertising companies who advertise on the screens or on the frame, making them part of the new market economy.

Conclusion

What should be concluded from this discussion of localness in Shanghai's public screen culture? First, one should hesitate before jumping too easily to any conclusions about the modern city as "generic." Although fixed moving image screens in public spaces may rarely help to fulfill dreams of an intellectually and politically engaged public, they are not uniform, and not uniform in a number of ways. Although we may take them for granted and think they are "everywhere," in fact they are far from ubiquitous. Furthermore, the type and size of the screens along with their particular location and the materials displayed on them varies according to particular local usages. Here, local specificity is determined by both genres of social function and site specificity, as discussed in the examples from Shanghai in this chapter. Second, the uptake of the screens is also shaped by the interaction with pre-existing locally specific practices.

This leads to my second and final general point about local specificity. Local specificity has been part of larger debates about the nature of the culture of globalization. While the culture of globalization is commonly assumed to have a homogenizing (or, some would say, Americanizing) tendency, others have argued that new hybridities produce new local forms, and that therefore globalization is heterogenizing.[14] Amongst the influential concepts associated with this understanding is "glocalization." In the business world, this term is associated with the practices of Japanese multinationals in their efforts to adapt to local conditions (and known in Japanese as *dochakuka*). Roland Robertson popularized this term as a way of understanding how the local ameliorates the force of the global (Robertson, 1995).

Is this framework of "glocalization" an appropriate one through which to see the local specificity of Shanghai's public screen culture? Appealing though it may at first seem, I would suggest that glocalization may not be adequate to the task in this case, and that therefore the local specificity of Shanghai's public screen culture also reveals something about a new kind of localism for media technologies under current conditions of globalization. The idea of the glocal presumes a global standard (usually associated with the West) that is ameliorated and adapted at the local level. For example, McDonalds is widely known not to use beef in India, and introduces variations on its offerings designed to satisfy local tastes. In this scenario, the pattern of imperial metropolitan centers versus peripheries continues into the era of globalization.

However, in the case of Shanghai's public screen culture, can it be said that there is a global standard that Shanghai's local culture is a variation away from? Perhaps not. Here, we may need to think about simultaneous and different appropriation and installation of new technologies according to local needs and adapted to pre-existing local patterns. In other words, in this situation, the local may not be a kind of resistance to or adaptation of a global standard but part of a pattern of coeval development. This coeval development occurs under conditions where some new media technologies are circulating too rapidly around the globe to think about a Western standard and local followers. Johannes Fabian famously argued that Western culture flatters itself by failing to see that others are in the same time as it but different, and instead tries to relegate them to the past, as lagging behind (Fabian, 1983). Instead of a global and Western standard, it might be possible to try to argue for an East Asian regional pattern of public screen usage and lightscapes, with Japanese city centers initiating the pattern. But even here the time difference would, I suspect, be difficult to prove. And, in the face of the far fewer and less elaborate installations of screens in the cities of North America and Europe, it might be tempting to reverse the usual patterns, and make claims about Shanghai and its East Asian peer cities as setting the standard for public screen cultures, with others "lagging" behind. However, perhaps it is more productive to ask if the emphasis on speed of circulation and the production of a global marketplace is not producing a situation where new media technologies are taken up in a manner that is at once local and coeval, leading to even greater levels of heterogeneity than are produced by glocal adaptation and variation alone.

Acknowledgments

The research presented in this chapter has been supported by grants from the Leverhulme Trust and the State Innovative Institute for the Studies of Journalism and Communications and Media Studies Society at Fudan University, Shanghai. I am very grateful for their support.

I would also like to thank my research assistant, Wu Dan, as well as Yu Wenhao, Wu Changchang, Lu Xinyu, Ma Ling and the staff at the various institutions in Shanghai who have offered assistance and cooperation.

Notes

1. The definition of what constitutes "public space" is a complicated one and deserving of separate consideration. For the purposes of this chapter and the research project it is derived from, a broad definition has been applied, extending beyond publicly owned spaced to privately owned spaces that the public have access to. Another way of understanding is based on the distinction between the public and the domestic.
2. The larger project is being conducted with Janet Harbord, Amal Khalaf and Rachel Moore. In Shanghai I worked with research assistant Wu Dan and photographer Yu Wenhao.
3. The political agenda of the Situationists has not been part of this project.
4. For example, "now boarding" might flash on and off in green or orange. However, we were unable to determine a consistent use of green and orange across the information screens in the station, nor were we able to find anyone who was able to explain this to us.
5. When I visited the station on October 20, 2009, an employee said that according to her memory, these numbers had not been there when the station first opened and that they were installed to solve problems encountered then. But when Chris Berry and Wu Dan conducted a March 25, 2010 interview with Professor Zheng Gang, the Vice General Manager and Chief Architect of the East China Architectural Design and Research Institute, who was one of the people in overall charge of the Shanghai South Railway Station project, he corrected this, explaining that the numbers had been an integral part of the design from the beginning.
6. In addition to numerous tourist materials that deploy this English name, the Wikipedia (2011) entry for the Yangpu District of Shanghai dates the name back to the construction of a farmers' market there in 1929. However, it does not give any sources. Zhong Song, whose company was commissioned to landscape design the site as part of its redevelopment, also uses this terminology in the translation he offers for the title of his own article (Zhong, 2009).
7. For further details on the redevelopment and construction of the entire five-road intersection, see Long (2010).
8. Where Schivelbusch emphasized the link between light and disenchantment as part of the process of modernity, I would emphasize the secular enchantment sparked by the "magic" of electric light. However, here his documentation and analysis of the prodigious investment in displays of light in the West support my argument for caution in discussions about cultural specificity on this point.
9. This "screen walk," as we referred to these exploratory investigations, took place on March 29, 2010.
10. Arthur Waldron has shown how the image of the Great Wall and its conflation with China itself was originally very much the work of Westerners

before being taken on board by many Chinese nationalists and patriots (Waldron, 1990).

11. Han provides a detailed overview of *pailou*. Although he does not have a specific chapter analyzing the inscriptions on *pailou*, the profuse illustrations throughout the book give many examples. According to Mark Elvin, the Qing dynasty helped to fuel a cult for chaste widows by subsidizing the construction of memorial arches in their honor (Elvin, 1984).
12. Today, plenty of advice is also available online (see Fan, 2008).
13. The original Chinese reads: "为别人指路时，应热情周到地向对方指引和解释。不要歧视外地人。不可指错路。自己不清楚或不确定是应致歉."
14. The best-known proponent of this argument is Arjun Appadurai (1996).

Bibliography

Appadurai, Arjun (1996) "Disjuncture and Difference in the Global Cultural Economy", *Modernity at Large: Cultural Dimensions of Globalization* (Minneapolis: University of Minnesota Press).

Arcagni, Simone (2009) "Urban Screens in Turin and Milan: Design, Public Art and Urban Regeneration", in McQuire, Scott, Martin, Meredith and Niederer, Sabine (eds.) *Urban Screen Reader* (Amsterdam: Institute of Network Cultures).

Beiguelman, Giselle (2009) "Public Art in Nomadic Contexts", in McQuire, Scott, Martin, Meredith and Niederer, Sabine (eds.) *Urban Screen Reader* (Amsterdam: Institute of Network Cultures).

Bolter, Jay David and Grusin, Richard (1999) *Remediation: Understanding New Media* (Cambridge: MIT Press).

Bounegru, Liliana (2009) "Interactive Media Artworks for Public Space: The Potential of Art to Influence Consciousness and Behaviour in Relation to Public Spaces", in McQuire, Scott, Martin, Meredith and Niederer, Sabine (eds.) *Urban Screen Reader* (Amsterdam: Institute of Network Cultures).

Brennan, Kate, Martin, Meredith and McQuire, Scott (2009) "Sustaining Public Space: An Interview with Kate Brennan", in McQuire, Scott, Martin, Meredith and Niederer, Sabine (eds.) *Urban Screen Reader* (Amsterdam: Institute of Network Cultures).

Casetti, Francesco (2008) "The Last Supper in Piaza della Scala", *Cinéma & Cie*, no. 11(Fall), 7–14.

China Daily (2010) "China's High-Speed Train Sets New Speed Record", *China Daily*, 28 September, http://www.chinadaily.com.cn/china/2010-09/28/content_11361177.htm, date accessed 6 March 2011.

Cubitt, Sean (2004) *The Cinema Effect* (Cambridge: MIT Press).

Dekker, Annet (2009) "City Views from the Artist's Perspective: The Impact of Technology on the Experience of the City", in McQuire, Scott, Martin, Meredith and Niederer, Sabine (eds.) *Urban Screen Reader* (Amsterdam: Institute of Network Cultures).

Dikötter, Frank (2007) *Things Modern: Material Culture and Everyday Life in China* (London: Hurst & Company).

Elvin, Mark (1984) "Female Virtue and the State in China", *Past and Present*, 104(1), 111–152.

Eppink, Jason and Arnold, Alice (2009) "Electric Signs: An Interview with Jason Eppink, the Pixelator", in McQuire, Scott, Martin, Meredith and Niederer, Sabine (eds.) *Urban Screen Reader* (Amsterdam: Institute of Network Cultures).

Fabian, Johannes (1983) *Time and the Other: How Anthropology Makes Its Object* (New York: Columbia University Press).

Fan, Wensou (范文搜) (2008) How to Produce a Successful Blackboard Newspaper (怎样办好黑板报), 17 January, http://www.fwsou.com/wenmizhishi/banbaosheji/2008-01-17/26773.shtml, date accessed 16 March 2011.

Foucault, Michel (1977) "Nietzsche, Genealogy, History", in Bouchard, Donald F. (ed.) *Language, Counter-Memory, Practice: Selected Essays and Interviews* (Ithaca: Cornell University Press).

Gibbons, Mike and McQuire, Scott (2009) "Public Space Broadcasting: An Interview with Mike Gibbons", in McQuire, Scott, Martin, Meredith and Niederer, Sabine (eds.) *Urban Screen Reader* (Amsterdam: Institute of Network Cultures).

Habermas, Jürgen (1989) *The Structural Transformation of the Public Sphere: An Inquiry into a Category of Bourgeois Society*, Thomas Burger (trans.) (Cambridge: MIT Press).

Han, Changkai (韩昌凯) (2008) *Chinese Pailou* (中华牌楼) (Beijing: China Construction Industry Press (北京：中国建筑工业出版社)).

Hsieh, Jiann and Chou, Ying-Hsiung (1981) "Public Aspirations in the New Year Couplets: A Comparative Study between the People's Republic and Taiwan", *Asian Folklore Studies*, 40(2), 125–149.

Huang, Youqin and Setha M. Low (2008) "Is Gating Always Exclusionary? A Comparative Analysis of Gated Communities in American and Chinese Cities", in Logan, John R. (ed.) *Urban China in Transition* (Oxford: Blackwell).

Huhtamo, Erkki (2009) "Messages on the Wall: An Archaeology of Public Media Displays", in McQuire, Scott, Martin, Meredith and Niederer, Sabine (eds.) *Urban Screen Reader* (Amsterdam: Institute of Network Cultures).

Koolhaas, Rem (1995) "The Generic City", in Koolhaas, Rem, Mau, Bruce, Sigler, Jennifer and Werlemann, Hans (eds.) *S, M, L, XL* (New York: Monacelli).

Lancel, Karen and Maat, Hermen (2009) "StalkShow", in McQuire, Scott, Martin, Meredith and Niederer, Sabine (eds.) *Urban Screen Reader* (Amsterdam: Institute of Network Cultures).

Long, Zhengxing (龙正兴) (2010) *Integrated Urban Engineering, Construction, Organization, and Design* (综合性市政工程施工组织设计) (Shanghai: Tongji University Press (上海：同济大学出版社)).

MacPherson, Kerrie L. (1990) "Designing China's Urban Future: The Greater Shanghai Plan, 1927–1939", *Planning Perspectives*, 5, 48–52.

McCarthy, Anna (2001) *Ambient Television: Visual Culture and Public Space* (Durham: Duke University Press).

McDonagh, Thomas (1996) "The Dérive and Situationist Paris", in Andreotti, Libero and Costa, Xavier (eds.) *Situationists, Art, Politics, Urbanism* (Barcelona: ACTAR).

McQuire, Scott, Martin, Meredith and Niederer, Sabine (eds.) (2009) *Urban Screen Reader* (Amsterdam: Institute of Network Cultures).

Nevárez, Julia (2009) "Spectacular Mega-public Space: Art and the Social in Times Square", in McQuire, Scott, Martin, Meredith and Niederer, Sabine (eds.) *Urban Screen Reader* (Amsterdam: Institute of Network Cultures).

Pierson, Michele (2002) *Special Effects: Still in Search of Wonder* (New York: Columbia University Press).

Robertson, Roland (1995) "Glocalization: Time-Space and Homogeneity-Heterogeneity", in Featherstone, Mike, Lash, Scott and Robertson, Roland (eds.) *Global Modernities* (London: Sage).

Roh, Soh Yeong and Nikos Papastergiadis (2009) "Large Screen and the Making of Civic Spaces: An Interview with Soh Yeong Roh", in McQuire, Scott, Martin, Meredith and Niederer, Sabine (eds.) *Urban Screen Reader* (Amsterdam: Institute of Network Cultures).

Saler, Michael (2006) "Modernity and Enchantment: A Historiographic Review", *The American Historical Review*, 111(3), 692–716.

Schivelbusch, Wolfgang (1995) *Disenchanted Night: The Industrialization of Light in the Nineteenth Century* (Berkeley: University of California Press).

Schuijren, Jan and McQuire, Scott (2009) "Putting Art into Urban Space: An Interview with Jan Schuijren", in McQuire, Scott, Martin, Meredith and Niederer, Sabine (eds.) *Urban Screen Reader* (Amsterdam: Institute of Network Cultures).

Shanghai Municipal Government (2011) Yangpu District's Investment Environment (杨浦区投资环境), http://www.shanghai.gov.cn/shanghai/node2314/node2318/node2376/node2391 /index.html, date accessed 8 March 2011.

Shanghai Science and Technology Museum (2011) Introduction, http://www.sstm.org.cn/kjg_Web/html/kjg_english/About_Introduction/List/list_0.htm, date accessed 9 March 2011.

Sortie des Usines (1895) Directed by Louis Lumière. Produced by Louis Lumière.

Waldron, Arthur (1990) *The Great Wall of China: From History to Myth* (Cambridge: Cambridge University Press).

Weber, Max (1988) "Science as a Vocation", in Lassman, Peter, Velody, Irving and Martins, Herminio (eds.), Michael Jon (trans.) *Max Weber's 'Science as a Vocation'* (London: Routledge).

Whissel, Kristen (2008) "Electric Modernity and the Cinema at the Pan-American Exposition: City of Living Light", *Picturing American Modernity: Traffic, Technology and the Silent Cinema* (Durham: Duke University Press).

Wikipedia (2011) Yangpu District, http://en.wikipedia.org/wiki/Yangpu_District, date accessed 9 March 2011.

Xin, Ge (2009) Interview with Chris Berry and Wu Dan. Shanghai, 22 October.

Yue, Audrey (2009) "Urban Screens, Spatial Regeneration and Cultural Citizenship: The Embodied Interaction of Cultural Participation", in McQuire, Scott, Martin, Meredith and Niederer, Sabine (eds.) *Urban Screen Reader* (Amsterdam: Institute of Network Cultures).

Zhang, Dajin (2010) Interview with Chris Berry and Wu Dan. Shanghai, 18 September.

Zhang, Tingwei (2009) "Striving to Be a Global City from Below: The Restructuring of Shanghai's Urban Districts", in Chen, Xiangming (ed.) *Shanghai Rising: State Power and Local Transformations in a Global Megacity* (Minneapolis: University of Minnesota Press).

Zhong, Song (仲松) (2009) "Landscape Design for the Pentagon Plaza, Shanghai" (上海五角场环岛下沉式广场景观设计), *Landscape Design* (风景园林), 3, 113–115.

Zhou, Wuji (周五级) (1952) *How to Produce a Successful Blackboard Newspaper* (怎样办好黑板报) (Shanghai: Beixin Press (上海：北新书局)).

Zhou, Yan and Bo, Jiang (周艳，姜波) (2002) *Successful Publication of Blackboard Newspapers* (出好黑板报) (Shanghai: Shanghai Calligraphy Press (上海：上海书画出版社)).

6
iPhone Girl: Assembly, Assemblages and Affect in the Life of an Image

Helen Grace

A small biography of the image

In August 2008 the world's attention was on China. The Beijing Olympics were reaching their climax, having already put into circulation a myriad of explosive images. A minor scandal followed the Zhang Yimou-directed opening ceremony when it was revealed that Lin Miaoke (林妙可), a pretty young girl, had lip-synched over the voice of the ostensibly less attractive Yang Peiyi (杨沛宜)[1] in a contemporary *Singing In The Rain* scenario (Spencer, 2008). In this volatile image-world of national spectacle, image was everything and images of beautiful young girls and women fueled the desire for the national in a global world, just as the image of woman has functioned in so many other contexts as a universal sign, producing desire for whatever product or nation-state is being promoted (Figure 6.1a).

On August 20, four days before the closing ceremony, a UK IT specialist reported in a blogpost to the *MacRumors* (2008) site that he had discovered on his brand-new iPhone a set of photographs of an attractive young worker at an iPhone assembly plant in China. At first he acknowledged that he felt angry because he thought the new phone was used or repaired, but then he realized that the images had been taken within the factory (Mitchell, 2008). The exchangeable image file format (EXIF) data of the original image records the images as having been taken on July 26, 2008 at 7.20 am – a Saturday morning. Its download to the buyer's computer took place on August 15, 2008 at 1.13 pm – a Friday afternoon – although he acknowledged that it took him the better part of a week before he decided to upload the images (ibid.). Based on the EXIF data attached to the image,[2] it thus took two weeks from the phone's completed assembly in China to its activation in the

a

b c

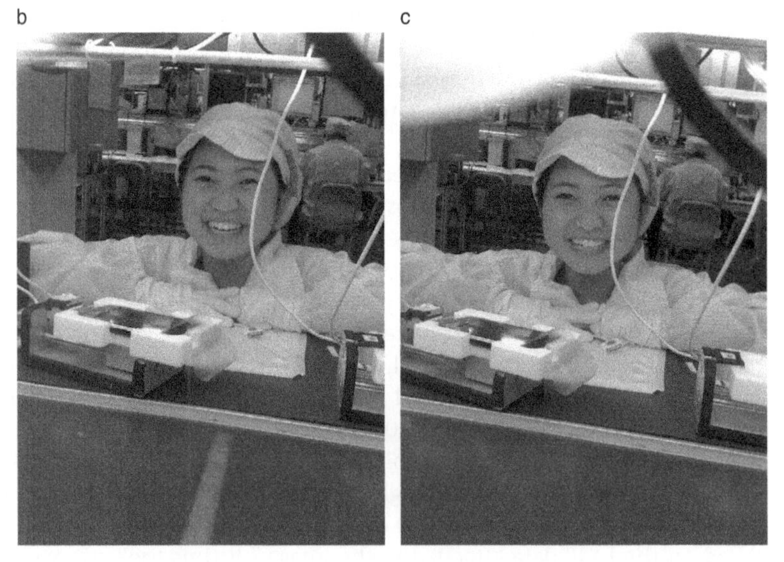

Figure 6.1 iPhone Girl
Source: MacRumors, http://forums.macrumors.com/showthread.php?t=547777

UK, so we have a trace of the image's "life" as a partial signature of the commodity's circulation.

In the most widely reproduced of the images, the young woman smiles directly at the camera, giving the "V" sign with both her gloved hands. She is in work clothes – a pink striped cap holding up her hair, a pink-striped uniform over her clothes. The image is hastily composed and the bottom half of it consists of the green surface of the workbench in front of her. In the immediate foreground we see two iPhones encased in polystyrene and between them an iPhone cable. A yellow line intersects the green work surface, pointing to the yellow tips of the young woman's gloved fingers. This configuration emphasizes the constrained energy of her gesture of freedom, a moment seized in the production process that otherwise absorbs all of her time and energy.

Behind her left shoulder we see other workers sitting in front of screens, but we do not see so much of the workplace and there is a sense that the body of the young woman is screening and containing the space within the world of this surreptitiously seized moment. She is bending forward and downward to meet the camera's gaze, located opposite her. It is an awkward gesture, in which there is a greater sense of presence than in the other two reproduced images in the series – even though in the other two we have a much broader smile and more relaxed pose, in a more extended moment of pause. It is the sense of reaction, the angularity of the composition, the reduced facial frontality and the fact that it is a more tightly framed picture that gives the first image its dynamism and force (Figures 6.1b and c).

In narrating the biography of this image, I want to emphasize that it is specifically located. Perhaps we can say it is brought forth by time itself, by a particular moment in a particular place when the image is especially animated and when visibility and energy seem to coalesce, engendering each other.

There can be no doubt that mediatized public space has had an impact on what we understand by physical space as a sphere and location of public intervention. But it is difficult to be precise about the nature of this impact or the ways in which we can measure it. In a city like Hong Kong, one hour from Shenzhen where these images were taken, physical public space experiences the constant expansion of commercial space. This expansion occurs in physical ways[3] and in the projection of the image into the sensorium of citizens, in the form of advertising messages on every conceivable surface, the reflection of self-images in mirrored surfaces, and the increasing use of the screen and projected moving images on public transport. To escape, people resort to the cocoon of other screens – the intimacy of the mobile phone or gaming console – or they tune out with MP3 players, as Michael Bull discusses in Chapter 11.

In this chapter my focus is on the intimate screen as a form of public screen. Although a proliferation of small screens – in mobile phones[4] and digital cameras, in commercial displays, in ticketing and ATM machines, and elsewhere – is less insistently visible than the large public screen, it is a much more ubiquitous phenomenon, setting up a contrast – and in some ways a continuity – with the large-scale insistent screen. We might regard the relation between the large and the small screen as a certain kind of assemblage (Ong and Collier, 2005), that is to say an ensemble of heterogeneous elements, enabling in this case the management of the everyday and the spectacular via scalar contrasts.

So the key questions to consider are as follows. Are new publics, new public processes and new public spaces being constituted? And how should we understand public communication? Is it only a matter of rational discourse, or does it also concern emotion, affect and fleeting perceptions? It is precisely this field of emotion, affect and fleeting perceptions that I want to deal with in talking about a very quotidian form of mediatized public space here. To do so, I focus on one image that I consider to be an emblem of some far-reaching changes that have occurred in the ways in which we might understand the relation between public and private, and virtual and real in their precise biopolitical intensities. In particular, in any reflections on the relation between public and private, it is necessary to consider the contradictions of an operational *privacy* within *public* companies (i.e. those listed on major stock exchanges, as opposed to private companies which are wholly owned by their proprietors) and the ways in which publicity itself forms a key part of public communication, supplementing forms of public mobilization, as understood in conventionally oppositional terms.

In order to present this small biography of an image, I first want to invoke the concept of "assemblage."[5] I then turn to the more mundane circumstances of actual *assembly* of products in China, substituting the concept of post-Fordism with that of super-Fordism to better describe the circumstances of contemporary production. Returning to the details and aftermath of the iPhone Girl image's circulation, I then speculate on significant changes to the image of labor and the relation between commodity and brand, through a discussion of Celia Lury's essay "Brand as Assemblage" (Lury, 2009), Siegfried Kracauer's "The Mass Ornament"

(Kracauer, 1995) and Evgeny Dobrenko's work on the political economy of socialist realism (Dobrenko, 2007).

The use of the word "assemblage" in my title is key. By drawing out in a more empirical way the networks of circulation of a particular image, embedded in a small screen, this small biography of the image will also note a certain impossibility of individual biography in the context of the assemblage form's dissolution of identities of this nature. Individual "biography" and "identity" in the singular sense are called into question by the concept of assemblage, since it designates a configuration of components which are interchangeable, rather than a fixed identity as such. So there is perhaps some irony in speaking of the "biography" of a non-organic thing like an image – although it is the notion of assemblage that allows for the configuration of the organic and the inorganic, forming something that might be said to have life (and hence "biography").

The turn to surface

Lury's essay deals with the concept of mass culture and the brand as mass product "in the sense that it is a medium in which the masses are continuously cut up, differentiated and integrated in the co-ordination of a more-or-less constant flow of products, services and experiences" (Lury, 2009, p. 73). She argues that this means that brands are thus "like other mass products, such as the crowd, the public, and the mass media, insofar as they are transient 'in the multiple sense of being evanescent, incomplete and moving on' " (ibid., pp. 73–74). In discussing the assembly of culture, Lury draws upon Siegfried Kracauer's "mass ornament" (Kracauer, 1995) as an instance of a "turn to surface" that is characteristic of mass products such as the hotel lobby, arcades, the Tiller girls, bestselling novels, cinema and photography – practices that "display an elective affinity with the surface" (Levin, 1995, p. 18, as cited by Lury, 2009, p. 76).

This "turn to surface" does not necessarily imply a lack of substance, and Lury argues that Kracauer is not opposing surface to mass. She suggests instead that surface might be understood as "a vector of the movement of mass," consistent with the non-linear logic of contemporary economy's organization and modes of calculation (Lury, 2009, p. 76). Presciently, for Kracauer, the logic of surface can only be seen from above (hence his point that the mass ornament "resembles *aerial photographs* of landscapes and cities in that it does not emerge out of the interior of the given conditions, but rather appears above them"

(Kracauer, 1995, p. 77). Lury uses a mathematical model to understand the nature of surface here, thinking about it in topological terms: surface does not emerge *in* space but is rather "a space in itself" (De Landa, 2002 as cited by Lury, 2009, p. 77). The notion of assemblage thus represents the implementation of the rationality of this new logic of space.

Because we are focusing on public communication and public space, I want to concretize this thinking through the image I have chosen. What enables the emergence of the image that is my focus here is the screen. But in this case it is not the large screen that commands attention but rather the small, dispersed screen. I take this dispersed screen to be a kind of equivalent to the large screen, by virtue of its combination of multiple small screens, gathered not in one material space but rather in virtual space. This combination constitutes a virtual photo mosaic that is mentally assembled from above in a virtual sense at least – which is to say, from a position of exteriority in relation to the individual image. We might therefore say that it is a form of the mass ornament itself.

The iPhone Girl image is emblematic, bringing together the production and consumption of mobile media in a way that is rarely seen, powerfully condensing questions of globalization, gender and labor within new mediated public processes and shifting interactions between public and private. Following W. J. T. Mitchell, we can say that pictures are, in a sense, life forms that place demands on us and we may be attracted to them by their very spectacularity (Mitchell, 2005). But here I am interested in a highly ephemeral image, discovered on a mobile phone at the end of its cycle of production and distribution and as it enters its cycle of consumption. At this point it acquires a new life form – a viral quality – and spreads rapidly for a time, but then dissipates.[6] In considering the nature of this ephemeral phenomenon, we turn to its source, rather than to the point of its transmission.

Super-Fordism

In Hong Kong,[7] with its high consumption of mobile media and image-making devices, the link with device production is never as far away as it is in Europe and North America. This proximity is the result of the central role that the city and its business have played in the development of Pearl River Delta industry since the establishment of Shenzhen as a special economic zone in 1980, and the subsequent massive expansion of industry in the region and the proliferation of large and small-scale factories. Therefore the concept of post-Fordism does not really make much sense regionally but instead there is the experience of what might be called "super-Fordism." Where post-Fordism implies high levels of specialization and flexibility almost to the point of customized production, super-Fordism suggests even greater scales of mass production than ever seen before. The term super-Fordism[8] is not new and emerged around the same time as the critical concept of post-Fordism but is less widely used (see Hall and Jacques, 1989; Drache and Gertler, 1991; Amin, 1994). Perhaps this is because the relocation of manufacturing away from Western Europe and North America in this period resulted in a specifically located experience of post-Fordism that has attracted most of the attention in critical scholarship in those places where manufacturing appeared to be in decline.

The phenomenon of super-Fordism is widely seen in the scale of Chinese factories. For example, Foxconn's Shenzhen "campus" is reported to have 400,000 workers (Hu, 2010, p. 3). It is also visualized in recent photography's fascination with the sheer scale of China's development (see Burtynsky, 2005). The visual abstraction of production and fascination with the surface patterns of development aestheticizes the phenomenon – and thus renders invisible the experience of labor that underpins this development, implying that it is capital and the state that principally enable the emergence of such transformations of landscape. This is not entirely new. Although in the history of photography the visualization of labor and laborers has always been present, it is a minor genre, generally involving an observation of "how the other half lives" rather than a self-projection by labor itself. The Worker Photographer movement of the 1920s attempted to put the image-making process into the hands of those previously only depicted by professionalized practices but, in general, relatively few workers were thus mobilized (Hoernle, 1978; Ohrn and Hardt, 1980; Ribalta, 2011).[9] It is only with the arrival of widespread user-created content in this area that a genuine "worker-photography" is emerging in the viral circulation of images.[10]

At the time of its initial circulation as a term, super-Fordism was understood as the realization of the capitalist dream of the factory without workers – full automation with robots replacing human labor. This was, however, seen as a too costly solution in the West. But the development of China since the 1980s realizes a form of super-Fordism in the robotization of workers (SACOM, 2010).

Labor as visual abstraction

The visual abstraction of labor in contemporary photographic representations of China takes on a troubling ornamental form. To explore this further, I want to draw on Siegfried Kracauer's highly relevant concept of the mass ornament in the context of my discussion of the iPhone Girl image – an image that emerges, either accidentally or deliberately, from a space of image interdiction. Viewed through the distributed circuits of its production and circulation, the image is emblematic of major shifts in labor relations in China. Although the image does not play a *causative* role here, its affective force forms one pole of an ensemble of emotional relations – between the image of a happy worker on the one hand and on the other a groundswell of developing activism in China, and suicide as protest against factory living and working conditions (Chan and Pun, 2010).[11]

To this extent the image I am focusing on, which appears on a small screen, can be seen as a part of the online life that extends the ephemeral nature of this image and others. The subsequent discussion overlaps with the online lives of workers in factories in China, especially after the suicide of Sun Danyong in 2009 and the online traces of life left by Sun and other workers (East South West North, 2009; Hinews.cn, 2009). These traces of emotional life in turn mobilized students and academics in Hong Kong, and internationally in groups such as Students and Scholars Against Corporate Misbehavior (SACOM), drawing attention to living and working conditions in Pearl River Delta factories.

Pressure brought to bear by the publicity generated in these initially local campaigns led Foxconn to organize its own counter-publicity, with mass rallies emphasizing the efforts it was making to address concerns.[12] The ways in which company publicity and PR mobilize to produce public "demonstrations" themselves constitute a new form of public communication, especially in China. This new form contradicts the established rhetoric and function of demonstrations and public manifestations, further appropriating images and symbols of revolutionary action thought to be the preserve of particular forms of oppositional political life.

A clear overlap between virtual and real space thus exists. Virtual space can be seen to generate new uses of public space, with an affective response initially appearing online, then spilling over into real spaces and generating new forms of tactics and campaigns.

Mobilization thus begins in an emotional response, prior to the formation of rational demands, and this emotion manifests itself in online discussions and social networking sites. There, confessional expression becomes public, leaving residues of pain, individually experienced but, by virtue of its poignant expression in online sites, giving voice to the worker, even after their death.[13] Subsequent discussion registered the impact of the suicides as a form of sacrifice made by the workers. As Liu Kaiming, head of the Institute for Contemporary Observation in Shenzhen, puts it, "We should thank those workers who committed suicide. They used their life to arouse introspection at Foxconn, Apple and even the general public" (He, 2010a, pp. A1, A5).

A bright spark

But before this happened, iPhone Girl appeared, presenting a rare individualized image of a worker. It is the very singularity of this image that remained as an afterimage, a spark that was later available for detonation, all the more so because iPhone Girl appeared as an object of desire, "humanizing" the otherwise dehumanized images of factory labor as machines in China.

After the story was reported on the *MacRumors* blog, it went viral, with 18 million Google hits for "iPhone Girl" in the first two weeks and another 903,000 on Baidu. The images were widely circulated, and there was widespread commentary, both offensive and inoffensive, with racist and sexist attitudes expressed, as well as pro- and anti-China views. Some suggest it was a case of child labor, others that it was merely a carefully managed publicity campaign on the part of Apple[14] (Moss, 2008), allegedly in the middle of negotiations between Apple and China Mobile to release the new 3G iPhone in China. Whether the image's emergence was sheer accident or carefully managed company PR remains uncertain. However, we can suggest that the image's destiny exceeded its capacity to be manipulated and it is the very quality of the image to float free that allowed it to be read as an emblem of some quite profound historical changes, the impact of which is just beginning to be felt.

Various news reports (Andrews, 2008), blog posts (Slattery, 2008) and company admissions confirmed that iPhone Girl – referred to as Xiao Li (literally "Little Plum") in online discussion on the mainland – worked as a testing section inspector in a Foxconn factory in Longhua, in the Bao'an District of Shenzhen, where 137,000 iPhones were being made each day (Balfour and Culpan, 2010). Foxconn Technology Group (富士康科技集团) is the largest Original Equipment Manufacturer (OEM) of computers and electronics in the world. Its parent company, Hon

Hai Precision Industry Co., Ltd. (鴻海精密工業股份有限公司), is Taiwanese, established in 1974 (Dean, 2007; Balfour and Culpan, 2010), and has manufacturing plants in the UK and the USA, as well as subsidiary operations in the Czech Republic, Hungary, Brazil,[15] Mexico and India. Its biggest plant is in Shenzhen and now has 400,000 employees (Hu, 2010, p. 3).[16] Apple is one of its key customers and, as is now well known, it makes the Mac mini, the iPod, the iPhone and the iPad. It also makes Intel motherboards, Motorola phones, Sony's Playstation, Nintendo's Wii, Microsoft's Xbox 360 and Amazon's Kindle.

Given that these are all clearly delineated brands in the marketplace, there is considerable secrecy and tight security surrounding the factory. This is necessary as a form of disavowal to conceal the perceptual disjunction between the sense of uniqueness and individuality in the marketing of such identity-expressive commodities and the fact of their mass production – in the same factory on a scale far exceeding that of Fordism in its heyday – and the very antithesis of the individuality claimed for the products in their consumption.

In 2006 a *Mail On Sunday* (UK) report alleged poor employment practices in the Foxconn factory complex, with 15-hour working days (*Mail Online*, 2006). For these long hours, the report claims that a worker earned £27 a month – "about half the wage [that] weavers earned in Liverpool and Manchester in 1805, allowing for inflation" (ibid.). Living conditions were sub-standard and workers were housed in military-style dormitories with no privacy. Work discipline was strict and workers were punished for minor infractions. The story was accompanied by striking photographs, the force and immediacy of which was intensified by their low-resolution camera phone quality – as if they were surveillance images or spy photographs (see *AppleInsider*, 2006).

Apple responded quickly to the story, carrying out an investigation. It posted the results on its website within two months and appointed Verité, an "internationally recognized leader in workplace standards dedicated to ensuring that people around the world work under safe, fair and legal conditions," to ensure that its "Supplier Code of Conduct" was being followed in the production and assembly of its products (Angell, 2006).

The key point here in a discussion of public communication is that firms are required to extend PR strategies into new spaces by reporting actions on their websites. In such ways they communicate more directly with customers, critics and the public at large. In the past, PR worked more in the background, placing stories in media outlets; now the firm itself is a media outlet as its actions are more closely scrutinized.

In the *Mail on Sunday* story, the moral reaction that condemned the working conditions was displaced by the instrumental reason that accepts normal business practice in a structure of disavowal: (We know very well that it's terrible, but all the same...). "It's the nature of big business today to exploit any opportunity that comes their way" (*Mail Online*, 2006). Within this normal business practice, the exploitation of labor is not only central to the production process but is also required by it. Labor must be made invisible, it must be effectively effaced in the process, so that the commodity – or more especially the brand – can become visible.

A bigger picture

iPhone Girl faded and the blog discussion receded by Christmas 2008, though her image remains as *affect*, influencing subsequent developments, I suggest. This is because this particular image is the best-known register of individual life that exists for this firm – even though the very secrecy surrounding the production of these devices for producing visibility denies any status to the image or to the worker. Less than a year later, a new Foxconn story emerged. On July 16, 2009, Sun Danyong, a 26-year-old man working in the logistics department at Foxconn, jumped to his death from a dormitory building, after having been accused of misplacing an iPhone G4 prototype and allegedly beaten up by security staff. It was the first of a spate of suicides (17 so far) and suicide attempts at the factory that became a huge story in Hong Kong – and more widely – intensifying especially between April and June 2010, with extensive media coverage and widespread online discussion on the mainland (Chan and Pun, 2010).

Foxconn was forced into damage control, massively increasing wages for its workers – unprecedented increases of 30% without formal demands. This raised the ¥900/month base level to ¥1200/month, not including overtime (He and Perez, 2010).[17] All of this occurred in a period in which there was extensive labor unrest on the mainland, with a widely publicized strike by Honda workers and increasing demands by unions and NGOs in Guangdong (*South China Morning Post*, 2010b, front page, A14). Counseling was increased and psychologists (referred to in some reports as psychoanalysts (He, 2010b, p. A4)) were appointed, as well as Buddhist monks and *feng shui* specialists (Chan, 2010, p. A4).[18] Safety nets were installed around the dormitories and factories to prevent workers from falling to their deaths (Ye, 2010), and mass motivational rallies were organized by the company and unions

(Tam, 2010).[19] Burson-Marsteller, a major global PR firm, was appointed to crisis-manage the situation, giving journalists unprecedented access to the factory "campus" in Longhua, and to Hon Hai chairman Terry Gou. A cover story about Gou appeared in *Businessweek* (Balfour and Culpan, 2010).[20] At the same time, Foxconn moved to relocate its operations further inland in China, where wages are lower (for example Chengdu, in Sichuan Province, and Zhengzhou in Henan Province) (*South China Morning Post*, 2010a, p. A5).

However, the impact of all this was far-reaching. Foxconn argued that the rate of suicides in its factories was lower than the national average and, though this does not excuse the number of deaths, it was probably true. There were also more suicides by young men than by young women. This gendered pattern is in keeping with global patterns, where generally speaking the rate of suicide of men is three times that of women (World Health Organization, 2011). The exception to this pattern is China, where more women, especially in rural areas, commit suicide, commonly by swallowing pesticides (Phillips *et al.*, 1999; Phillips *et al.*, 2002). However, the cold facts are not as important as the symbolic value that the cluster of suicides had. The emotional intensity of the suicides and suicide attempts by young workers galvanized a response, and far more effectively than attempts to organize workers by more traditional means.[21]

As noted earlier, some online discussion on the mainland thanked the suicide victims for their sacrifice and martyrdom that led to profound changes. In a November 2010 story in the *Financial Times*, for example, there were suggestions that the Foxconn suicides were an epoch-making event, potentially representing the end of dirt-cheap labor, and triggering "a rethink of the entire factory-town system on which 30 years of Chinese economic growth has been built" (Pilling, 2010). An optimistic view suggested that there may be much more tolerance of unions and workers' rights by the Beijing authorities. This impact is certainly being felt in pressure on many Hong Kong firms across Guangdong for better wages and conditions, linked to the establishment of minimum wage standards in Hong Kong.[22] Important here is that the movement that has enabled these changes has been virtual as much as real. Certainly the low-level non-governmental organization (NGO) activity that has been going on quietly in Shenzhen for some time has been greatly enhanced by the online movement of a remarkably active netizenry in China. This local, small-scale and long-term activity is really the main story on this issue, and it tends to be overlooked in the often more sensationalist coverage that has appeared with increasing rapidity in major Western news reports since 2010.

A feature in *Wired* magazine in March 2011 began by emphasizing the nets surrounding Foxconn buildings designed to break the fall of potential suicides, and it ended by downplaying consumer responsibility:

> When 17 people take their lives, I ask myself, did I in my desire hurt them? Even just a little?
> And of course the answer, inevitable and immeasurable as the fluttering silence of our sun, is yes.
> Just a little.
>
> (Johnson, 2011)[23]

In January and February 2012, a series of feature articles on Apple and Foxconn appeared in the *New York Times* focusing less on factory life and more on the pressures of global production and the loss of American jobs (Duhigg and Barboza, 2012a–c; Greenhouse, 2012).[24] US TV networks have also covered the issue, with a recent ABC News promo story beginning: "Okay." "Okay." "Okay." The voices are robot feminine and they never shut up, each chirp a surreal announcement that another new iPad is about to be born: "Okay." "Okay." "Okay." (Weir, 2012).

The sensationalism of the coverage reached a particular low point in March 2012, when it was revealed that an episode of the US radio program *This American Life*, entitled "Mr. Daisey Goes to the Apple Factory," which aired on January 6, contained fabricated information (Milian, 2012). It was based on Daisey's theatrical monologue "The Agony and the Ecstasy of Steve Jobs," which itself fabricates the context in conventional orientalist fashion: the innocent abroad arrives in Hong Kong and goes into Chungking Mansions, where he is offered drugs and sex of all kinds, though he is only interested in finding a *shanzhai* (fake) iPhone.[25]

The general context of the most recent outpouring of feature articles on Apple and Foxconn is the release of the iPad 3 on March 6, 2012 and the simultaneous efforts by Apple – in order to protect sales of the new product – to sanitize its production processes by joining the Fair Labour Association and inviting its inspectors to tour the Foxconn factories. Apple announced its efforts on its website (Apple Press Info, 2012a). SACOM suggested that these announcements warned Foxconn to relocate underage workers within the factories (Farrell, 2012). In any case, the global concern for factory workers in China has not impacted on sales, with 3 million iPads sold on the first weekend of the release

(Apple Press Info, 2012b).[26] And the attempt to sanitize the production process also failed, though the report indicating breaches of labor and health and safety conditions was not released until after the blockbuster release[27] of the new iPad (Garside, 2012).

The virgin product and the invisibility of labor

Earlier I mentioned the necessity of the effacement of labor as a precondition for the emergence of the brand, and it is this very necessity that partly explains the shocked response to the image of a worker on a device.[28] Labor must be ghost-like and invisible so that the commodity – and the brand – can appear as a magical thing, a creation born in a process of "value-adding," a pristine object, pure, innocent and untouched by human hands before the new owner takes possession of it, tearing off the sealed wrapping guaranteeing its newness. The branded object is always a virgin in this sense. That the object has already been *touched* in the production process – that indeed it cannot be made without being made of material and by a process involving manual labor – is disavowed in the language of magic which characterizes the marketing process, where the empty shell of the generic product gains the fullness of the brand's meaning. In discussing the brand as assemblage, Celia Lury acknowledges this aspect of the brand's emergence: "Brands are the outcome of diverse professional activities, including marketing, graphic and product design, accountancy, media, retail, management, and the law, with each of these professions having multiple histories..." (Lury, 2009, p. 67).

Production labor is notably not included and has, in this account, little to do with it. The production of the brand is the result of *professional* activities, rather than of low-level manual labor or trades, which only exist as vestiges of earlier configurations, especially in the marketing of luxury brands. It is the sphere of *salaries* rather than wages, though in practice the same fragmentation of labor that occurs in production and assembly appears in creative industries (Pun and Chan, 2008).[29]

Similarly, Paulo Virno notes that "social prosperity is no longer produced by labour time, but by knowledge, by a general knowing, by 'general intellect', and as a result social prosperity and labour time are no longer directly connected" (Lavaert and Gielen, 2009). This perspective, from the point of view of post-*operaism*[30] and in the context of its Euro-Communist emergence, underlines an experiential shift in the relation to labor. This shift is marked by its partial transformation and by the displacement of manual labor with immaterial labor (Fortunati,

2007).[31] Of course, manual labor never disappears; it is just increasingly performed by invisible laborers.

The production of the brand is the result of another form of *immaterial* labor – such as the consumer's "recognition, communication, and identification" (Lury, 2009, p. 67) – and labor processes are further abstracted by reference to "the supply chain" as the intermediary sphere or network structure within which the factory disappears.[32] The total fragmentation and atomization of production is given a fluid presence, enabling the smooth flow from assembly in China to activation by the consumer in the UK in two weeks in this case – as if the speed of transportation itself has been accelerated to match the immediacy of information transfer. Space–time co-ordinates thus shift in the passage of the brand from one place to another within such a short time-frame, these shifts seeming to mirror in some ways the very shifts in the nature of matter itself, arising in the high-energy phenomenology of experimental physics, in its nanotechnological applications within electronic products.

There is thus no distinction between production and consumption, as both are mere stages in the life of the object or brand. In fact, production no longer really exists at all, but has been replaced by the *assembly* of components, the result of earlier processes of flexible configurations within modular design in the rationalization of production. Nothing is thus *made* because the material transformations have already occurred in component production (deferred, outsourced) or in design and marketing.

Happy workers: the image of labor as product

The image of the "happy worker" that is my focus here might be regarded as a type of propaganda image.[33] However, the heroic possibilities of this image are reduced by technology itself and in particular the technology of the camera phone, which condenses everything – every moment – into something ordinary, ephemeral. For the heroic worker image to have its power, it needs to have the appearance of eternity, to be classical. This was the point of Stalinist classicism. In the Soviet context, the glorification of labor had a paradoxical character – an essential irrationality. As Evgeny Dobrenko puts it, "the Soviet cult of labour is based on the abolition of a fundamental rational component of any labour – its result" (Dobrenko, 2007, p. xviii). Labor must therefore become visible because production (or, more accurately, products) does not exist. Labor is thus aestheticized: it becomes beautiful as a product in itself – the only product of Soviet socialism – serving to provide the image of productivist desire as the substitute for a reality (socialism) that only existed in such an image.

However, in the Chinese context the glorification of labor is unnecessary because socialism has been fully realized (and class ostensibly eliminated – even though the official line of the Chinese Communist Party is that China is still in the early stages of socialism). Instead it is the nation that becomes the glorious image and the generic product that displaces the image of labor.[34] Notwithstanding the subsumption of class discourse, what has undoubtedly enabled the success of the Chinese economy has been above all the very *collective* investment of bodies and hearts and minds in full enthusiasm of a kind only imagined in earlier failed utopian projects. It is, in other words, pure communism in its realization, a pure communism implemented by neoliberalism. Although it is undoubtedly the case that necessity rather than enthusiasm drives labor to take the risks it does, there is nonetheless an enthusiasm in risk-taking (and the history of enthusiasm in all its risk, necessity and desperation is still to be written). Much is made of venture capital in the development of new economies and technologies, but it might be appropriate to speak of "venture labor" as a particular historical experience in the Chinese context. Venture labor is that large-scale and personally risky phenomenon of migration from one part of the country to another – or from one country to another – in order to transform life.[35] It is venture labor that draws capital to China and without it venture capital would not have a purpose. Venture labor involves much greater risk than venture capital because it risks life itself.

The mass ornament of production

In some sense, then, a production process within which labor is not included – in the sense in which it is not included in Lury's discussion of the brand's emergence – means that, on the scale we see in the Chinese context, we therefore have a mass ornament of production rather than consumption. In his well-known essay, Kracauer claims of the somewhat Fordist entertainment industry that "These products of American distraction factories are no longer individual girls, but indissoluble girl clusters whose movements are demonstrations of mathematics" (Kracauer, 1995, p. 76).

Chinese factory assembly realizes this image of indissoluble girl clusters as demonstrations of mathematics on a far greater scale than US "distraction factories" were able to manage. Nonetheless, in spite of the almost total control of the production regime in its super-Fordist form, time is surreptitiously appropriated from the machine. The iPhone

Girl image is just such an appropriation, rare but significant. Kracauer writes further: "A current of organic life surges from these communal groups – which share a common destiny – to their ornaments, endowing these ornaments with a magic force and burdening them with meaning to such an extent that they cannot be reduced to a pure assemblage of lines" (ibid., p. 76).

The iPhone Girl image elicits an online response that recognizes this "current of organic life." There is a sense in which a continuity could be said to exist between the young woman, the device she is assembling and testing in the factory, and the end user and his potentially "ornamental" use of the device to take subsequent pictures. One respondent writes: "This girl's smiles are so lovely, it seems she enjoys her work and life. I feel happy just looking at her smiling. Wish all the best to her" (France 24, 2008).

Undoubtedly the image and the phenomenon of its circulation serves Western consumers well: by looking at the image they are able to overlook the circumstances of the devices' production. But at the same time, the imagined connection between the young woman – as image – and the end user is a powerful condensation of energies across time and space that disrupts the order of clear separation between production and consumption. There is certainly a banality to much of the discussion online, in response to the image's circulation, but the story has an impact by virtue of its viral life that indirectly impacts upon the broader perception of the brand. Although Foxconn has deservedly borne the brunt of public criticism of working conditions so far, it is a matter of time before the circumstances of production impact on Apple more fully.

The key point here is that in the new forms of public communication emerging via online discussion and viral circulation, an emotional space is opened up, which influences the formation of new public spaces and activities within them. This applies most directly to the activism that has arisen around the Foxconn case in China, in which the voiceless experience of migrant workers is given voice in online discussion.

"Just an image" as a just image?

By coincidence or by careful calculation, the iPhone Girl image emerged from the Shenzhen factory on July 26, 2008 – the day that Terry Gou, Foxconn's founder, married his girlfriend, Tseng Hsin-Ying, in Taipei in a relatively subdued reception at the Grand Hyatt, attended by major political figures and business leaders (*China Post*, 2008).[36] Is there a moment of lightness on the factory floor on the day the boss is getting married? Does the venture laborer dream of another life? It is an ephemeral and surface detail, but perhaps, as Kracauer suggests, "The position that an epoch occupies in the historical process can be determined more strikingly from an analysis of its inconspicuous surface-level expressions than from that epoch's judgments about itself" (Kracauer, 1995, p. 75).

It is easy to assume, as does Kracauer, that in the context of mass society, "Community and personality perish when what is demanded is calculability" (ibid., p. 78). Yet the iPhone Girl image cracks the wall of mathematical lines and topological surfaces, not to reveal an individual personality but to remain merely an image. Because it is a strong image and a hopeful image, especially in the context of so many stories of suicide and despair, it sparks something, though it has not *caused* anything. What follows in its wake is a widespread movement demanding better living and working conditions. The worker is personified through an image, though not identified. And the image floats away, unable to be captured. Apple and Foxconn cannot claim it because it represents a glitch in the process. The new iPhone owner cannot claim it because its EXIF data locates it at its source. It is thus a strangely free image. Godard had famously noted, within a radical expectation that the image could change things, that it was not a "just image" but "just an image" (Hartley, 1994). However, in this case, it might be that although it is just an image, it also becomes in some ways a just image, or an image in whose wake justice might flow.

Notes

1. The then five year-old Peiyi has become a minor celebrity in her own right, appearing in 2009 in a Hong Kong shopping mall to sing songs (Sun, 2009).
2. EXIF data record camera settings and scene information as well as date and time of capture. The EXIF data, recording this image's time of capture, as well as its time of download, is preserved when it is uploaded from the iPhone to the blog-site and we can rely on the machine intelligence of the device to obtain the image's "signature," and hence "biography." EXIF data are not preserved when images are uploaded to social networking sites, such as Facebook, and their "biographies" are lost to this extent.
3. This was clearest in March 2008, when a controversy arose over the use of public space in the Times Square shopping mall. In a case of an effective "public space theft," which is relatively common in property developments in Hong Kong, the owners, Wharf Holdings (who also own the Star Ferry and, until February 2010, the Hong Kong Tramway), had leased to Starbucks an area of the mall designated as public space, under the Deeds of Dedication, which allowed the site's redevelopment in the early 1990s (on what had been the Hong Kong tramways original depot). The issue was then

further publicized and taken up by pro-democracy groups (Gentle, 2008; Lee, 2008a, b). Subsequently the site became the focus for pro-democracy protests, directed at the mainland on the 21st anniversary of the Tiananmen Square "Incident" in June 2010 (Leung and Tsang, 2010a–c). Local academics, architects and activists used the controversy to continue public debate on the topic of public space (Designing Hong Kong, 2010a–c).

4. Hong Kong has the highest mobile phone penetration rate in the world at 221.6% (July 2012) (Office of Telecommunications Authority, Hong Kong SAR (Special Administrative Region), 2012).
5. De Landa's concept of assemblage draws upon Deleuze and Guattari's use of the notion in *A Thousand Plateaus* to designate something more than a desiring machine, since the assemblage can be both machinic and enunciative (Deleuze and Guattari, 1987; De Landa, 2006).
6. At the time of writing, much of the discussion is still accessible online, though the *MacRumors* thread runs dry in December 2008; the images are still widely accessible in various forms, some cropped, and the originals are still available in the *MacRumors* iPhone Girl thread (MacRumors, 2008).
7. The research from which this essay is drawn was undertaken in Hong Kong under a Research Grants Council, General Research Grant awarded in 2008 when I was employed at the Chinese University of Hong Kong.
8. Lyberaki argues that "super-Fordist" productivity gains were made in Western industry as early as the 1960s (Lyberaki, 1991). For a more recent discussion of regional labor conditions, see Chan (2012).
9. This is made especially clear in the recent – and very important – exhibition entitled "A Hard, Merciless Light: The Worker-Photography Movement, 1926–1939" (2011), which brings together arguably the largest collection of such work that has ever been assembled. But, although the work of many of the major figures in modernist photography is assembled, true "worker-photographers" are largely absent.
10. In Shenzhen, a number of NGO groups have been working with migrant factory workers to record living and working conditions. One such group, Grassroots Pixels, supplies workers with cameras, donated by Hong Kong supporters, equipping the workers with photography skills and encouraging them to record their own circumstances. Remarkable images have been produced, drawing upon the qualities of everyday image-making and the experience of migrant workers (Ngai and Qiu, 2010).
11. Between January and December 2010, 17 workers at the Foxconn factory in Shenzhen attempted suicide; 13 succeeded and the remaining 4 survived with serious injuries (SACOM, 2010).
12. "... an Alice in Wonderland spectacle of floats, blaring vuvuzelas, and workers dressed up as Victorian ladies, geishas, cheerleaders, and Spider-Men. This was followed by a two-hour rally inside a vast sports stadium featuring acrobats, musical performances, fireworks, and life-affirming testimonials punctuated by chants of 'treasure your life' and 'care for each other to build a wonderful future' " (Balfour and Culpan, 2010). The authors are explicit in their identification of leading PR firm Burston-Marsteller's briefing in the writing of the story, indicating the extent to which PR firms direct business news journalism.

13. Chan and Pun (2010) quote the poignant words of a worker's blog: "Perhaps for the Foxconn employees and employees like us – we who are called *nongmingong*, rural migrant workers, in China – the use of death is simply to testify that we were ever alive at all, and that while we lived, we had only despair."
14. *Imagethief* is William Moss, a Beijing-based blogger who is Director of Communications, Asia-Pacific, for Motorola Mobility. The original story – no longer available on the site, but downloaded by the author and archived – speculates on whether the iPhone Girl "event" was a carefully calculated publicity stunt of a particular type that has become a phenomenon in China, but he concludes – on the basis of Chinese blogosphere evidence available to him – that it appears to be an accident rather than Apple or Foxconn PR. See also Ma Jun (2008), an English-language version of an original story published in *yWeekend*, a supplement of *Beijing Youth Daily*. This story appears to be a key source for both blogposts.
15. More recent reports suggest that Foxconn is considering expansion of operations in Brazil because of the cost of labor in China (Colitt and Winter, 2011).
16. The figure is put at 400,000 in a 2010 *Sunday Morning Post* report (Hu, 2010, p. 3). Taiwanese reports of further expansion in 2010 put the figure at 1.3 million employees overall in China (Chang and Huang, 2010).
17. SACOM claims that, notwithstanding the media announcements of pay increases, by October 2010 the workers had not been told of the pay raises – and had presumably not received them (SACOM, 2010).
18. The report notes that experts are to be offered annual salaries of between ¥200,000 and ¥600,000 – on average 32 times the wages of the workers (Chan, 2010, p. A4).
19. For a good selection of images of the rallies, see Bloomberg TV (2010) and ChinaSMACK (2010).
20. Burson-Marsteller is one of the world's largest PR firms and crisis-managed the Bhopal Disaster in India in 1984 for Union Carbide, as well as the Three Mile Island accident in 1979 for Babcock and Wilcox, the plant's manufacturer. In 1985 it partnered with a subsidiary of Xinhua News Agency to provide PR services for foreign firms in China and for Chinese firms internationally (Hooper, 1985, p. 22). More recently it has been implicated in planting false information to discredit Google in order to protect Facebook (see Bazilian, 2011; Murphy, 2011).
21. As a result, the workplace is less likely to be the location of organization and the public/private realm of the workers' dormitories has become a locus of intensification within the greater biopolitical dimension of the *dagongmei/zai* experience (see Pun and Chan, 2008).
22. A minimum wage bill – set at HK$28/hour – came into effect in Hong Kong on May 1, 2011 (see Cheung *et al.*, 2010, p. A4; Chan and So, 2011, p. B2; Tsang, 2011, p. B1; Yau *et al.*, 2011, p. C1).
23. Johnson acknowledges Burson Marsteller briefing in his visit to the factory (see Farrell, 2012).
24. The stories do not appear to have received a Burson Marsteller briefing, but, as a result of publication, the *New York Times* subsequently lost access to Apple's pre-release briefings on its new Mac operating system (Slivka, 2012).

25. The script is available on Daisey's blog and readers are invited to download and adapt it for widespread use, thus maximizing self-promotion (Daisey, 2012).
26. Apple controls all of the information on the release of sales figures and no independently verified data on actual sales figures appear to exist because of the control that the company maintains over all aspects of the sales and marketing process.
27. The release of new products now takes on all of the features of the marketing of blockbuster films.
28. The IT specialist who uploaded the image to the *MacRumors* site expressed initial concern that the presence of the images on the phone indicated that the phone was not new or had been repaired (Mitchell, 2008).
29. See also, in particular, the contradictions of a subsumption of class discourse even as a new class of peasant workers – *dagongmei/zai* – appears.
30. Post-operaism (from the Italian *opera* – "work") refers to the theorization of post-industrial labor, developed in the work of André Gorz, Maurizio Lazzarato, Antonio Negri, Enzo Rulani and Antonella Corsani (see Virno, 2004; Chukhrov, 2010).
31. On the pre-operaist sources of the concept of immaterial labor, see Fortunati (2007).
32. The Foxconn complex is referred to as a "campus" rather than a factory, as if it is primarily a place of learning.
33. A bookstore on the Foxconn factory site sells volumes of founder Terry Gou's aphorisms, which include "work itself is a type of joy," "a harsh environment is a good thing," "hungry people have especially clear minds," extending the language of socialist realism and the cultural revolution into the motivational language of neo-liberalism.
34. In this regard, Ai Weiwei's *Sunflower Seeds* installation in the Tate Modern's Turbine Hall (Ai, 2010) also seems emblematic of a displacement and aestheticization of labor, notwithstanding the artist's own emblematic status as globally known dissident superstar (Brown, 2010).
35. Pun provides one of the best and most engaged accounts of the intricacies of labor migration in its starkest and most emotional/affective – and biopolitical – sense (Pun, 2005). More recently, Ku has presented a detailed biopolitics of Filipina laborers in Taiwan (Ku, 2011).
36. Gou and Tseng met when she was hired to teach him the tango for a company Chinese New Year function (Balfour and Culpan, 2010).

Bibliography

Ai, Weiwei (2010) *The Unilever Series: Ai Weiwei*, 12 October 2010–2012 May 2011. London: Tate Modern.

Amin, Ash (ed.) (1994) *Post-Fordism: A Reader* (Oxford: Blackwell).

Andrews, Robert (2008) " 'iPhone Girl' Finds Fame and Fear on the Production Line", *Washington Post*, 28 August, http://www.washingtonpost.com/wp-dyn/content/article/2008/08/28/AR2008082800571.html, date accessed 30 September 2008.

Angell, L. C. (2006) "Apple Posts Report on iPod Plant Investigation", http://www.ilounge.com/index.php/news/comments/apple-posts-report-on-ipod-plant-investigation/, date accessed 29 April 2010.

Apple Hot News (2006) "Report on iPod Manufacturing", 17 August, http://www.apple.com/hotnews/ipodreport/, date accessed 29 April 2010.

Apple Press Info (2012a) "Fair Labor Association Begins Inspections of Foxconn", 13 February, http://www.apple.com/pr/library/2012/02/13Fair-Labor-Association-Begins-Inspections-of-Foxconn.html, date accessed 30 March 2012.

Apple Press Info (2012b) "New iPad Tops Three Million", 19 March, http://www.apple.com/pr/library/2012/03/19New-iPad-Tops-Three-Million.html, date accessed 20 March 2012.

AppleInsider (2006) "Photos: Inside Foxconn's 'iPod City' ", 14 June, http://www.appleinsider.com/articles/06/06/14/photos_inside_foxconns_ipod_city.html, date accessed 29 April 2010.

Balfour, Frederik and Tim Culpan (2010) "The Man Who Makes Your iPhone", *Bloomberg Business Week*, 9 September, http://www.businessweek.com/magazine/content/10_38/b4195058423479.htm, date accessed 5 July 2011.

Bazilian, Emma (2011) "Burson-Marsteller PR Reps Caught Spreading Fake Google Stories", *Adweek*, 11 May, http://www.adweek.com/news/technology/burson-marsteller-pr-reps-caught-spreading-fake-google-stories-131523, date accessed 30 March 2012.

Bloomberg TV (2010) Foxconn "Treasure Your Life" Rally at Longhua Campus, http://www.youtube.com/watch?v=i5vTXt8mlEM, date accessed 5 July 2011.

Brown, Mark (2010) "Ai Weiwei's Turbine Hall Installation Closed 'Over Health and Safety Concerns' ", *The Guardian*, 14 October, http://www.guardian.co.uk/artanddesign/ 2010/oct/14/ai-weiwei-turbine-hall-installation-closed, date accessed 14 October 2010.

Burtynsky, Edward (2005) *China: The Photographs of Edward Burtynsky* (Göttingen: Steidl).

Chan, Chris King-Chi (2012) *The Challenge of Labour in China: Strikes and the Changing Labour Regime in Global Factories* (London: Routledge).

Chan, Jenny and Pun, Ngai (2010) "Suicide as Protest for the New Generation of Chinese Migrant Workers: Foxconn, Global Capital, and the State", *The Asia-Pacific Journal: Japan Focus*, http://japanfocus.org/-Jenny-Chan/3408, date accessed 20 February 2011.

Chan, Minnie (2010) "Foxconn Recruiting 2000 Experts to Help Stop Its Suicide Problem", *South China Morning Post*, 24 May, A4.

Chan, Quinton and So, Peter (2011) "Firms Face Inflated Minimum Wage Bill", *South China Morning Post*, 9 February, B2.

Chang, Liang-chih and Huang, Frances (2010) "Foxconn Plans to Increase China Workforce to 1.3 Million", *Focus Taiwan News Channel*, 19 August 2010, http://focustaiwan.tw/ShowNews/ WebNews_Detail.aspx?ID=201008190012&Type=aECO, date accessed 22 March 2012.

Cheung, Gary, Nip, Amy and Lee, Ada (2010) "Minimum Wage Law to Help 310,000", *South China Morning Post*, 11 November, A4.

China Post (2008) "Tycoon Gou Gets a Better Half, Marries Girlfriend", *China Post*, 27 July, http://www.chinapost.com.tw/print/167294.htm, date accessed 27 March 2012.

ChinaSMACK (2010) "Foxconn Rallies: Employees Pledge To Cherish Their Lives", 23 August, http://www.chinasmack.com/2010/pictures/foxconn-rallies-employees-pledge-to-cherish-their-lives.html, date accessed 25 May 2011.

Chukhrov, Keti (2010) "Towards the Space of the General: On Labor Beyond Materiality and Immateriality", *e-flux*, no. 20, http://www.e-flux.com/journal/towards-the-space-of-the-general-on-labor-beyond-materiality-and-immateriality/, date accessed 27 April 2012.

Colitt, Ray and Winter, Brian (2011) "Apple iPhone-Maker Foxconn Ponders Big Brazil Move", *Reuters UK*, 12 April, http://uk.reuters.com/article/2011/04/12/us-brazil-foxconn-idUSTRE73B6BD20110412, date accessed 10 July 2011.

Daisey, Mike (2012) Mike Daisey, http://mikedaisey.blogspot.com/, date accessed 30 March 2012.

De Landa, Manuel (2002) *Intensive Science and Virtual Philosophy* (London and New York: Continuum).

De Landa, Manuel (2006) *A New Philosophy of Society: Assemblage Theory and Social Complexity* (London: Continuum).

Dean, Jason (2007) "The Forbidden City of Terry Gou", *Wall Street Journal*, 11 August, http://online.wsj.com/public/article/SB118677584137994489.html?mod=blog, date accessed 29 April 2010.

Deleuze, Gilles and Guattari, Félix (1987) *A Thousand Plateaus: Capitalism and Schizophrenia* (Minneapolis: University of Minnesota Press).

Designing Hong Kong (2010a) 1. City Speak XIV: Privatised Public Space: Do New Guidelines Solve the Problems?, http://www.youtube.com/watch?v=h23WvTwZAqA&feature=related, date accessed 27 April 2012.

Designing Hong Kong (2010b) 12. City Speak XIV: Privatised Public Space: Do New Guidelines Solve the Problems?, http://www.youtube.com/watch?v=xn41_oYWHnI, date accessed 27 April 2012.

Designing Hong Kong (2010c) CitySpeak XIV: Privatised Public Space: Do New Guidelines Solve the Problems?, http://www.designinghongkong.com/cms/index.php?option=com_content&task=view&id=27&Itemid=12, date accessed 26 April 2012.

Dobrenko, Evgeny (2007) *The Political Economy of Socialist Realism* (New Haven: Yale University Press).

Drache, Daniel and Gertler, Meric S. (1991) *The New Era of Global Competition: State Policy and Market Power* (Montréal: McGill-Queen's University Press).

Duhigg, Charles and Barboza, David (2012a) "How the U.S. Lost Out on iPhone Work", *New York Times*, 21 January, http://www.nytimes.com/2012/01/22/business/apple-america-and-a-squeezed-middle-class.html?pagewanted=all, date accessed 26 April 2012.

Duhigg, Charles and Barboza, David (2012b) "In China, Human Costs Are Built Into an iPad", *New York Times*, 25 January, http://www.nytimes.com/2012/01/26/business/ieconomy-apples-ipad-and-the-human-costs-for-workers-in-china.html?_r=1&scp=1&sq=%22in%20china,%20human%20costs%22&st=Search, date accessed 26 April 2012.

Duhigg, Charles and Barboza, David (2012c) "Pressure, Chinese and Foreign, Drives Change at Foxconn", *New York Times*, 19 February, http://www.nytimes.com/2012/02/20/technology/pressures-drive-change-at-chinas-electronics-giant-foxconn.html?scp=1&sq=%E2%80%98Pressure,%20Chinese%20and%20Foreign'&st=Search, date accessed 26 April 2012.

East South West North (2009) The Suicide of Sun Danyong, http://www.zonaeuropa.com/ 20090724_1.htm, date accessed 24 May 2010.

Farrell, Nick (2012) "Foxconn Hires Burson-Marsteller to Hit Out at Underage Worker Claims", *TechEye*, 24 February, http://news.techeye.net/business/foxconn-hires-burson-marsteller-to-hit-out-at-underage-worker-claims, date accessed 20 March 2012.

Fortunati, Leopoldina (2007) "Immaterial Labour and its Machinization", *Ephemera: Theory and Politics in Organization*, 7(1), 139–157.

France 24 (2008) "Fifteen Minutes of Fame for the 'iPhone Girl' ", *France 24 International News*, 29 August, http://observers.france24.com/content/20080829-iphone-girl-apple-factory-photos, date accessed 25 May 2011.

Garside, Juliette (2012) "Apple's Factories in China are Breaking Employment Laws, Audit Finds", *The Guardian*, 30 March, http://www.guardian.co.uk/technology/2012/mar/30/apple-factories-china-foxconn-audit, date accessed 31 March 2012.

Gentle, Nick (2008) "Mall Sued Over Public Space Rents", *South China Morning Post*, 18 June, A1.

Greenhouse, Stephen (2012) "Early Praise in Inspection at Foxconn Brings Doubt", *New York Times*, 16 February, http://www.nytimes.com/2012/02/17/business/early-praise-in-foxconn-inspection-brings-doubt.html?_r=2, date accessed 31 March 2012.

Hall, Stuart and Jacques, Martin (1989) *New Times: The Changing Face of Politics in the 1990's* (London: Lawrence and Wishart).

Hartley, Hal (1994) " 'In Images We Trust': Hal Hartley Interviews Jean-Luc Godard", *Filmmaker*, 3, no. 1 (Fall), http://cinemagodardcinema.wordpress.com/interviews/hartly/, date accessed 30 April 2012.

He, Huifeng (2010a) "Foxconn Largesse Raises Suspicion", *South China Morning Post*, 8 June, A1, A5.

He, Huifeng (2010b) "More Anxiety and Fear at Foxconn Factory", *South China Morning Post*, 28 May, A4.

He, Huifeng and Perez, Bien (2010) "Foxconn Staff to Get Second Pay Rise", *South China Morning Post*, 3 June, front page.

Hinews.cn (2009) "Foxconn Employee Sun Danyong's Suicide Blog and Chat Record Revealed" (富士康員工孫丹勇自殺 博客曝光聊天記錄), http://wwwbig5.hinews.cn/news/system/ 2009/07/21/010523658.shtml, date accessed 24 May 2010.

Hoernle, Edwin (1978) "The Working Man's Eye", in Mellor, David (ed.) *Germany: The New Photography 1927–33* (London: Arts Council of Great Britain).

Hooper, John (1985) "China Brushes Up on Public Relations", *The Guardian*, 2 September, 22.

Hu, Fox Yi (2010) "Family Demands Truth Behind Teen's Death", *Sunday Morning Post* (Hong Kong), 18 April, 3.

iPhone Girl (2008) *MacRumors*, http://forums.macrumors.com/showthread.php?t=547777, date accessed 30 April 2012.

Johnson, Joel (2011) "1 Million Workers. 90 Million iPhones. 17 Suicides. Who's to Blame?" *Wired*, 28 February, http://www.wired.com/magazine/2011/02/ff_joelinchina/all/1, date accessed 27 April 2012.

Kracauer, Siegfried (1995) *The Mass Ornament: Weimar Essays*, in Levin, Thomas Y. (ed., trans.) (Cambridge: Harvard University Press).

Ku, Yuling (2011) *Our Stories: Migration and Labour in Taiwan*, in Ding, Naifei and Parry, Amie Elizabeth (eds.), Agnes Khoo (trans.) (Petaling Jaya: SIRD).

Lavaert, Sonja and Pascal Gielen (2009) "The Dismeasure of Art: An Interview with Paolo Virno", *Open*, 17, http://classic.skor.nl/article-4178-en.html, date accessed 1 May 2009.

Lee, Diana (2008a) "Democrats Enter Fray in Times Square Rent Row", *The Standard*, 6 March, http://www.thestandard.com.hk/news_detail.asp?pp_cat=11&art_id=62639&sid=17926300&con_type=1&d_str=20080306&sear_year=2008, date accessed 22 May 2010.

Lee, Diana (2008b) "Pushy Times Square Guards Raise Hackles", *The Standard*, 5 March, http://www.thestandard.com.hk/news_detail.asp?pp_cat=11&art_id=62525&sid=17904294&con_type=1&d_str=20080305&sear_year=2008, date accessed 22 May 2010.

Leung, Ambrose and Tsang, Phyllis (2010a) "Police Back Down Over Protesters' Art", *South China Morning Post*, 1 June, A1.

Leung, Ambrose and Tsang, Phyllis (2010b) "Statues Released and Placed in Victoria Park", *South China Morning Post*, 2 June, A3.

Leung, Ambrose and Tsang, Phyllis (2010c) "Students Give Statue a New Home", *South China Morning Post*, 5 June, C1.

Levin, Thomas Y. (1995) "Introduction", in Kracauer, Siegfried *The Mass Ornament: Weimar Essays* (Cambridge: Harvard University Press).

Lury, Celia (2009) "Brand as Assemblage", *Journal of Cultural Economy*, 2(1), 67–82.

Lyberaki, Antigone (1991) "Crisis and Restructuring in Greek Small Scale Industry: A Case of Flexible Specialisation?", *Capital & Class*, 15(2) (Summer), 35–48.

Ma, Jun (2008) "Was iPhone Girl a Planned Beauty?", *East South West North*, 4 September, http://www.zonaeuropa.com/20080905_1.htm, date accessed 30 March 2009.

MacRumors (2008) "MacRumors iPhone Girl Thread", http://forums.macrumors.com/showthread. php?t=547777, date accessed 12 November 2010.

Mail Online (2006) "The Stark Reality of iPod's Chinese Factories", *Mail Online*, 11 June, http://www.dailymail.co.uk/news/article-401234/The-stark-reality-iPods-Chinese-factories.html, date accessed 29 April 2010.

Milian, Mark (2012) "How a Google Search Unraveled Mike Daisey's Apple-Foxconn Story", *Bloomberg: Tech Blog*, 16 March, http://go.bloomberg.com/tech-blog/2012-03-16-how-a-google-search-unraveled-mike-daiseys-apple-foxconn-story/, date accessed 16 March 2012.

Mitchell, Mark (2008) "Fifteen Minutes of Fame for the 'iPhone Girl' ", *France 24 International News*, 29 August, http://observers.france24.com/en/content/20080829-iphone-girl-apple-factory-photos, date accessed 24 May 2011.

Mitchell, W. J. T. (2005) *What do Pictures Want? The Lives and Loves of Images* (Chicago: University of Chicago Press).

Moss, William (2008) "China's iPhone Girl: Brilliant Apple PR or Lucky Accident?", *ImageThief*, 6 September, http://news.imagethief.com/blogs/china/archive/2008/09/06/china-s-iphone-girl-brilliant-apple-pr-or-lucky-accident. aspx, date accessed 30 March 2009.

Murphy, David (2011) "Burson-Marsteller Caught Deleting Facebook Criticism; Facebook Delivers Statement", 14 May, http://www.pcmag.com/article2/0, 2817,2385394,00.asp, date accessed 30 March 2012.

Museo Reina Sofía (2011) *A Hard, Merciless Light: The Worker-Photography Movement, 1926–1939*, 6 April–22 August 2011. Madrid: Museo Reina Sofía.

Ngai, Lung Tai and Qiu, Jack Linchuan (2010) "Grassroots Pixels: Simple Digital Camera and the New Imagery of Migrant Workers", *Image, Hyper-Production, Value, Event: Researching Mobile Images and Everyday Experience*, conference at the Chinese University of Hong Kong, 15 June 2010.

Office of Telecommunications Authority, Hong Kong SAR (2012) Key Telecommunications Statistics (March), http://www.ofta.gov.hk/en/datastat/key_stat.html, date accessed 22 March 2012.

Ohrn, Karin B. and Hardt, Hanno (1980) " 'Who Photographs Us?' The Workers Photography Movement in Weimar Germany", *63rd Annual Meeting of the Association for Education in Journalism*, conference in Boston, 10–13 August 1980.

Ong, Aihwa and Collier, Stephen J. (eds.) (2005) *Global Assemblages: Technology, Politics and Ethics as Anthropological Problems* (Malden: Blackwell).

Phillips, Michael R., Li, Xianyun and Zhang, Yanping (2002) "Suicide Rates in China, 1995–99", *The Lancet*, 359, March 9, 835–840.

Phillips, Michael R., Liu, Huaqing and Zhang, Yanping (1999) "Suicide and Social Change", *China, Culture, Medicine and Psychiatry*, 23, 25–50.

Pilling, David (2010) "Foxconn's Milestone for a Rising China Price", *Financial Times*, 17 November, http://www.ft.com/cms/s/0/8e061c46-f285-11df-a2f3-00144feab49a.html#axzz1EZCIYzvF, date accessed 17 November 2010.

Pun, Ngai (2005) *Made in China: Women Factory Workers in a Global Workplace* (Durham: Duke University Press; Hong Kong: Hong Kong University Press).

Pun, Ngai and Chan, Chris King-Chi (2008) "The Subsumption of Class Discourse in China", *Boundary 2*, 35(2) (Summer), 75–91.

Ribalta, Jorge (2011) *The Worker-Photography Movement 1926–1939* (Madrid: T.F. Editores, S.L.C).

SACOM (2010) *Workers as Machines: Military Management in Foxconn*, http://www.sinoptic.ch/ textes/rapports/2010/20101012_PPP-SACOM_Report_Foxconn. Workers.pdf, date accessed 10 February 2011.

Slattery, Brennon (2008) "iPhone Girl Becomes Internet Superstar", *PC World*, 29 August, http://blogs.pcworld.com/staffblog/archives/007631.html, date accessed 29 April 2010.

Slivka, Eric (2012) "Apple Shuns The New York Times in OS X Mountain Lion Coverage Over Foxconn Reporting", *MacRumors*, 17 February, http://www.macrumors.com/2012/02/17/ apple-shuns-the-new-york-times-in-os-x-mountain-lion-coverage-over-foxconn-reporting/, date accessed 20 March 2012.

South China Morning Post (2010a) "Foxconn Building US$100m Plant in Henan", *South China Morning Post*, 3 August, A5.

South China Morning Post (2010b) "Strike a Critical Turning Point in Development of Mainland Labour", *South China Morning Post*, 4 June, front page, A14.

Spencer, Richard (2008) "Beijing Olympics: Faking Scandal Over Girl Who 'Sang' in Opening Ceremony", *Daily Telegraph*, 12 August, http://www.telegraph.

co.uk/sport/othersports/ olympics/2545387/Beijing-Olympics-Faking-scandal-over-girl-who-sang-in-opening-ceremony.html, date accessed 29 April 2010.
Sun, Celine (2009) "Peiyi Not Bitter Over Olympic Snub", *South China Morning Post*, 11 January, C1.
Tam, Fiona (2010) "Foxconn Rallies Urge 800,000 to 'Treasure Life' ", *South China Morning Post*, 18 August, A5.
Tsang, Denise (2011) "Wage Increases Spark Rise in Factory Prices", *South China Morning Post*, 28 January, B1.
Virno, Paolo (2004) *A Grammar of the Multitude* (New York: Semiotext(e)).
Weir, Bill (2012) "A Trip to The iFactory: "Nightline" Gets an Unprecedented Glimpse Inside Apple's Chinese Core", *ABC News* (US), 20 February.
World Health Organization (2011) Mental Health: Suicide Rates per 100,000 by Country, Year and Sex (Table), http://www.who.int/mental_health/prevention/suicide_rates/en/, date accessed 30 April 2012.
Yau, Elaine, Wong, Martin and Nip, Amy (2011) "March of the Minimum Wage Victims: Labour Day Protest Centres on New Unemployed Who Were Valued at Less Than HK$28", *South China Morning Post*, 2 May, C1.
Ye, Juliet (2010) "Foxconn Installs Antijumping Nets at Hebei Plants", *Wall Street Journal*, 3 August, http://blogs.wsj.com/chinarealtime/2010/08/03/foxconn-installs-antijumping-nets-at-hebei-plants/, date accessed 25 May 2011.

7

In Transit: Between Labor and Leisure in London's St. Pancras International

Rachel Moore

Screens today proliferate in all manner of public settings, from the iconic bank machine through rail station advertisements, Tube escalators and information panels to museum displays. They are, by turns, tools to get money and information; platforms to advertise, entertain, instruct and inform; and media to attract, occupy, preoccupy and distract your attention. Their presence or absence is an indication of modernity, tackiness, concern or suspicion. Built into them is a random spectator whose momentary glance whilst hurrying through their everyday resists the scrutiny and rich theorization traditionally enjoyed by visual studies of art or cinema. Who or what in these scenarios is the subject and who or what is the object? The address is not to one and everyone but to anyone. Infecting every facet of the urban experience, taken as a whole, they amount just so much visual noise, pulling your attention this way and that, repelling or seducing you with the warm glow of the commodity fetish. Despite the fact that we are dealing with moving images, investigating their medium specificity, their internal formal structures and the ingenuity of their siting, will not, on its own, suffice to understand the impact of this phenomenon on our daily experience of the city. The cinema that once might have satisfied the losses associated with modernity, when experience and contemplative thought were losing ground to representation and the fragmentation of perception, bears no straightforward relation to contemporary public screens. For classical film theorists, the paucity of bodily felt and contingent experience put pressure on cinema to recover what was being lost in daily life. Jean Epstein's reeling paragraphs produced a version of cinema that went straight to the nervous system; Balázs' communion with the screen brought back bodies and faces to communicate those things language would not, and the haptic apperception of Benjamin's optical unconscious responded to the modern condition by hitting the spectator between the eyes (see Moore, 2000, pp. 12–25, 96–106, 62–72). In all, cinema brought a nearness otherwise unavailable. That pressure now falls on public spaces, to a large degree, to fill the new losses brought with the twenty-first century. While this has led to a range of laudatory claims for Internet activity in a virtual public forum, there is an increasing interest on the part of institutions, researchers and artists in the enlivening of physical public space, and screens are no less prevalent in these endeavors.

While this investigation represents a change in the object of study, it is worth remembering that many of the classical film theorists who addressed cinema as it grew to be recognized as an art form did so in the context of the changing nature of labor. In different ways, Benjamin, Kracauer and Epstein noted that the shift from artisanal to industrial labor changed the way we occupied our world and left room for the cinema to meet the new form of attention engendered by new work rhythms. For Kracauer, the new laborer was distracted, their attention pulled this way and that, but matched shot for shot by the mechanics of the cinema screen. For Benjamin, the tactile ballistics of the cinema screen could circumvent the diffuse business of everyday demands and go straight to our senses. Jean Epstein saw the new laborer in a constant state of mental strain which he called "fatigue." That fatigue left us as open receptors for the cinema. While their theories may be of little use in understanding the place of, say, a bank teller machine today as regards our attention, it is nonetheless the case that the way in which we labor affects how and what we perceive. This chapter thus takes the changing nature of labor today as fundamental to understanding how we occupy and preoccupy ourselves with regard to screens in public spaces. Industrial labor is increasingly pushed to the periphery of the cosmopolitan urban dweller's worldview, condensing its exploitation to inhuman proportions (see Helen Grace, Chapter 6). At the same time, the defining characteristics of industrial labor have all but disappeared from the first-world urban scene. To look at the way in which media feature in our attention today requires that we address the shift away from mechanical labor and its time clock toward the immaterial labor that predominates today. "Immaterial labor" is a term deployed by Maurizio Lazzarato to describe a phenomenon begun in the 1970s wherein work became cerebral rather than manual, defined as "the labor that produces the informational and cultural content of the commodity" (Lazzarato, 1996, pp. 132–146). Aided by cybernetics and computer control, immaterial labor diffuses the measurement of labor time as well as the definition of labor itself to give, in Lazzarato's thinking, the corporate structure a new, hidden and even firmer hold on the worker. London's St. Pancras Station is a place designed for such laborers, and it is in this light that it appears to offer an insight into the current relationship between labor and leisure, which have always been intertwined, but never more so than now. In line with the cultural value such labor produces, St. Pancras Station preserved the historic Victorian shell of the building only to house within it the super modern complex of shopping, eating and transport establishments, constructed in steel and glass, readily replicated in any number of contexts, famously referred to now via Marc Augé as "non-places" (1995). The changes in labor associated with modernity have been dramatic, as have the theories that they instigated. Far from that drama and noise, our current labor situation leaves us scrutinizing to find those moments when we are not working, and what, if anything, we can do with that time. This chapter will explore the interstices of a rail station, to see how its screens fit into our quotidian urban experience, where not only is our sense of place increasingly indeterminate but also at a moment when our understanding of our labor time is ever more vague.

In the shift from the study of cinema in its classical large-screen iteration to the proliferation of varied moving images in formats large and small, addressed to audiences that are isolated or randomly convened, Brecht's maxim to "take your cue not from the good old things, but from the bad new ones" looms large (cited in Benjamin, 2002, p. 350). To meet this challenge, we began a research project to understand the impact of moving screen imagery on daily life by spending a good deal of time observing them in specific environments.[1] This article addresses St. Pancras Station, chosen because it was recently built, with screens as an integral part of its design, not merely retrofitted or added onto an existing scene. Added to this, the station is part of a major redevelopment project of the King's Cross area, an all-out makeover of an area famous for its unsavory nature, and highly contested because of the many displacements such upheaval wrought upon its population. The research involved informal walks through the area and hours of personal observation in the station, as well as highly organized observation at peak moments of the commuting day by paid investigators placed at key sites in the station. Once these key sites of activity had been determined, researchers watched the amount of attention paid to screens, and how often and how long people looked at them, as well as noted what it felt like to be in each situation. While this may appear overly empirical, the liminal nature of train stations, not to mention the peripheral place screens occupy in daily routines, seemed to demand that we get at least a snap shot of the attention paid to them amidst a scene of continual movement.

Eschewing the customary idea that train stations function primarily as sites of temporary homelessness, the newly renovated St. Pancras Station is designed to be "Europe's destination station" with a "unique identity" also reflected in the design, content and technological innovativeness of signage there. The official station website states that "St. Pancras is not just the key destination for the Eurostar and high-speed rail in the UK – but a truly grand retail and hospitality destination – a great place to meet" (Passenger Focus, 2010). This additional convivial aim of the designers surfaces in subtle and not so subtle ways, from the reduction of aural and visual noise, to the monstrously scaled bronze statue of a couple embracing that hovers over the elegant dining section of the upper level. With its glass ceiling, it has the feeling of an outside that is inside, light and airy, but also safe and secure. Built to the specifications of various and many demands, the shell of the building envelops not only an entire world but also a world that is a manifestly secure one; indeed, the safest by a long chalk in all of London.[2]

Originally constructed in 1868, the station is eminently new in many ways. The eight large departure and arrival screens at its entrance are designed to disperse passengers immediately to one of the four separate rail terminals. Those going to the East Midlands, Eurostar, Southeastern and First Capital are variously dispatched so that there is no danger of being touched by or touching a stranger, and no chance of that intrusion of the foreign which we fear from others and for which we immediately beg our pardon. There is also no danger of a crowd forming, a crowd being that amorphous mass with an energy of its own whereby bodies touch tightly together in such a way that they are anonymous and require no apology. The fears and pleasures regarding touching strangers that Canetti identified in *Crowds and Power* play no part in the swift rationing out of bodies to take their places, and watch and wait (Canetti, 1984, pp. 17–18). This also leaves no spectators to watch the one moving screen that sports a bland feed of Sky news, weather and advertisements. In the many hours of observing people entering the station, we have not witnessed so much as a glance in its direction. Indeed, compared with other London rail stations, St. Pancras is screen poor, at least with regard to spectacle. The information screens subtly placed about its four sections show locations in and around the station, train schedules and business advertisements. Designed to be used interactively, one person at a time, these screens are small and address the individual rather than the crowd. Not only is visual noise at a minimum but the soundscape is also meagre. The only announcements are confined to the Eurostar in both English and French, and on rare occasions English when a national train's departure needs to be amended. One is therefore completely dependant on one's sight to get to the track on time, aided by the departure screens installed in every shop and restaurant. Even at the busiest of times, the sound of footsteps – the definitive metonym for the laborer – performs the only narration of your passage. Visually austere and aurally quiet, the environment fosters relaxation where normally anxiety would feature.

While the intensity of surveillance and control systems, along with the fairly obvious address to a middle-class consumer – pretty much everything listed on the website "Stuff White People Like," even a "Farmer's Market"[3] – might tempt a simple interpretation of exclusivity and control, the enterprise participates in a much larger context. According to architect and theorist Alejandro Zaera Polo, such spaces as St. Pancras are "bubbles" which through their ability to maintain fluidity against the pressing march of monolithic globalization can be spaces of either freedom or control (Zaera Polo, 2008, p. 78). As an envelope, the exterior walls of the building not only perform the basic task of separating the outside from the inside to provide shelter but enclose an entire world. This is true of many new builds designed for public use that are private public partnership ventures, where it is crucial that the public feels included, and that there are multiple activities accessible to everyone (not just those who have a ticket for the Eurostar). These sites must be multi-functional, and must create an "experience" and "a sense of place" (Hammond, 2006, pp. 24–25). While the feeling of an enclosure congenial to social gathering is new compared with other stations in London, this does not conflict with its basic function as a transportation hub where people are caught in the liminal transition between work and home, or between labor and leisure.

It is in this most prosaic of functions, and the screens associated with rail travel, where the nature of labor and its relationship to time that attention to the experience of St. Pancras might be illuminating. Modernist social theory has trained us to understand that the nature of our labor determines, to a significant degree, the way we treat the concepts of space and time. Georg Lukács in his highly influential 1923 essay "Reification and the Consciousness of the Proletariat" went so far as to say that because of the thorough rationalization of time through industrial labor, time becomes space. In his description of a reality wherein all value has become abstract he writes,

> Time sheds its qualitative, variable, flowing nature; it freezes into an exactly delimited, quantifiable continuum filled with quantifiable 'things' (the reified, mechanically objectified 'performance' of the worker, wholly separated from his total human personality): in short, it [time] becomes space... [In this] environment, at once the cause and the effect of the scientifically and mechanically fragmented and production of the object of labor, the subjects must likewise be rationally fragmented.
>
> (Lukács, 1971, p. 90)

Lukács' 'abstract totality' left a world of fragmented subjects whose perceptual capacities were no less so. Thus for classical film theory, the shift from artisanal to industrial labor meant that the unrationalized time and perceptual relaxation necessary to contemplate things was gone. The neurasthenia that then took over left us, for Kracauer, victims of continual distraction; for Jean Epstein, in a state of constant fatigue that made us excellent receptors for the art of film (see Epstein, 1977, p. 13; Kracauer, 1995, p. 332; Moore, 2000, pp. 96–106). Since then, however, labor has changed significantly. Work has become quiet, often silent, and even though every device you own now has a clock somewhere in it, labor time is far more elastic than during the industrial period. The temporal rationalization of labor that would lead to a world that was totally abstracted from meaning that Lukács described is not the way much of labor is measured today. Increasingly, a kind of degraded communism which mimics the lifestyle of the bohemian or the artist, the person for whom the distinction between work and life does not exist, has become the norm for many kinds of labor, labor known as immaterial labor. Lukács may still be relevant, however, because of the way in which the measurement of time has infected all aspects of work and play, to the extent that it may be the case that time, with rare exceptions, is never our own.

According to Stefano Harney, the kind of labor whose value can be immediately measured is the labor of the financier, who can look up at the screen and immediately see their productivity go up or go down (Harney, 2010). The worth of performative labor, on the other hand, is more difficult to measure. The value of immaterial labor is always deferred. Advertisers, artists and academics, for example, do not immediately, if ever, know where their labor's value lies. Given that it is the ethics of the financier that dictate value today, but also that workers' ability to measure their labor's value is hindered by those severe standards, workers must remain constantly vigilant about their labor's value. Because they cannot ever know for certain, they just work all the time, endlessly performing so as to be deemed productive. This leads to a situation in which the financier gets from the laborer what they call "total commitment" and a blurring of the boundary where work ends and the rest of life begins. But that finance world is not the world of performativity's other, according to Harney; its other is free time. Unlike the financier who earns their free time, the laborer's free time is "time to the side." With the world of productivity constantly pushing the world of performativity, free time is the exact opposite of something like a vigilance of productivity. Unlike leisure, which is something that is earned, free time is unproductive time – time for wandering, random time, time to get lost, time you cannot and do not account for. Hence the complaints that people on benefits, for example, have too much free time (Harney, 2010).

Free time, time to the side, is under attack from all quarters. As if to extend the reification of labor time to absurdity, every second is captured with the efficiency only paralleled by London's surveillance cameras. Time is measured but rarely quantified; the only point is that it is not your time anymore. Like the hourglass that turns over and over as you wait for your debit card's pin number to be ratified, whose time is that? How much time is it? The move from analog to digital clocks began it all, whereby time was no longer shown on a dial so that its position relative to the day was instantly graspable, and counting instead was the initial abstraction. Now, such devices as the ever-turning hourglass and the various spinning graphics on computers and phones habituate us to hand over our time, without even counting it. This is analogous to the always-on-hold time, common now in the immaterial labor work force at large, that is the final blow in the rationalization of life formerly theorized through, and largely associated with, the proletarian labor of the industrial age.

It is against the backdrop of this increasingly common labor situation of the UK's cities, I would argue, that the belly of St. Pancras Station, the area known as "The Arcade," where you are only a ticket barrier away from Europe, extends its invitation. The laborer, who effectively works all the time, steals 20 minutes or so at some point in their unrationalized day on their way to or from somewhere, to enter this new station. Many of the features normally associated with a train station are gone. Noise, crime and crowding have all but disappeared. The assaults and distractions that modernist theory had maintained prevented us from contemplation, from losing ourselves in ourselves, from the state of mental relaxation that could lead to profound boredom, seem to have been largely eliminated. Instead a retail promenade, with its discrete advertising, shops for luxury and novelty goods, fixed waiting seating in the center, endless variations of quality coffee and, of course Wi-Fi, quietly invite speculation.

So for some of us, the casual amounts of time when we cannot work, as the imperative to work more and more so that it might be valued increases, those 20-odd minute slots of time become moments of non-productivity, moments to meander. The question then arises whether this is an invitation to leisure time, in which work and play are all of a piece, time that is merely the mirror image of labor, or genuinely free time; time that is off to the side of a daily ritual, time that is markedly unproductive. Or is it another kind of time altogether? The division between work and play is increasingly dissolving for most people, given that the prosthetic devices we use daily, such as the laptop, the mobile phone and the iPod, blur that divide as a rule. And every device, from cooker to computer, has a digital clock somewhere, further injecting a constant sense that your time is being counted. This ubiquitous temporal monitor forms a silent backdrop as one steps out into the urban everyday as well, forging the immateriality of labor and the abstraction of time together with each screen encounter.

The arcade section of the station would suggest a bit of both leisure and free time, since (claims for *flâneurie* notwithstanding) to shop and to buy can be activities of leisure rather than free time, and to sit with a cup of hot drink may or may not lead to having time that is really stolen out of that ever blurring maze of work and life. In all, this arcade could easily function as one of Agué's non-places servicing the lone wanderer, with its singular address, and the way in which the historical place of magnificent Victorian architecture has been reamed of its insides to make way for glass and plastic surfaces that would be at home in any airport or shopping mall.

The monotony of sameness Augé described alongside the many critiques of globalization caught the attention of the authors of *The New Survey of London Life and Labour* (1934), who also saw the growing habit of transport as something that had done much to level prices, tastes and classes. One could easily shop, work and live in different places because of the growth of transport (which initially primarily carried the goods), and they see the social effects of travel as healthy, allowing, for example, people living in poor conditions increased opportunities to move into decent surroundings. They conclude their section on transportation with their comments on its social effects:

> But there have been other and subtler results. Thus the visible signs of class distinctions are disappearing. Chokers, Derby coats and ostrich feathers are rarely to be seen. The dress of the younger generation of working men and women, so far from having any distinctive note of its own, tends merely to copy, sometimes to exaggerate, any particular fashion current in the West End. In the same way paint and powder, once regarded in this class as the marks of the prostitute, are freely used by respectable working girls... The Cockney dialect and rhyming slang are slowly disappearing while Cockney twang is spreading to other classes. In fact the whole demeanour of the different social classes has tended towards a closer approximation in the past generation.
>
> (Smith, 1935, p. 289)

The parallels with today in terms of fashion and language are remarkable, where today middle-class mimicry of working-class accents prevails, and fashion trends now readily traverse the borders between the elite and the street in both directions. Whether their following conclusion has a parallel today is far less obvious:

> It is not suggested that the general improvement of economic conditions and of education, and the influence of the Press, have not been powerful factors in this change. But the change would certainly not have taken place so rapidly had it not been for the much freer mingling of the classes, which has resulted from the increase of travel. In so far as it represents a levelling up of opportunities and a breaking down of class barriers, the change is indeed to be welcomed, but perhaps a word of regret may be allowed to escape for the passing of something original and colourful in the drab monotony of a great city.
>
> (Smith, 1935, p. 289)

The drab monotony of which they speak surely foreshadows Augé's ethnography, but the way they align that with the leveling-out of class in general does not fit our current situation. Nonetheless, it reflects something of what we observed in the station, which aspires to serve the working person with a modest surplus of time and money ready to hand.

Much care has been given at St. Pancras to do away with drabness; the airiness and light, the openness of the space with the ceiling permitted to shine through to the ground floor, which render the passage bright at all hours. The absence of large screens, and the visual and aural clutter that characterize most train stations and increasingly airports, point to an attempt at least to permit a person to have some control over their own perception, and allow an opening for the senses to let down their guard. The signature technology for the growing mechanization and facelessness of contemporary life – the cash machine – is hidden away at the far end of the arcade, barely noticeable as if to elude Marc Augé's fictional ethnographer of non-place, Pierre Dupont (Augé, 1995, p. 1). Although the place has lost the noise, grit and permeable architecture of a traditional rail station, the efforts to avoid the worst of airport anonymity in the arcade causeway are noteworthy. For instance, the Foyles bookshop, the elaborate flower stall and the expensively recreated Victorian clock are testimony to the effort to distinguish the station as a real place. In losing the crowds and clamor of a traditional rail station, it has become the public's favored terminal. According to the 2010 Passenger Focus Survey, "St. Pancras continues to be voted passengers' favourite (94% satisfied) of Britain's busier railway stations" (Passenger Focus, 2010). Can we so easily dismiss it?

The criteria that would make this a place in Agué's terms would look to the possibility for what one fancifully imagines as his character embarks on a trip:

> surely it was in the crowded places where thousands of individual itineraries converged for a moment, unaware of one another, that there survived something of the uncertain charm of the waste lands, the yards and building sites, the station platforms and waiting rooms where travellers break step, of all the chance meeting places where fugitive feelings occur, of the possibility of continuing adventure, the feeling that all there is to do is to "see what happens".
>
> (Augé, 1995, p. 2)

This sort of longing may voice the romance we anticipate momentarily when entering a rail station, but it is too subjective, too contingent to measure and does not really speak to what might constitute the kind of break from the continual labor that dogs the contemporary worker.

A better measure might be to ask what happens to people's attention in this environment, what happens to their time and what it does to stave off anxiety. Boredom, a highly prized state of mind for thinkers from Warhol to Agamben, whose meaning varies widely, is one thing to look for. For Walter Benjamin, because of the shift from artisanal to industrial labor, boredom had become impossible. Boredom, he writes, "is the dream bird that hatches the egg of experience" (Benjamin, 1969, p. 91). It is the same sort of relaxation for the mind that sleep is to the body. Kracauer too remarked upon the loss of mental relaxation in his contemporary Berlin brought on by neon signs and the like in his essay "Boredom" written in 1924 (1995, pp. 331–334). He calls those who "do their business by inclination," those laborers who would now fall into the category of immaterial laborers, "unhappy types" precisely because of the confusion of attention that such ill-defined labor time creates, singling out their emptiness and woes for particular derision. What he calls "radical boredom" (ibid., p. 331) is increasingly difficult to attain because "the world is too interested for one to find the peace and quiet necessary" (ibid., p. 332). The search for boredom begins by wandering through the city in the evening:

> In the evening one saunters through the streets, replete with an unfulfillment from which a fullness could sprout. Illuminated words glide by on the rooftops, and already one is banished from one's own emptiness into the alien *advertisement.* One's body takes root in the asphalt, and, together with the enlightening revelations of the illuminations, one's spirit – which is no longer one's own – roams ceaselessly out of the night and into the night.
>
> (Ibid., p. 332)

Outside, an advertisement pulls your attention with its "thousand electric bulbs out of which it constitutes and reconstitutes itself into glittering sentences," likewise the radio and the cinema, loudspeakers in cafés chase at one, such that one's spirit is in danger of being lost all together. Boredom then becomes the only possible way to combat this onslaught: "Boredom becomes the only proper occupation, since it provides a kind of guarantee that one is, so to speak, still in control of one's own existence" (ibid., p. 334). At the end of the article he suggests that to find boredom "one would do best to hang about in a train station or, better yet, stay at home, draw the curtains..." (ibid., p. 332).

For Benjamin our ability to achieve boredom is lost with the quiet, unrationalized time of artisanal labor, and for Kracauer, the ascendance of an aggressive media environment. The new labor and media environment of their 1920s modernity signaled a loss of our ability to achieve boredom and, with it, our very access to genuine experience.

Andy Warhol's 1960s boredom is predictably simple. The subject comes up when he discusses the screening of *Sleep* that Jonas Mekas had arranged at the Gramercy Arts Theatre. It is a film with a duration of 5 hours and 20 minutes that depicts a person sleeping, but it is actually faked by looping footage. When hearing what was going to happen, one person said he would not sit through it for anything, so Jonas got a piece of rope and tied him to a chair to make an example out of him. Warhol, however, left after a few minutes: "Sometimes I like to be bored, and sometimes I don't – it depends what kind of mood I'm in. Everyone knows how it is, some days you can sit and look out the window for hours and hours and some days you can't sit still for a single second" (Warhol and Hackett, 1980, p. 50). Warhol goes on to explain:

> I've been quoted a lot as saying, "I like boring things." Well, I said it and I meant it. But that doesn't mean I'm not bored by them. Of course, what I think is boring must not be the same as what other people think is, since I could never stand to watch all the most popular action shows on TV, because they're essentially the same plots and the same shots and the same cuts over and over again. Apparently, most people love watching the same basic thing, as long as the details are different. But I'm just the opposite: if I'm going to sit and watch the same thing I saw the night before, I don't want it to be essentially the same – I want it to be *exactly* the same. Because the more you look at the same exact thing, the more the meaning goes away, and the better and emptier you feel.
>
> (Ibid., p. 50)

While Warhol does not touch on what might prompt a need for boredom, his description of the way repetition creates the condition for its realization adds a significant property to media that Kracauer had described. Rather than wrenching and jolting our attention so that life when at its mercy is never our own, media's repetitive nature might exhaust its seduction, and instead aid in emptying meaning, leaving us feeling the better for it.

Could Andy Warhol get bored at St. Pancras? That is to say, could he stare at something in such a way that the meaning disappears and the mind is emptied, leaving it completely untethered? There are no windows to stare out of on the ground level. There is one repetitive large screen that runs in a cycle: an animated advertisement for E.ON energy, an advertisement for IBM, a few seconds of Sky news, which does not change frequently and has the weather framed on the right with the printed newsfeed running along the bottom of the screen, back to animated adverts for British Gas, showing business events such as musicals and the like, to long, live action adverts for a Wilkinson Sword Shaver and Volvo, and a pitch for Turner Classic Movies. The screen, having been poorly installed for its size and distance from the spectator, is heavily pixelated, which he probably would not mind, but he could not get bored there because he would have to stand in an awkward place, and mental relaxation requires physical relaxation. The information screens would require standing, moreover, while the images change: Neuhaus Chocolates ("When Chocolates meet seduction"), security warnings about bags or smoking, and notification of free Wi-Fi, and no cycling or skateboarding. These screens do not move in themselves – they have no pensive allure. I think the most promising place I could park Andy Warhol at St. Pancras, if he was in the mood to be bored, would be sitting askew to watch the small demonstration screens at the security gate for the Eurostar, which show how to get through the security check in dull monochrome rigid live action. There are eight of them and they are all "exactly the same," but they are not working (ibid., p. 50). This ground floor is largely marginal to the actual business of train travel (with the exception of the diesel odor that permeates the arcade), as the trains themselves depart from above and below ground level. Here the energy level is low, allowing the laborer who never starts or stops working to lull about, neither captivated nor bored, left to wander in the in-between that also defines their labor situation.

The mood intensifies as you take the escalator to the upper level, where the station is pared down to the bare essentials. Trains, platforms, a large departure screen, fast-food shops off to the side without display windows and a row of waiting seats constitute the waiting area for the East Midland Trains, in the southwest section. The researcher who stayed there reported a feeling of "killing time," "boredom" and an environment hostile to sociability. Up here the tedium and anxiety associated with the business of catching a train are fully visible. Here people wait. They wait and they look at the departure screen continually to monitor the gate. I have watched people stand and wait for a half an hour, paralyzed. Giorgio Agamben had something to say about boredom, and for him (or, I should say, for Agamben channelling Heidegger) it goes through stages, much in the way that is implied by Warhol, for this emptying to occur.

For Heidegger, there are three stages before you can reach "profound boredom," which are condensed into two structural moments. The first is a when a person is left empty, abandoned by their environment. Heidegger's description of this state is the classic emptiness we know in different formulations, looking down the dark Tube tunnel for the train, so fixated on its absence that you cannot think, you cannot do anything but wait. His version:

> We are sitting, for example, at the tasteless station of some lonely minor railway. It is four hours until the next train arrives. The district is unattractive. We do have a book in our rucksack, though – shall we read? No. Or think through a problem, some question? We are unable to. We read the timetables or study the table giving the various distances from this station to other places we are not otherwise acquainted with at all. We look at the clock – only a quarter of an hour has gone by. Then we go out onto the main road. We walk up and down, just to have something to do. But it is no use. Then we count the trees along the main road, look at our watch again – exactly five minutes since we last looked at it. Fed up with walking back and forth, we sit down on a stone, draw all kinds of figures in the sand, and in doing so catch ourselves looking at our watch again – half an hour – and so on.
>
> (Heidegger, 1995, p. 93)

One's own version of this may vary, but the essential mood is that we try to divert ourselves from the fact that we feel empty to no avail. Things are still there, but they do not offer any real interest, yet we cannot get free of them. You look at the posters for all of the movies as you wait for the Tube, but you do not get anything to think about from them, you look at the Tube map, you read the adverts across the tracks, or watch the video, but you return your gaze to the black tunnel, you look up at the screen for the minutes yet to wait. Insofar as the nothing of the black tunnel displaces interiority, you abandon yourself. You are entirely bound over to what is external to you, but bound to nothing. As Agamben puts it, "in boredom we suddenly find ourselves abandoned in emptiness" (Agamben, 2004, p. 64). But in this emptiness, things are not simply "carried away from us or annihilated"; they are there, but, "they have nothing to offer us"; they leave us completely indifferent yet in such a way that we cannot free ourselves from them, because we are riveted and delivered over to what bores us: "In becoming bored by something we are precisely still held fast by that which is boring, we do not yet let it go, or we are compelled by it, bound to it for whatever reason" (Heidegger, 1995, p. 92).

Arriving at Charing Cross or Victoria Station at rush hour, who has not been shocked by the mass of people staring up in the air, not even glancing at those of us leaving the turnstiles, not moving an inch to make way for us? They have a concrete emptiness upon which to fixate, which might offer up the platform number at any moment. What goes through your mind then? For we have done it as well. Our minds are completely blank in the face of something that is not there, or, as Heidegger puts it, "open to a closedness" and we are exposed. In this forced exposure to that which is in a sense alien to us, says Agamben, we are like a feral animal in captivity (Agamben, 2004, p. 65). Forced or compelled by such circumstance, there is nonetheless a Warhol-like freedom in this pure emptiness, the black hole of the Tube line where you look, the space where the platform number will drop at some point, where you are bound to nothing. At St. Pancras Station, it is in these most quotidian of screens that the laborer finds his or her free time.

Notes

1. The entire project, "Tracking the Moving Image, Mapping the Screen," funded by the Leverhulme Trust, studied a host of environments in Cairo, London and Shanghai, with four principle researchers: Chris Berry, Janet Harbord, Amal Khlalaf and me.
2. Under the scheme's accreditation criteria, railway stations must get crime down to just one incident per 20,000 people using the station. St. Pancras not only achieved this minimum target but bettered it four times over with just one incident for every 80,000 people using the station. The design of the refurbished station was singled out in the police assessment as contributing significantly to the prevention of crime and anti-social behavior in the station (High Speed 1, 2012).
3. 1. Coffee; 5. Farmer's Markets; 6. Organic Food; 34. Architecture. As the site itself indicates, the association of a kind of taste with race is shorthand substitution for the young and well to do with time and money to spare/waste (Lander, 2008).

Bibliography

Agamben, Giorgio (2004) *The Open* (Stanford: Stanford University Press).

Augé, Marc (1995) *Non-Places: An Introduction to Supermodernity*, John Howe (trans.) (London and New York: Verso).

Benjamin, Walter (1969) *Illuminations* (New York: Schocken).

Benjamin, Walter (2002) *Walter Benjamin: Selected Writings*, Volume 3: 1935–1938, Eiland, Howard and Jennings, Michael W. (eds.), Edmund Jephcott (trans.) (Cambridge: Belknap Press).

Canetti, Elias (1984) *Crowds and Power*, Carol Stewart (trans.) (New York: Farrar, Straus and Giroux).

Epstein, Jean (1977) "Magnification and Other Writings", Stuart Liebman (trans.), October, 3, Spring, 9–25.
Hammond, Michael (2006) *Performing Architecture: Opera Houses, Theatres and Concert Halls for the Twenty First Century* (London and New York: Merrell Publishers).
Harney, Stefano (2010) "Talk at the James Taylor Gallery", London, 17 October. http://london.indymedia.org/system/file_upload/2010/10/20/292/stefano.mp3, date accessed 26 May 2012.
Heidegger, Martin (1995) *The Fundamental Concepts of Metaphysics* (Bloomington and Indianapolis: Indiana University Press).
High Speed 1 (2011) www.highspeed1.com/news/?page=1&id=241, date accessed 2 November 2011.
Kracauer, Siegfried (1995) *The Mass Ornament*, Thomas Levin (trans.) (Cambridge and London: Harvard University Press).
Lander, Christian (2008) "Stuff White People Like", http://stuffwhitepeoplelike.com/full-list-of-stuff-white-people-like/, date accessed 26 May 2012.
Lazzarato, Maurizio (1996) "Immaterial Labour", Paul Colilli and Ed Emory (trans.) in Virno, Paolo and Hardt, Michael (eds.) *Radical Thought in Italy* (Minneapolis: University of Minnesota Press).
Lukács, Georg (1971) *History and Class Consciousness: Studies in Marxist Dialectics* (Cambridge: MIT Press).
Moore, Rachel (2000) *Savage Theory, Cinema as Modern Magic* (Durham: Duke University Press).
Passenger Focus (2010) "Press Releases – Rail, Bus, Coach and Tram: More of Britain's Rail Passengers are Satisfied to New Year Fare Freeze and More On-time Trains", www.passengerfocus.org.uk/news-and-publications/press-release.asp?dsid=4095, date accessed 26 May 2012.
Sleep (1963) Directed by Andy Warhol.
Smith, Hubert Llewellyn (ed.) (1935) *The New Survey of London Life and Leisure*, vol. 9 (London: P.S. King and Son).
Warhol, Andy and Hackett, Pat (1980) *POPism: The Warhol '60s* (New York: Harper & Row).
Zaera Polo, Alejandro (2008) "The Politics of the Envelope: A Political Critique of Materialism", Volume, 17, http://c-lab.columbia.edu/images/0128.pdf, date accessed 26 May 2012.

8
Encountering Screen Art on the London Underground

Janet Harbord and Tamsin Dillon

For the past 40 years, the material form of public art works has included media of various kinds. The use of film and video in public art practice breaks with a tradition of fixed, monumental public art, the memorial culture that writer W. G. Sebald describes as the official sanctioning of forgetting (Sebald, 2005). In a culture of moving image public installations, by contrast, the architectural fabric of the city becomes dynamic, uncertain and a fluid surface suggestive of the contingency of urban life. Each time we encounter a video screen the images may vary, depending, for example, on the particular intersection of a looped program and a finely timed daily commute. As time-based media, the presence of moving image screens in the city mixes with the various temporal flows of urban space. Each artwork is, of course, functioning in relation to a given environment, drawing on a tradition of site-specific art practice that became prominent in the 1970s (Kwon, 2003). The majority of what might be called intermedial public artworks has been commissioned for a particular location, negotiating with factors of history and neighborhood, material properties and environmental atmosphere, and the habitual and exceptional uses of a space by various communities, commuters, tourists and individuals. Site-specific art as it was conceived over 40 years ago challenges a heritage of timeless and universal public art, inserting into urban contexts artworks that surprise and engage; perhaps most significantly, many of these artworks can only be understood within the dynamic situation of their context (Finkelman, 2000).

The spectacle of moving images on the surface of walls at a public site remains an urban curiosity. As Alan Kaprow has argued of video more generally, it retains a novelty in the shift of a domestic medium into a public space (Kaprow, 2008, p. 118). Public screen works potentially create a slippage in our sense of private and public technologies and worlds. In addition to this schism, these moving images "dislocate" in another way.[1] In public space they move alongside us as our uncanny doubles; images (and words) travel with the rhythmic movement of bodies, cars, trains and goods circulating through the vectors of a city. Such artworks may or may not, of course, impinge on our consciousness, and if they should do so, they may or may not register as art. In *Pixels and Places: Video Art in Public Space,* Catrien Schreuder argues that it is possible to distinguish two types of practice defining screen art in urban space, one concerned with the work and its street location, and the other, a modern form of *Gesamtkunstwerk,* a work of overlapping interests of artists, architects and urban planners (Schreuder, 2009). This latter form of public art is found on the London Underground, where artworks are conceived at the intersection between the values and public commitments of a transport system, and the reflexive practice of artists from an international context. Screen art on the Underground exists within a culture of eclectic display, alongside information screens, ambient time-filler loops and advertising, sometimes discreetly, at other times prominently and spectacularly. Here, Tamsin Dillon, Head of Art on the Underground, talks about the program.

JH: Why is art commissioned for the Underground system? What's the broadest remit for what art might be doing in these spaces of transport and transition?

TD: Art on the Underground commissions art to enhance the Tube's customer journey experience. The program is funded by London Underground as part of its customer service program. On that level it's a very small budget. With that as a starting point and within those limitations, I think it's important to say that we create a credible world-class art program. Over the years we've established a set of criteria, aims and objectives around which the program is based. So it's about enhancing journey experience in the first instance, but presenting art to a very diverse audience, most of whom are not necessarily familiar with visiting art galleries or encountering art in their everyday lives. Presenting the most stimulating art that we can in that context reflects London as a cultural city. We produce and present work by artists whose work you might easily encounter in galleries in the city as well.

JH: When you're talking about enhancing the journey experience by exposing people to art, particularly people who may not necessarily go to galleries, does the principle of presenting art on the

Underground belong to some kind of socialist tradition, or is that too big a claim?

TD: I don't think it's been explicitly a socialist tradition but it builds on the London Underground's legacy of commissioning art and design of the highest quality as part of its brand. That was developed in the early part of the twentieth century. A man called Frank Pick, famous for being one of its pioneering managing directors, commissioned people like Charles Holden to design modern new stations for the Piccadilly line. He commissioned Harry Beck to design the Tube map. He also commissioned artists like Man Ray, Edward McKnight Kauffer, László Moholy-Nagy, some of the best artists in the world, to design posters that went into the Underground to promote the journey itself. He's also responsible for some of the technical innovations that were happening, like the new pneumatic doors or escalators. His vision was embedded in the unifying principle of "total design", bringing together all these different elements.

JH: When does that date from?

TD: Arguably it dates from right at the beginning of the twentieth century, but Frank Pick was bringing that work together in the 1920s and 1930s. It's a very long and rich heritage that we're building on.

JH: It's interesting to think about the modernist dimension of this legacy, of architecture and transport, and art and design, being part of a shared concept of how people should live in urban contexts. Were there models for art on the Underground in other countries that may have influenced the UK, or was the UK an influential force in this respect?

TD: That's an interesting question. The combination of art and Underground travel is certainly something that you will find in other metro systems globally. London Underground is the first underground railway system in the world, in fact it's about to celebrate its 150th anniversary in 2013, so its obviously a pioneer and innovator in all sorts of ways of how an underground railway system could work. So bringing art and good design into that environment was part of its ambition, and art is a connecting factor between national and international colleagues. I think London Underground has prided itself on being pioneering and influential rather than imitating other models.

However, you've talked about how it comes out of a modernist tradition bringing together all sorts of disciplines, and certainly the way London Underground developed in the mid twentieth century was very influenced by European modernism. Frank Pick and Charles Holden in particular were influenced by journeys that they took together in Europe, and they came back thinking about how to bring a modern European design ethic into the way that they designed buildings and systems for London Underground.

Now it seems to be an activity in many global contexts to place art within travel systems. It's something that many travel authorities think about, the question of how to incorporate good design and art into their systems. It depends on the funding model, I suppose. Most travel authorities commission permanent works as part of capital projects because that's the most cost efficient way to do it. Art on the Underground is delivering some projects as part of certain capital projects that are happening on the Underground, and they're funded by part of the budget for those capital projects. A program that presents largely temporary projects in such an environment is relatively rare; I think one reason for that is that it's more of a challenge to defend funding for temporary projects, particularly in the current economic climate.

JH: Are you saying that funding for permanent artworks is seen to be a better investment than temporary exhibits that form part of an experience but one that's only offered for a limited amount of time?

TD: I suppose it could be seen like that. Having something more permanent, that seems to be a longer-term investment, is perhaps always going to be looked upon as a safer bet, as long as it's maintenance-free, of course.

JH: Does that frustrate you: that funders (internally or externally) are happier to support something that is permanent, a monument if you like to art, rather than something that is less enduring but more experimental?

TD: Yes, the cost benefit scenario tends to have greater resonance when projected over the long term. I've spent a lot of time making the benefits clear for a program of temporary projects. It helps that London Underground has a robust customer service strategy, which the objectives for the Art on the Underground program can link to.

JH: Because the customer service strategy is about addressing people's experience, the more human aspects of travel, rather than the pragmatic ones?

TD: Exactly, but that has to be carefully realized in terms of cost benefits as well. At London Underground, this is done by measuring customer experience, how people felt about their last journey, and how they feel about London Underground in general. These measures are taken through surveys to give an annual score for London Underground's reputation. Art on the Underground can contribute to that scoring process.

JH: Listening to you talk about it in those terms it seems really quite endearing, a part of a public service culture that's disappearing, "taking care" of people as they go to work. The Underground system moves people round the city fairly efficiently, but often in very crowded, oppressive situations, so the project of art in this context might be thought of as taking care of people's psyches. I wonder if this is also a legacy of modernism, the sense that urban life brought anxiety and neurosis, and to which Anthony Vidler (2001) has more recently added agoraphobia and claustrophobia as psychopathologies of urban space? (Vidler, 2001)

TD: Yes definitely, and it's seen as compatible with good business because London Underground wants to improve its reputation, or be seen to have a good reputation for that.

JH: Thinking comparatively, can you name a few cities that have renowned art on the Underground programs and the sorts of work that they commission?

TD: There's quite a strong program in New York, the Arts for Transit, and they certainly focus on permanent artworks as part of their capital projects, although they also have a small temporary program, which goes on some of their trains as well. Then there's Stockholm, Munich, Lisbon and further afield, Taipei, where I visited quite recently. I'd say most metro systems globally have in some way considered how to bring an art aspect into the way that they work. Art on the Underground differs mainly in its focus on bringing a contemporary art program – something that you might encounter in a gallery or in another cultural organization – into a transport environment. In terms of the artists and the artworks we produce, the standard and quality [are] the same as galleries.

JH: So it's an ambitious experiment with contemporary artworks and their relationship to environments, rather than reinforcing conventional ideas about art?

TD: Yes, rather than presenting something decorative, we offer artists an opportunity to make a new work and customers an opportunity for a new encounter with art. This has been acknowledged as a challenging approach but I think it's important not to compromise on what we can deliver. The starting point is the artists that we invite and what they want to present.

JH: Can we bring screens into the discussion here in two respects? One is that earlier on when you were talking about maintenance costs, I'm interested in the pragmatics of getting screens into these places and types of regulations and obstacles that have to be observed or overcome. Second, related to what you were saying about challenging people's ideas about art in public space, I imagine that screen art is something of a surprise for a lot of your customers in various ways, either because they anticipate that screens will be advertising something, or because we still expect framed images in public spaces to be still images. Were you the first person to commission screen art on the Underground or does it pre-date your time?

TD: I've been developing Art on the Underground for about eight years or so and the program existed for a couple of years before that. There hadn't been any work on film or screens with the exception of some small projects on the website, which is perhaps the easiest presentation mode without a dedicated physical space for viewing moving image works. Many contemporary artists work with moving images in many different ways, so we had to consider how to incorporate that area into the program. At the same time as we began to think about it, CBSO, the company responsible for selling the advertising space, started to bring moving image screens into the Tube. However, those screens weren't the first opportunities for Art on the Underground to present film through the network; instead we built bespoke screen-based spaces, working opportunistically in the way that we've worked with many of our projects.

For example, at Gloucester Road Station, we have commissioned many large-scale artworks on the redundant platform simply because it is available and no advertising, information or signage is in the way. We took a similar approach when we started presenting moving image works as part of the program. One of the first artists we worked with to present moving images was Stephen Willats, for a commission as part of a series for the Piccadilly line. The film was made between and presented at two stations at one end of the line. The film reflects on the different ways that people communicate with each other. We found sites within the two stations to situate the three-screen works that Willats produced. One was installed in an old shop unit with the screens facing out onto the ticket hall (Figure 8.1), and the other was installed in an old information unit within the station itself.

Figure 8.1 Assumptions and presumptions by Stephen Willats (2007)
Source: Image courtesy of Art on the Underground. Photograph by Andy Keate.

JH: These were situated at Rayners Lane and Sudbury Town stations?

TD: Yes, where we commissioned the works especially.

JH: And what was your sense of what the public thought of the screens, and how do you solicit feedback?

TD: Getting feedback to know how people are responding is one of our biggest challenges. We use various methods; the simplest one is to invite people to leave comments on our website. We have a line on all our promotional materials asking for feedback via our website. Spending a day on the network interviewing customers to get feedback sounds simple and straightforward but it requires further resources, so we only do it infrequently.

In terms of the Willats commission in particular, Tube users would have seen something unusual, not what they might expect to see in a ticket hall. They would either have engaged with it and looked a bit closer, or not. There would have been information near the work, leaflets and a notice suggesting more information can be found on our website. We need to make it easy for people to get more information if they want it. I assume the audience would either watch the film, understand it, enjoy it and move on, or possibly look for more information and engage with it further. The opportunity to see the work is there, the presentation is very high quality, and it looks like something unusual, out of place even, so attracts attention that way. I think the people that use the Tube are frequently underestimated. They're constantly interpreting complex messages through advertising and signage, and they're negotiating their way through a quite complicated environment all the time. So, even if we present a work that's quite subtle or conceptual, we always get some kind of feedback. People either understand it and respond to it very positively or we get less positive feedback but any response is important – it shows that the work has engaged people.

JH: Is there anything that particularly characterizes the feedback you get from screen artworks?

TD: I have learnt that, particularly in the Tube environment, people really respond if they see something more than once and more than one place. Certainly companies that advertise on the Tube have understood that. What they'll do is place an advert for something on an escalator, say a film or some new technological device, then another advert for the same thing with the same message in a different place in the station. So people follow a trail of adverts that reinforce the message. I think if you don't do that, people are less likely to pick up on what you're trying to do. We use that opportunity through by promoting our projects with posters across the Tube network, and using the idea of the network as routes. We can do this in two ways, by using one poster in each station, and also by using unsold advertising space. The feedback that we get is always more dense, there's more of it and its more engaged, when we've had an opportunity to put more information out there. It's as simple as that.

JH: So you might have one work in one location but you have lots of trailers for it in other sites?

TD: Yes, in terms of a screen work the one that we did that may have had more feedback than anything else was by Dryden Goodwin. It was a piece that we did as part of the Jubilee line series where he drew over 60 members of staff from across the Jubilee line. He represented every single station and every single level of staff by drawing portraits, and he filmed the drawing being created and he recorded the conversation with the sitter. Each drawing took between half an hour to an hour. Dryden edited all of the films down to two or three minutes each including the conversations. You can see these on our website and the conversations are *really* engaging because they're so revealing. We also had the opportunity to use unsold advertising space on the digital screens, particularly on the escalator panels.

Dryden edited the films down to five seconds or so, so that you see the drawings appear extremely quickly. That had a really powerful impact on promoting the work and encouraging people to visit our website, which is another way that we monitor impact and engagement (the hits to our website always go up when we first launch a project or campaign). Using advertising screens in a creative and meaningful way, is something that we would always want to try to do. But for many reasons we don't get the opportunity on a regular basis – the spaces are sold for advertising and otherwise many other messages have to take priority (Figure 8.2).

JH: With Dryden Goodwin's project, a screen on the Underground would lead you to another screen after your journey, extending the narrative of your travel?

TD: Yes, we've learnt that it works well if we can use the network in this way. By "network" I mean the literal Tube network and also the accompanying information network. We create layers of programming, involving different ways that people can encounter art works. They can see them as site-specific works in a particular station, and also in the system of posters they encounter. There are also interventions via other information. For example, our Tube map cover series, which inserts an artwork on to the front cover of a piece of travel

Figure 8.2 Linear by Dryden Goodwin (2010)
Source: Image courtesy of Art on the Underground. Photograph by Daisy Hutchison.

information is another way we've engineered an encounter with art. The artists we work with are also keen to exploit these different ways of working. In 2008 we commissioned 100 artists to make a new artwork using the London Underground logo. With those images we could make 100 new posters that we could use all over the network. We also presented the original images in an exhibition off-site, which allowed us to connect with people in another way. We also had an auction of the first prints of the artworks. I think that, like a lot of organizations with different methods of working, we've recognized that the way that you can communicate with a huge diversity of people is to operate in lots of different spaces.

JH: Do you think people might ever mistake artworks for adverts? I'm thinking about those screens on the escalators where my expectation is that they will be carrying adverts and I may only glance at them. Do you think that there's a blurring of genre because the device of screens could be for either?

TD: I think that undoubtedly happens. It is another thing that the artists we work with are interested in exploiting. They're highly aware of the context and that it's a space that is conventionally used for advertising, for getting some kind of message out to encourage people to spend money, to buy something. I think what artists like about that is that they can play with that space and that it's a way of punctuating, or literally puncturing, that space with something unexpected, a different kind of encounter. I think that's why we get a lot of positive feedback; because it gives people something else to see. So I think that the blurring that you mention happens but that people do see that there's something different there. The punch line isn't "and this is where you can buy these things," it's offering a different kind of engagement.

JH: I can see how both advertising and conceptual artwork are operating with the idea of enigma to a certain extent. But with those particular screens where you're moving on the escalator and the screens are moving too, is there anything about the dynamism of the situation that has appealed to artists? I'm thinking of the doubling of mobility.

TD: I'd certainly think that it gets used that way all the time by the advertisers. The problem for Art on the Underground is the cost of commissioning work that could use that space in that way. I think it would be a fantastic thing to do. I suppose, going back to Dryden's work and the way his five second drawings films were presented; they were set up so that as you moved up the escalator you were seeing a different portrait as you went past each screen. So there's definitely a way of playing with that and I do think that multiple screens offer endless possibilities. It's time and money that's required to exploit this of course.

JH: Thinking about the way that transport systems are about the efficiency of movement, what does it mean to have moving images within that environment? When you stand on the Tube platform or you're walking along and you catch sight of something moving on the wall opposite, and a train comes in that is moving as well, the screens seem to be mimicking the process that you're involved with. With travel you're rarely static unless something has gone wrong. It seems to me that part of the appeal of having screens in that context is that they're reproducing the dynamism of flow.

TD: We seem to be heading for a world like *Blade Runner* where you can't escape the moving image. Perhaps that sounds a bit pessimistic or Luddite of me but more often than not, I'm disappointed by the quality of the advertising that I see, that the space has not been understood very well. I think the site where a moving image is projected across the track is a place that calls for a very site-specific intervention and that artists are very well placed to be able to engage with that. There's an organization that has been bringing together existing artworks to present on these cross-track projectors, but its been done in a rather unsophisticated fashion. They've brought together a random range of cultural work representing myriad cultural organizations but I'm not sure it worked together so well in that context.

JH: Do you think that this organization is using very conventional forms in this very dynamic situation?

TD: Yes, the opportunity to reflect that dynamism has been missed. I think the situation demands something quite specific to work in that space.

JH: I want to talk about a work that you commissioned, the piece *Oil Stick Work* installed at Canary Wharf (May 2010–2011), which operates in different ways to what we've just been describing. It's much more about spectacle, with a huge screen – quite cinematic in scale – being given prominence within the station. Can you talk about how you came to exhibit this work, and whether you chose the work for that site, or whether the idea of the site inspired a work of this scale? (Figure 8.3)

TD: We're talking about a work by John Gerrard. It wasn't commissioned specifically for that particular site, John was invited to

Figure 8.3 *Oil Stick Work* by John Gerrard (2008)
Source: Image courtesy of Art on the Underground. Photograph by Andy Keate.

present it there as part of the Jubilee line series. The theme for that series was the value of time, so many of the works we presented were time-based works. *Oil Stick Work* is a digital piece that unfolds over a period of 30 years. It's a very slow piece of work featuring a grain silo on a Midwest prairie and a man who comes to work and, each day, paints a 1 m black square on the silo with an oil stick crayon.

JH: And this character is going to do this for 30 years, until 2038, is that correct?

TD: Yes, it operates in real time so what you see is a virtual world that's moving along at the same speed as our world. As it's set in America, when you see the work at nine in the morning London time, it's still dark. When the character, Angelo, arrives at work in the morning, it's round about 1.00 pm in London. He literally paints a square meter of the building in a black oil stick and the point is that it's going to take him 30 years to paint the entire building, which is estimated as the time when the oil supplies in the country are predicted to run out.

JH: Can I just ask, is there really a building in Kansas that this is modeled on or is this a creation?

TD: I think so, yes! John Gerrard makes these works using gaming technology. As I understand it he's been to this place and taken thousands of photographs, which are used to model the artwork; this includes photographs of a person. In this way it's possible to put together a whole menu of different actions that this person can take, thousands of them. The artwork is set up to make him randomly do a range of things, such as stopping to look at his work, over a day.

JH: Is there a connection between the work and Canary Wharf Station?

TD: The work was presented at the Venice Biennale 2009 and we thought that it would be interesting to present it at Canary Wharf Station because of its political references; its reference to time, to the huge financial sector and that connection to oil reserves and Canary Wharf being at the center, or one of the centers, of that in London. So that's the conceptual connection. But on a physical level, we had to think about how people would encounter the work. The space at Canary Wharf Station in the ticket hall seemed ideal. It's a huge building in scale and size not unlike the Turbine Hall at Tate Modern. At one end there's an entirely redundant space, planned as an exit from the building but now just a dead end. The space is a great opportunity to present work but it requires the audience to go and look rather than walk past. People come and go from quite far away so the setup needs to allow them a glimpse from a distance that might encourage them to take a closer look. This is why we installed such a large screen. We worked with John on the scale and dimensions of the screen. It's built with very robust walls in order to be compliant with a working train station. We planned to present the work for one year out of its 30-year life span – so we couldn't use a temporary screen – we had to build something almost permanent.

JH: So the artwork took on something of the physicality of the station as a robust installation. What other considerations were there?

TD: If we had presented something as a temporary event we probably could have just erected a temporary screen. But because this was going to be a 24/7 projection event we had to produce something very solid, and something that couldn't be easily vandalized or tampered with. Other considerations in developing the project included the projection tower and the projectors, which needed to be powerful enough to deal with the light levels in the space. It was a significant challenge to maintain the work in those conditions but we've had some fantastic feedback and it did look stunning.

A particular challenge was how to maintain the interest of people who regularly use the station. We wondered if the work unravels too slowly for those people. How to engage people with a work over time is something we will keep exploring.

JH: Otherwise people walk past in a habitual dreamworld, ignoring the artwork much as we ignore monuments. Is narrative an important element for keeping the attention of daily commuters?

TD: Possibly, I'd always want to invite an artist to consider that rather than come up with the answer myself. The presentation of *Oil Stick Work* has come to an end now. The next phase for that area will be a new screen program in that site. We're collaborating with a whole range of arts organizations to think about and provide the content for that site, so each organization will get a season each.

JH: What kind of organizations?

TD: We're tending to work at first with organizations that are specialists with moving image work, such as London Film and Video Umbrella (FVU) and LUX. We're also talking to Animate And the BFI (British Film Institute), and so on. Each organization will get a three-month period to program for this very specific site. It's complicated because they need to think about how to maintain interest over a period of time.

JH: Given the repetition of journeys undertaken daily. Does this mean that works for this screen will be selected from archives rather than commissioned?

TD: Yes, very few of these works are going to be commissioned specifically.

JH: So there will be a mix of experimental film and film traditionally seen in cinemas, making the identity of this screen explicitly cinematic. That seems quite different from the real-time virtual artwork of Gerrard.

TD: Yes, the idea is to create a new venue to see artists' film, offering a different kind of encounter between artists' film and audiences and a new opportunity for artists to think about how their work might be seen. We're launching in 2012, and I think we'll probably have quite a lot to learn about how this engagement might work. We'll think about special screenings – special events – as well as having films on a looped program running for people to go and see as they go on their journeys.

JH: So you're anticipating that people will actually go to Canary Wharf to be an audience in that space?

TD: From time to time yes.

JH: And in those moments to transform that part of Canary Wharf Station into a cinema?

TD: Yes, in a way. One challenge is how we're going to deal with sound, particularly when you're constantly buffeted by messages from the station speakers about the Tube service for example! It's imperative that people can hear those announcements in case of any kind of emergency situation, but we are putting in a sound system. So we'll see how well that works. There will be plenty of material that we would be able to present without sound, but we're very keen to experiment with that.

JH: Cinema used to automatically assume, and produce, a collective audience or a crowd. By putting film into a transport space where there are crowds, whether people like to be in a crowd or not, it's quite an interesting inversion of what cinema used to be. I imagine that the majority of people won't be viewing films curated by the LUX or the FVU accidentally, but will be there specifically because they know that this is happening in the station.

TD: What I'm hoping is that it will build up both of those audiences, the planned and the accidental. I think the program in general will always draw a knowing audience and that's quite deliberate, but if it doesn't have an impact on the unknowing audience as well then I'm not doing my job properly as far as London Underground are concerned. That's always been a key part of this job for me – that people will encounter something new and interesting in an unexpected context.

JH: In an interview with the artist John Gerrard, he talks about the audience on the Underground not being receptive. Audiences are crowds hurrying and blind, which reminds me of Walter Benjamin's celebrated remarks about a work of art being "consummated by a collectivity in a state of distraction" (Benjamin, 1969). Is that the way that you think about a lot of the audiences for your works in different sites (in a state of distraction), or do you have more of a diverse sense of how people might come across screen works?

TD: I think there are different speeds or paces at which people are going to encounter what we put in front of them. When they are standing waiting for a train, that is the place to put something that demands a bit more contemplation and I think that a lot of artists are very keen to have that opportunity. But when people are hurrying through the stations, hurrying to get from one end of their journey to the other, that's where I think the idea of the repeated message that we talked about before is important. Anna Barriball did a great series of works based on that concept. She produced a series of texts for posters using the New Johnson font, the font that you would expect to see on the Tube. They looked like traditional London Underground posters, but they featured little phrases that Anna had discovered on the back of a set of photographs that she found in a junk shop. The phrases referred maybe to someone's portrait: "wearing a nurse's uniform," or to a holiday snap or a landscape: "looking back the way we had come." The poster featured only the phrases – the images were absent. We produced six or seven different posters, carrying these tiny little snippets of phrases, that you might have seen on different parts of your journey. It worked as a way of getting into people's heads from a range of places.

JH: I'm going to ask you a little bit about the dream project, but could you tell me first about the Stratford Gaff?

TD: Yes that's another way that we presented a film work by developing a bespoke screen set-up. The Stratford Gaff is a project by Matt Stokes for Stratford Station. It's a big and airy station that lends itself well to the presentation of screen-based art works. We've been commissioning a series of works there to reflect the way Stratford has been going through a massive transformation, particularly since the Olympic bid was won. We've invited artists to come in and produce projects that start with an engagement with the people who use the station and who live and work in the area. Matt Stokes predominantly works with film and video; he was invited to consider the history of the area, which is famous for its music hall history and the fact that it's the home of "cheap entertainment." Matt discovered a key form of entertainment that development there in the Victorian era was the "Penny Gaff," where people paid a penny to be entertained by magicians, escapologists, singers and so on. He then found people in Stratford who are entertaining their audiences in similar but contemporary ways. He decided to make a film that presented the work of all these entertainers in a modern take on the Penny Gaff. So what you encounter at Stratford Station is a three-screen film showing a range of set pieces by the entertainers, one by one going through their acts. There's an opera singer, an escapologist, a magician, dancers, a rap artist and so on. People using the station regularly will hopefully see a different entertainer each time they pass through.

JH: Is that a permanent work?

TD: No it's a temporary work, there for one year as part of the Jubilee line series.

JH: And could you say something about the Dream...

TD: Daria Martin's project?

JH: I'm thinking about the way in which we've been talking about the different experiences that people have as they're traveling on the Underground and the way in which artists are trying to engage with multiple psychic states. Daria Martin's project is a direct attempt by an artist to find out what people are thinking, not just to engage but to get inside the heads of travelers. Could you describe the contours of that project?

TD: It was also one of the Jubilee line series commissions and therefore based on the concept of time. Daria's aim was to discover what people do when they are spending time on the Underground, what's going through their heads. She started thinking about this because at one end of the Jubilee Line is the Freud Museum, which made her think about the psychology of people as they are traveling underground. The project explores what it's like to be in a dark gloomy place, not a natural situation, and what daydreams people might have to take themselves out of that situation. We worked with the Freud Museum and took photographs from inside it. Using these images, the project began with a series of posters inviting people to log on to our website and let us know what their daydreams were about. We were quite astonished by the range of response we got. We also interviewed people in stations to ask them about their daydreams. Something like 600 face-to-face interviews took place. Some were undertaken by the artist, some by the Art on the Underground team, and some by a consultancy. We got an unusually high response rate; perhaps when people are not being sold something, they are more willing to be interviewed. I think what Daria, and what many of the artists we work with, are interested in is how to set up a dialog with the people using the Tube, and then what you can do with that information in terms of feeding it out again and stimulating ideas about travel.

JH: From reading through a selection of the responses on the website, people are far more positive in their thoughts than I might imagine they would be. I'm thinking about the conditions of underground travel as being quite frustrating, and crowded and marked by unwanted intimacy, and yet people are quite often dreaming utopian thoughts. I also noticed that there are a number of comments that are about using a number of media to create the experience of travel. For example, one says: "I often daydream about the trailers or adverts for films according to what music I'm listening to and I put myself in them." And there's another one: "listening to the words of the song on the iPod, sometimes I'm in the song which is enveloping everyone." So there seems to be a way in which we're using personal devices to create our own experience combined with other cues from the environment, the adverts and maybe the screen works, to make something more fictional.

TD: That seems symptomatic of the fact that this is around us all the time, it doesn't surprise me at all.

JH: I'm thinking of the ways that screen contents play into, or encourage, a sense of a fictional world. Most screens, be it advertising or artworks, don't have sound in these spaces, so whatever kind of dialog you're having in your head with someone else or listening to a song could be fitted to those images. I wonder if that is part of how screens operate on the Underground, that they are facilitators enabling these sorts of daydreams to connect the personal with the public.

TD: Yes, it must work somehow like that. I think the artists we work with are very much aware of that. They are not offering an opportunity to visit an art gallery and have an exclusive one-to-one experience with a painting or a sculpture, but they are aware that whoever is going to encounter the work that they are presenting is also in the middle of quite a complex situation; they're traveling, they're having to think about all sorts of other things. So whatever artists are presenting is going to be something that has to address that as well as helping travelers to escape from that situation or take their minds in a different direction.

JH: It would seem that the televisual, that kind of domestic, bounded way of experiencing screen media often used to relay live events, isn't represented on the Underground. Your commissions are much more cinematic, which audiences might then match with personal devices. Would it be fair to say that the screens on the Underground are more cinematic than they are televisual? The question that I have here on my sheet is whether screens on the Underground attempt to make the city cinematic, by which I mean larger than life, romantic, spectacular. Reading through some of the comments from Daria Martin's project, there seems to be a way in which screens invite people to inscribe themselves into some kind of romantic story that includes image, and sometimes image and music combinations.

TD: I just think it's symptomatic, that that's the way we think or the mindset that people are in when they are moving through London.

JH: Is that romanticisation of the self in the world a feature of the encounter of screen works on the Underground, do you think, or more generally the way that people move through transport systems?

TD: Possibly transport generally, but I like to think it's a feature of the Underground.

Note

1. On the value of dislocation in urban space see Tschumi, (1996).

Bibliography

Benjamin, Walter (1969) "The Work of Art in the Age of Mechanical Reproduction", in Arendt, Hannah (ed.) *Illuminations*, Harry Zorn (trans.) (New York: Schocken Books).

Blade Runner (1982) Directed by Ridley Scott. Produced by Michael Deeley.

Finkelman, Tom (ed.) (2000) *Dialogues in Public Art* (Cambridge and London: MIT Press).

Kaprow, Alan (2008) "Video Art: Old Wine, New Bottle", in Phillips, Glenn (ed.) *California Video: Artists and Histories* (Los Angeles: Paul J. Getty Museum).

Kwon, Miwon (2003) *One Place After Another* (Cambridge: MIT Press).

Schreuder, Catrien (2009) *Pixels and Places: Video Art in Public Space* (Rotterdam: Nai Publishers).

Sebald, Winfried G. (2005) *Campo Santo*, Anthea Bell (trans.) (London: Penguin).

Tschumi, Bernard (1996) *Architecture and Disjunction* (Cambridge and London: MIT Press).

Vidler, Anthony (2001) *Warped Space: Art, Architecture and Anxiety in Modern Culture* (Cambridge and London: MIT Press).

Artworks cited

Gerrard, John (2008) *Oil Stick Work.*

Goodwin, Dryden (2010) *Linear.*

Martin, Daria (2010) "Jubilee Line Customer Daydream Survey", http://art.tfl.gov.uk/file-uploads/fck-files/file/PDF%20doc%20for%20Daria%20Martin.pdf, date accessed 27 May 2012.

Stokes, Matt (2010) *The Stratford Gaff: A Serio-Comick-Bombastick-Operatick Interlude.*

Willats, Stephen (2007) *Assumptions and Presumptions.*

At this very moment a plane is touching down in Vienna. When will you start packing?
VIENNA
Vienna
from £136

9

Direct Address
A Brechtian Proposal for an Alternative Working Method

Marysia Lewandowska

The invention of the printing press and the resulting availability of printed, yet often unauthorized theatrical productions, allowed theatre companies to produce plays without having seen a performance, or having consulted the playwright. Writers included "margin notes" — didascaliae — to guide actors rehearsing from their scripts. The *Direct Address* project explores how contemporary uses of social media engage with the tradition of annotation and commentary by making them live, participatory and open to public scrutiny. How are our lives and desires represented in public space with the proliferation of media screens, the immediacy of access to products and services, linking us to an ever-expanding network of consumption while in transit? What would happen if we reclaimed and renegotiated access to some of those spaces? What if we could overwrite the corporate signature by introducing a different voice and consolidating a different civic agenda?

In the rich landscape of our urban experience, social exchanges are increasingly directed by the presence of media. Hand-held, touch-screen devices guide our moves and moods through the city as we encounter informational image displays and silent screen messages, all plucked from global news streams. The screen and the city appear as a continuous present, creating a blur between pre-recorded adverts, live broadcast and life itself. We observe how the constitution of the public cannot be separated from that of the media, as it is the media that makes the public truly public, but it also generates other effects.

By using Twitter as a contemporary means to publish, exchange and share, *Direct Address* explores the possibility of staging a play generated by live Twitter feeds from actors rehearsing in a London theatre with those of travelers passing through one of London's railway stations. As people gather in front of timetables and watch the adjacent media screens, they will be able to follow and interact with the "Twitter play" appearing on the screen, a space normally reserved for the promotion of brands and services. The opportunity to turn the screens into a live platform of embodied presence — open to all — establishes a new relationship with the public. By introducing the possibility of wide participation and the alternative use of privately owned screens, the project intervenes in a closed system while confronting the ubiquitous culture of "texting" habits, and adapting them as a tool for public attention.

The project attempts to replace conspicuous consumption with conspicuous creativity. Brechtian in its origins, it pays tribute to his Great Method by focusing on the existing uses of mobile technologies and the role they play in our understanding of active citizenship. The very nature of mobile communications foregrounds the places of transition in which media screens appear. The project also serves as a reminder of how corporate presence remains unchallenged as it spills into sites which many of us still associate with public ownership, or at the very least, sites we presume are held in common. ✕

↗

Extracts from *Brecht and Method*, Verso, 1998 by Fredric Jameson, "retweeted" by Marysia Lewandowska, 2011.

Fredric Jameson Fredric Jameson Marysia_Lewandowska
[...] as I want to retain the connection between #Brecht's 'usefulness'
for us today and a whole range of #possibleactivities into...

An interview with Glen Wilson, Posterscope UK Managing Director. London, July 18th, 2011

Marysia Lewandowska/ Antonia Blocker: Our understanding of Posterscope is that it is a media agency advising corporate clients on how to engage with Out-Of-Home (OOH) opportunities provided by the use of a variety of media, such as public digital screens and live interactions. Most of your work relies on mediating between the corporate client and the companies owning advertising sites, such as billboards, bus shelters and media screens across major world cities.

Glen Wilson: We see the Out-Of-Home space as the medium; we help advertisers communicate with their customers when they're OOH. So we deal with anything the consumer might encounter when they are OOH. Most consumers are networked and so our 21st century concern is to try and understand the dynamic between what people think, feel and do when they are OOH, and how their behavior is changing. The communication landscape has become more interconnected and convergent. We at Posterscope need to think of what might be on people's minds and what forms would best engage them. Our interest is in tracing the patterns that emerge when people interact and share via mobile devices. Since we can access anything anywhere through said devices, and as people become location neutral, we are developing ways to best help brands to connect with people when they are Out-of-Home.

Essentially people's lives have become more fluid. Companies do not own their brands, people do.

ML/AB: Where does the term "Out-Of-Home" originate?

GW: The term used to be "outdoor," and it generally referred to posters. As advertising has begun to operate in a broader space, a new term has been developed to better describe this phenomenon. The term itself has been in use for the past 10 years or so, and is most likely to be an "Americanism."

›

Fredric Jameson Fredric Jameson Marysia_Lewandowska
... expected to energize us. [...] This amounts to saying that
'the idea of #'Brecht' is as important as his individual texts;

WHSmi

›

<u>ML/AB:</u> *Can you talk about how the idea of public utility, such as bus shelters, is reinvented for commercial purposes?*

<u>GW:</u> You would have to go back to the beginning of the development of outdoor advertising. The space has grown alongside the content. Previously you could buy space in an editorial or program space, so in a newspaper or on television, but outdoor is different. The concept of using a public utility for commercial purposes was developed by the French entrepreneur Jean Claude Decaux. In the early 1960s, he approached his local authority with a proposal to use bus shelters, newsstands, toilets, etc., suggesting he would pay to build them as long as his company, JCDecaux, could in return sell space to advertisers.

The introduction of digital media has dynamically changed the content; this change combined with the availability of data has created unprecedented opportunities. All kinds of data can be pulled in from online sources such as Twitter and Facebook and remixed and then transmitted elsewhere. Tweets can be aggregated, or the density of photo uploads can be carefully monitored. Collecting and analysing this data via OOH allows for this information to be represented back to people.

<u>ML/AB:</u> *You mentioned earlier that if an artist were to engage with the advertising space on one of the JCDecaux screens, for example the newly installed screens at Euston Station, the project would have to include a "positive publicity." What does this mean?*

Fredric Jameson Fredric Jameson Marysia_Lewandowska
the multiple paralyses in which we are all now historically
seized, [...] the notion of enablement is still not a bad one
for the release...
Fredric Jameson Fredric Jameson Marysia_Lewandowska
of #newenergies we have in mind here. @fredricjameson;
#brecht and #method @Verso 1998, page10

› GW: A collaboration with an artist would potentially help them (in this case JCDecaux but it could be any media partner) to merchandize what is technically and aesthetically possible within this new space. Artists are often the first ones to adopt new technologies, before they are used for commercial purposes.

Fredric Jameson Fredric Jameson Marysia_Lewandowska
But it is also a #symbolic @re_enactment of multiple hesitations,
and #alternative possibilities within interpretation itself [...]

For example, data visualization can be understood as absolute and empirical, relating solely to the commercial, and

yet when viewed under different circumstances its appeal is much wider. When things are relatively new, it takes a while for people to develop an understanding and a desire to use them, as most people's framework is what has happened in the past, rather than what will happen in the future. Companies such as JCDecaux need help with exploring and utilizing the flexibility and potential of digital media. Commercially, it is important for JCDecaux to be engaged with the greater variety of solutions to a communication problem that digital media can provide.

Their motivation and your motivation in attracting public attention is different, but what could your contribution look like without compromising your artistic practice? Can a mutually acceptable result be reached?

ML/AB: You previously explained that a railway station is a "managed environment." What do you understand by this term?

GW: A "managed environment" is somewhere enclosed to a certain extent (although not necessarily physically) rather than being outdoors and in the open air; like a railway station or the Underground. Namely, there is another managing body that has a particular point of view on that environment, so there are additional parameters and more rules and regulations. A managed environment has a distinct audience with expected behaviors.

ML/AB: What do you think it is that Posterscope produce? What is your product?

GW: We don't make anything; we don't physically produce anything. We produce value, which could be defined in many different ways. It could be simplistic, in a monetary sense, or it could be seen as the value of insight and knowledge through proprietary research. Efficiency also has value.

The advertising industry is mindful of the broader effects of its presence in people's lives, the social effects, which can be negative. There is an awareness of this and a sense of responsibility that comes with it. We at Posterscope don't make ads, but we are part of the same industry, and it can be challenging on a personal level, sometimes a personal moral dilemma emerges. Anything in the public domain is potentially controversial, it can be hard to anticipate how the public will react to something (like the Yves Saint Laurent Opium advert) and the environment is less controlled, there is a diminished sense of context. In certain environments there is a contextual appropriateness. OOH has a capacity to be viral. You have to be extremely conscious of the potential impact of certain imagery.

Fredric Jameson Fredric Jameson Marysia_Lewandowska
...it does not spill out into the #formless; on the other hand, it incites the @spectator to form further thoughts and test them...
E RACK

ML/AB: What acts as an inspiration for this work?

GW: If you have a broad range of interests, advertising allows you to indulge those: an interest in people, for instance, and in understanding their behavior. There is a juxtaposition of magic and logic. There is a scientific aspect, through analysis, but then there is a huge magic component.

There are rules, but then it is equally important to break the rules, introducing a dynamic between the two. We don't know why we do a lot of the things we do, there is a lack of rationality and logic. Consumers are better informed thanks to widespread availability of information; that allows them a greater insight.

›

Fredric Jameson Fredric Jameson
...gestures and postures of the actors trying out their roles [...] F. Jameson, page11-12
13 minutes ago

Fredric Jameson Fredric Jameson
...traces of #production itself have been made to disappear) #Brecht opens up this surface and allows us to see back down into the #alternative...
15 minutes ago

rogermiller9 roger miller
Brecht on Wall Street – http://t.co/kb4xnJI4
19 minutes ago

Fredric Jameson Fredric Jameson
The well-made #production is one from which the traces of its #rehearsals have been removed (as from successfully reified #commodity the...
22 minutes ago

roxanamjones Roxana Jones
Because things are the way they are, things will not stay the way they are. – Bertolt Brecht
23 minutes ago

Fredric Jameson Fredric Jameson
...which is their #pretext. F. Jameson page73
26 minutes ago

OOH media language — Statements from the Posterscope website:

"JUST WHO IS AN OUT-OF-HOME CONSUMER? EVERYONE IS."
www.posterscope.com

ML/AB: *Surely it is more complicated than that? You must have particular groups in mind? They would be those with a disposable income, so not "everyone." Should it say that it's everyone who has a purchasing capacity?*

GW: Potentiality, we want to sell OOH solutions, we understand how people behave better than anybody else.

It is important to talk to people who might never buy your product because you want to generate approval of those who *can* buy it. You want to trigger an aspiration.

"TRADITIONALLY THE PAST DROVE THE PRESENT. IN TODAY'S WORLD, THE FUTURE DRIVES THE PRESENT."
www.posterscope.co.uk

ML/AB: *What kind of future do you imagine drives our present?*

GW: We are dealing with networked individuals, how will this change our behavior? Before the Internet, people displayed heritage behavior. The past was their reference and brought re-assurance. Today, we are always "on," we are "connected," and we don't yet fully understand how it impacts our thinking and behavior. We are already using technology in ways that weren't intended; this will happen more and more.

One of the effects is that this new connectivity empowers us both as individuals and collectively. Everyone's a broadcaster, everyone's a publisher. The "nowness," the immediacy of response aided by social media, is very important.

"PUTTING CONSUMERS AT THE HEART"
www.posterscope.com

ML/AB: *Putting consumers at the heart of what? Is the consumer and citizen the same person?*

GW: We start with the consumer when presented with a communication problem. Consumer is just a term, we are talking about people, citizen and consumer are the same.

"WE MAKE THE SMART STUFF ACCOUNTABLE. FROM THE IDEA CREATION THROUGH TO PROJECT MANAGEMENT, HYPERSPACE TRANSLATES OUR PLANNING, BUYING AND ACCOUNTABILITY PRINCIPLES OF TRADITIONAL OUT-OF-HOME MEDIA INTO WORKABLE SOLUTIONS FOR NEW AND DIGITAL OUT-OF-HOME FORMATS."
www.posterscope.com

ML/AB: *We don't understand this, can you explain? Can you tell us more about your relationship with Hyperspace?*

GW: Hyperspace is part of Posterscope. They specialize in the innovative aspect. They represent the more cutting edge of what the medium can do in terms of planning and buying space.

›

"FROM THE VERY MOMENT WE STEP FOOT OUTSIDE OF OUR HOMES, WE ARE SURROUNDED BY OUT-OF-HOME MEDIA."
www.posterscope.com

ML/AB: *What is the boundary between home and out-of-home? With the invasive presence of media penetrating the home, is this division becoming less clear?*
GW: The boundaries are blurring, the business context creates the boundary. It is anything outside the front door. Due to the heritage of the business, we have to define it in business terms, although for a consumer it is less important or less clear, or simply different. Perhaps the difference lies in what is not permission-based.

People see OOH as "opt-in," they can choose to look or ignore its presence. Younger people see it as part of the fabric in which they live, it would be strange if advertising screens weren't there. The linking of various media creates an integrated urban experience with coherent messages, which saturates contemporary life.

"WE KNOW IT IS IMPORTANT TO DEMONSTRATE SUCCESS."
www.posterscope.com

ML/AB: *How do you demonstrate success? What platforms do they need in order to demonstrate success?*

Fredric Jameson Fredric Jameson Marysia_Lewandowska
It is that the properly utopian features of #Brecht's
#collectivework and of @collective and #collaborative-
work of all kinds, are occulted...
Breakfast from £3.99
THE BRITANNIA BAR
M&S SIMPLY FOOD

Fredric Jameson Fredric Jameson Marysia_Lewandowska
...and repudiated; yet this is one of the most exciting
features of this #workingeneral, and one of the unique
sources of excitement it has...

› GW: We don't succeed unless the advertisers deem the project successful; so the question is what are their measures of success. It can be massively complex and their approaches vary. They might simply want to sell more, or change public opinion, or launch a new product or process.

There are many ingredients, all contributing to a complex set of relations. Some objectives are more measurable, such as website visits and data trails, some are ephemeral but still traceable because we are all networked.

Accountability and proof are a science, all Posterscope can do is contribute to that and understand that contribution more fully. We are in the business of changing consumer behavior, powered by the latest technologies. ×

The Direct Address project has been developed in collaboration with curator Antonia Blocker and designer Luke Gould, with thanks to Aram Mooradian.

Fredric Jameson Fredric Jameson
...return in #futuregenerations, however unfashionable
it may feel to @contemporaries in the current age of
the #market. F. Jameson; #brecht and #method
@Verso 1998, page10
×

10

Domesticating the Screen-Scenography: Situational Uses of Screen Images and Technologies in the London Underground

Zlatan Krajina

Proposing a grounded approach to everyday interactions with urban screens, in this chapter I present findings of my ethnographic research conducted on the London Underground, which investigated people's encounters with a range of screens, including conventional poster advertising as well as newer LED screens showing moving images. Dominated by tunnels, the architectural design encourages passengers to move forward, but the surfaces, covered almost entirely with advertising screens, invite passengers to look around. As I aim to demonstrate, passengers nonetheless routinely compensate for their lack of control over advertising screens by employing ethnomethods[1] of appropriating the screens for their own situational ends, contrary to the advertisers' conception of passengers as "captive audiences." Silently progressing through what the respondents termed "scruffy," "narrow" and "crowded" space (a price many must pay in order to move through their city efficiently), passengers develop what I will call "situational uses of urban screens." Passengers make use of screens as representations of more pleasant looking elsewheres, as points of concentration to avoid the gaze of others, and to focus their own thoughts, or as providers of potentially useful information. Perfecting these skills of appropriation to a level of taken-for-granted habit allows passengers to move routinely through the changing screen-scenography[2] and to "domesticate" it (see Silverstone and Hirsch, 1992; Berker *et al.*, 2006) as their everyday travel space.

Such negotiations of the mediated travel space take the form of incidental media consumption (episodic encounters with screens), which itself is contingent upon the particular micro-social situations of passing through (crowds, movement, waiting). Since, in the Underground's tunnels, there is much space that contains representations of other space, passengers can, while interacting with the screens, temporarily escape not only advertisers' messages but also the underground space itself.

I shall take a broad starting point and use as a conceptual background the widely circulated viewpoint in media studies that the contemporary mediated everyday is an environment crowded by quickly changing stimuli (Gitlin, 2001), to which people are assumed to respond either with fascination or in distraction (McQuire, 2006; McQuire *et al.*, 2009). I will argue that this assumption about people's responses to excessive mediations is unsuitable for explaining actual everyday situations in the mediated cities, such as those analyzed in this study. I will then describe the research undertaken on the Underground, and sketch out the basic conceptual assumptions about everyday life in mediated public spaces, informed by perspectives from phenomenological geography (Buttimer, 1976; Relph, 1976; Tuan, 1977; Seamon, 1979; Moores, 2006, 2007, 2012) and studies of media consumption and domestication (Certeau, 1984; Lull, 1990; Silverstone and Hirsch, 1992; Berker *et al.*, 2006). Turning to my respondents' accounts, I will describe their time–space routines (moving efficiently) and site-specific visual cultures (looking away from others), which principally form a context of what I consider to be practices of appropriation (situational uses) and the habituation of the screen-scenography (domestication of screens). I conclude by suggesting that commuters experience the changes of screen images and technologies as *spatial* changes, which make their habituation of the Underground laborious, requiring continuous domestication. Moving through spaces constrained by pre-arranged changeability, commuters must keep glancing at new images and technologies (while looking where they are going) in order to maintain familiarity with the space of their everyday travel.

The everyday and "everywhere-mediation"

Contemporary debates in media studies suggest that media abundance is a central characteristic of modern everyday life. Albeit to a greater degree in some cultures than others,[3] it has become difficult to imagine the everyday without media (Gitlin, 2001; Bird, 2003; Couldry, 2005), as the presence of communication and information technologies is increasingly prevalent not only in the home but also in urban space (Friedberg, 2006, pp. 6–7; McQuire, 2008, p. 130; Huhtamo, 2009, p. 15). Citizens are surrounded by a variety of screens in public space to such an extent, so the argument goes, that they are immersed in an overwhelming excess of stimuli (see Krajina, 2009). As Gitlin asserts, "never have so many communicated so much, on so many screens, through so many channels, absorbing so many hours of irreplaceable human attention" (Gitlin, 2001, p. 4). Users are invariably "bathing [themselves] ... in images and sounds" and they keep "return[ing] for more" (ibid., pp. 6–8).

In this implicitly technological determinist argument (which equates the very presence of media technologies with an actual interaction), Gitlin rightly draws our attention to the rising statistical figures of measurable forms of media consumption (such as hours spent watching TV), and the fact that the diversity of contemporary media landscapes is greater than ever (ibid., pp. 15–20). Yet none of this gives us reason to assume that citizens are always, everywhere and, equally strongly, "eager" media consumers (ibid., p. 160). The screen in public space is not always positioned for the passers-by in the same way that it is for those who study it: an interface that occupies the central spot in the place (as it does in our study of it). The screen, though largely unavoidable, does not appear to passers-by as central on a day-to-day basis. If we are interested in *everyday* interactions with urban screens, it would be misleading to isolate the events of interactions from social situations in which they actually happen (such as moving through crowded space). It would also be unproductive to ignore instances of non-interaction, which are part of everyday life in technologically mediated cities. Let us rather ask how it is that people live with urban screens in the actual circumstances of passing by, and in day-to-day routines of moving through. For those who find themselves surrounded by them every day, the "excessive" screens (whether conventional large poster adverts or newer LED screens showing moving images) are in fact *standard equipment*. They are the everyday environment for commuters, who more often than not give screens little overt attention. The challenge in these instances is to understand the nature of the work people do to make the glossy electronic imagery expected and taken-for-granted, and thus not overly disruptive in the routine of the everyday commute.

Before exploring commuters' practices in more depth, let us clarify one other starting assumption, that *both* the activity of moving through sites such as the Underground, *and* the urban screens people pass while doing so, share a certain *spatiality*. Walking and traveling, as well as waiting to travel, are fundamentally spatial activities (Certeau, 1984). Yet if urban screens are not only located in but also partly constitute public spaces, we must recognize the *environmental* quality of urban screens too. Screens are not merely media technologies; they are also integral components of "perceptual environments" in "everyday urban arenas through which people move" (Larkin, 2008, pp. 2–3). Finally, the city is "inconceivable without the space it unfolds in: its empirical dimension is above all spatial" (Augé, 1999, p. 109; *cf.* Soja, 2003). In other words, studying interactions with urban screens means exploring spatial experiences. Assuming that "from the perspective of experience, landscape cannot be understood merely as an assemblage of objects," but can be better examined in terms of "meanings they have for those who are experiencing them" (Relph, 1976, p. 122), I take an interpretive approach to spatial routines, as developed in phenomenological geography, and as reviewed in media studies by Moores, for a study of "apparently automatic *uses of media in the habitual movements of the daily round*" (Moores, 2006, original emphasis).

Rejecting the positivist traditions of researching the relations between people and environment solely by measuring behavior (as stimulus–response relations) and cognition (as conscious productions of mental maps of space), human geography endeavors to elucidate the "daily world of taken-for-grantedness" (Seamon, 1979, p. 153). This world includes skilled and sophisticated quotidian activities, such as walking to the corner shop or driving to school, which can evolve "without intervention of conscious attention" (ibid., p. 38). Everyday life is inconceivable without these pre-conscious routines: attending to the surroundings habitually gives daily life in them a sense of meaningfulness and stability. Habits of interacting with space form the basis of how space is inhabited and intimately known. Its components typically only come to the inhabitant's "explicit attention" when something in the space as known changes (ibid., pp. 48–49, 58, 117).

Seeking to understand how a newly installed screen becomes taken for granted, I find especially helpful those studies of media consumption (Silverstone and Hirsch, 1992; Berker *et al.*, 2006) that have demonstrated that the negotiation of new technologies and texts in familiar spaces has the status of *domesticating* media. As has been demonstrated in studies of households, media technologies and texts are, through consumption and use, gradually incorporated into the architectural and social interior: they are allocated domestic spaces, while interactions with texts gain the status of household routines.[4] If "the work of inhabiting space involves a dynamic negotiation between what is familiar and unfamiliar" (Ahmed, 2006, p. 7), encounters with urban screens in the spaces of daily routines involve not only responding to institutions' (e.g. advertisers') repeated invitations to communication but also rendering those invitations familiar. In encountering mutable screens in spaces that are host to repeated traversals, Underground commuters seek a sense of stability while lacking the ability to materially manipulate the screens.

Encountering the presence of changing surfaces, such as new poster adverts or LED screens, complicates the "inhabitance" of everyday space. If I see an image of a waterfall where I expect to see a wall, I must re-negotiate the space as a space mediated by an electronic image of an elsewhere (see Berry *et al.*, 2008), in order to continue with my everyday life in that space. Let us then recognize that urban screens both *occupy* space as technological artefacts and *represent* other space as images and texts.[5] Moving through everyday spaces in contemporary cities is eventful because, alongside encounters of other kinds, it involves encountering and negotiating change in the familiar environment: when an image or the screen changes, a piece of familiar space changes, too. However, in order to move around routinely and without too much disruption, commuters have to avoid giving each message close attention. In order to habituate to the space of travel, in other words, commuters must do the work of *making* the continually changing screens expected (invisible) in the intimate horizon of experience, and in doing so they have to deal with the fact that, unlike the screens at home or at work, urban screens allow no material manipulation (they cannot be moved around or shut down).

In her pioneering study of "ambient television," McCarthy discusses the absence of remote controls in transport spaces in terms of the forms of civic action (such as complaints to managers) needed to protect individuals from the mediations "imposed" on individual "body, or at least the sensorium" (McCarthy, 2001, pp. 109–110). In this study, I found myriad *other* ways in which people routinely reject the screen's address. In interpreting these, I adopt de Certeau's viewpoint that citizens, by way of mastering their walking through urban space in endless variety (rushing, slowing down, pausing, disregarding traffic signs, leaning on fences, etc.) "form the space of the other" to the institutions that arrange the space (Certeau, 1984, pp. 31, 37). The "clandestine" and "quasi-visibl[e]" tactics of use run in parallel with the institutions' strategies of creating space and prescribing patterns of behavior in space. Although initially used widely in studies of popular culture (see Fiske, 1989a, b; Silverstone, 1989; Poster, 1992), de Certeau's theory has also been criticized for its romanticizing view of resistance, which offers no tangible way of transforming the pre-arranged spaces in relation to which such practices are developed (see Buchanan, 2000, p. 91; Gardiner, 2000, p. 179; Ahearn, 2001; Massey, 2005, pp. 46–47). Nonetheless, de Certeau's concept remains useful in understanding the situational repurposing of screens designed for commercial communication (1984, p. 31). It acknowledges a political dimension – no matter how minor – of everyday practice that I find lacking in what is still another important approach to interactions with screens: Lull's idea of "social uses of television" (Lull, 1990). Lull developed his approach in studying home TV viewing, where screens are often "handy expedients which can be exploited by individuals" in pursuing a variety of communicative goals (such as avoiding or encouraging communication with those co-present) (ibid., p. 29). The "social uses of television" emerge in this chapter as "situational uses of urban screens": forms of appropriating screens for purposes relevant to the individual in the micro-social situation of passing through. This is to emphasize one final conceptual point: I take interaction to be a situation "tied to particular *occasions* and to *other participants* in the situation," rather than merely dependant on "the attributes of single actors," the commuters (Knorr Cetina, 1981, pp. 9, 17, original emphasis). I study interaction as *"the immediate social event of communication"* (Vološinov, 1973, p. 47, original emphasis) whereby a screen "hail[s]" the passer-by and the passer-by negotiates the "hail" (Althusser, 1971) in the specific social context, such as avoiding communicating with an approaching other or imagining being in a nicer place. I explore such situations by comparing what people do (as seen in observations), what they say they do (in interviews) and what they experience as they do what they do (in diaries).

Research outline

The Underground provides a form of transportation not only on its trains but through and within its architectural totality, which consists of tunnels designed for the circulation of both passengers and trains. In such contexts, passengers typically prioritize personal time–space efficiencies over situational curiosities and incidental detours. Asking people I encountered on the Underground to allow me to join them on their trips, and then to give up two hours of their time for me to ask them questions about their experiences, was only achievable through a method of "snowballing" (Bloch, 2004, p. 177). The qualifying criterion for personal recommendations of participants was possession of some previous travel experience on the set route. I sought to include both those relatively familiar and unfamiliar with the space ("insiders" and "outsiders") (Relph, 1976). If the knowledge of space informs the variety of attention to the surroundings (see Moores, 2007; Moores and Metykova, 2009, 2010), "outsiders" may be more likely to notice things that, for the "insiders," have become experientially invisible. The following individuals participated, with their age indicated in brackets, followed by years of residence in London (taken as a sign of their "insideness" and "outsideness"): Nicola (32/1 month), David (28/5), Brian (35/6), Alena (30/7), Edward (32/7), Igor (45/18), Emma (25/19), Mario (43/20) and Peter (49/49).

All participants took the same route in central London, from Charing Cross to Baker Street. I gave them a voice recorder to produce "diaries" about their trips. I instructed them to note on the recorder whatever they noticed during their journey and how they felt about it. I did not tell them that I was interested in their responses to screens until after they had finished their journey and we talked about what they had and had not mentioned. I chose a highly frequented route that included characteristic architectural structures that direct passengers and position screens differently (station entrances and exits, escalators, corridors, interchange tunnels and platforms). The route also included a variety of moving image screens: large screens with live news in the foyers of interchange stations; sets of small moving image screens installed next to escalators; moving image screens in the corners of corridors; and cinematic projection screens on the platforms.[6]

Situational interaction and screen-uses

If interactions with screens only ever exist in combination with other daily activities, it is only by " 'decent[ering]' the media from our analytical framework" that we can seek "to better understand the ways in which the media processes and everyday life are interwoven with each other" (Moorley, 2006, p. 200). In this section, I will first explore interaction with screens in relation to the particular social situations in which it typically happens, and which it helps to articulate and transform. To paraphrase Hall, such a perspective is not "determinist," but it is also not "without determination" (Hall, 1994, p. 261). The research here is less about how the different kinds of screens might "affect" the passengers but rather emphasizes the ways in which space and circumstance frame the range of possible interactions.

Site-specificity, as McCarthy observes in her study of "ambient television," and circumstance, identified in this research, both frame interactions with screens by providing opportunities for and restrictions from interactions. According to Edward, "going down the escalator you can't watch [the videos] if you're walking... and at [the] platform there's usually something on and then the train usually arrives half-way through it, and then they cut it off." Tunnels prioritize continuous circulation. Stopping for looking is out of question, because when on the Underground "you're rushing... you have to move," there is "a sense of urgency that you have to be fast" (Nicola). Only when the corridors are less busy is it "OK to look at images." In the busy corridors one must respect the fact that only one person can be in one spot at a time. The presence of screens can complicate this premise by offering encounters with representations of others. As Nicola explained, "I turn my head behind my shoulder to see them as I walk." Or, as Emma put it, "I'd stick with [the screen] by the time it's out of my view." Those situational "orientations" matter inasmuch as according to Sara Ahmed, they "shape the contours of space by affecting relations of proximity and distance between bodies" (Ahmed, 2006, p. 3). When a corridor is busy, "you focus on minding your step" instead of "reading the screens" (Nicola).

A screen can also be a passenger's focus, as part of their tactical resistance to the screen. While waiting for the train, Brian said he looks at a billboard in front of him. As he explained in the interview, while the "loud" and "huge" multiple screens in spaces such as London's Piccadilly Circus invite "a sense of confusion" with "endless movements," the printed still images on the Underground "in some way ask you to think." Rather than merely interacting with the advertisers' offers, Brian was also engaged in a critical exploration of "what it is they do" in order to draw his attention. Rather than turning his head away, he studied with curiosity the design strategies that advertisers employ. Emma, Nicola and Peter similarly talked about the habit of critically assessing the adverts; they can "appreciate the layout that's got a bit of design or thought or care behind it." Nicola, in fact, remembers posters by their pictorial and chromatic creations: "I remember the one for the insurance company, [with] a beautiful sunset. I don't remember the product of the other one, maybe it was a perfume, but again it had beautiful colors." Through their analyses of graphic designers' work, Peter and Nicola make use of posters as aesthetically pleasing parts of the underground space. Emma's habit is even less related to the content of screens and billboards: she engages with posters on platforms by drawing on their size, location and mode of operation. She makes use of clearly visible, fairly large, (still) billboard images to focus her thoughts. While waiting for the train, she makes a mental note of things to do later and finds it helpful, in order to focus her thoughts in the busy surroundings, to find a familiar poster, and to make use of it as a safe spot to anchor her eyes. Emma suggested that this "anchorage" could be compared to holding a bar on a moving train. As she explained, she usually makes use of the screen as a focal point in "looking at something" while "thinking of something else." With a change of thoughts, she moves on to another known poster.

Passengers are involved in skilled cost–benefit calculations in deciding which train line at which time and for which location one finds most "practical." Alena spoke about her tactical positioning of taking "my own spots" on the platforms "where I board the train." She chooses the carriage that is likely to stop "at the right exit [to the linking corridor] so that if you're late, you don't have to move [far] on the platform after leaving the train." Edward's tactics include intentionally taking "the wrong" corridor. It is worthwhile moving against the signs "just because I *know* there is a quicker way to get out!" Heedless of surveillance, Edward lives de Certeau's "common hero" figure (Certeau, 1984) in a victorious *joie de vivre* of re-working architectural constructions by ignoring institutional signage. In this context, commuters may find encounters with advertising imagery useful in seeking to travel efficiently.

Being on the Underground for up to two hours a day raises a question about how one manages one's time. Part of what constitutes a "successful" trip is the ability to match the immediate activity of travel with other, especially home and work-based, activities, such as reading, typing or thinking about work. Reading "useful" information on advertising screens is one such form of the doubling-up of activities. Alena and David, for instance, reported "checking" that they are "not missing out on any interesting movies, books or exhibitions." Advertisers seek to capitalize on the institutional arrangement of orderly movement (promoted with signs such as "stand on the right," "do not run" and "stand away from the platform's edge") and seek to suggest to passengers where to look. As Alena said, "you're bored, you're waiting, and there's a picture; and it attracts you, you're hoping to get something interesting out of it." If travel time is to the commuters "wasted time," screen-viewing is offered as a time-filling activity (see Moore, Chapter 7). It promises that the time in between work and leisure can be spent "efficiently," as part of the long standing Taylorist encouragement in technologically saturated societies to spend not only work but also leisure time productively (see Spigel, 2005; Berry and Hamilton, 2010, p. 121; *cf.* Lyons and Urry, 2005; Moores, 2005, p. 99). Commuters may find advertising screens useful not only in gathering potentially relevant information but also in seeking to "have something done" while "doing" the travel. As Edward put it, "you're not there because you want to (be)... the images are *something to see while you're looking around*" (my emphasis). Since it is difficult not to notice screens while moving through space covered with them, we can only understand interactions with screens as part of the situation of "looking around."

While owners promote their moving image technologies and poster sites to potential clients as addressing passengers "when they are actively looking to be distracted and engaged" (CBS Outdoor, 2010; *cf.* Cronin, Chapter 12), according to my respondents "engagement" is largely a matter of circumstance. The Underground space is a playfield for vision, in which looking, seeing and noticing, as well as not seeing and not noticing *even while* looking, are the key forms of participation. Similar to the situation described by Bausinger of a husband pretending he is watching TV to avoid communicating with his wife (Bausinger, 1984), Underground passengers also find useful looking *toward* screens when avoiding exchanging glances with others. "These ads come very handy when you find yourself across someone who's looking at you in a way you find uncomfortable," says Mario. He adds: "I bet those [advertising] companies send people to do that. Just staring at others up to the point when they just have to start looking at the ads." Mario's joke plays with the perceived complicity of typical looking practices on the Underground and the ubiquitous advertising; it also explains my description of the Underground screens as "screen-scenography": screens form the scenography for the local visual cultures of looking at, with and away from others.

As the escalators take one up or down, one can read from each screen little more than a second of the video narrative. Rather than containing one long screen, the walls are pierced by many smaller monitors. In order to follow a given narrative (not all screens show the same advert), one must switch from one screen to another, and "work through" the interruptions between the screens. This is why many passengers, while looking *away* from the screens positioned on their side, look *toward* the screens on the opposite side.[7] As Paul reported, "you can see people coming towards you... sometimes they look at you, and then you quickly look at something else." Such situational circumstances often conflict with advertisers' expectations. Emma looked at the video shown next to the escalator on the opposite side of the tunnel, but

Figure 10.1 Where to look?
Source: All photographs by Zlatan Krajina.

many of the people standing there looked toward the video played by Emma's escalator. Having thus fallen into the visual "trap," Emma spent the remainder of her trip on the escalator looking at the back of the person standing in front of her (and not at the screens) (Figure 10.1).

Though unavailable for analysis in mere observations, such intimate encounters in underground travel spaces form what Brunsdon calls "public privacy" (Brunsdon, 2010, p. 199) whereby underground travel exists, in Augé's words, as "[a] collectivity without festival and solitude without isolation" (Augé, 2002, p. 30). In such social contexts, the fleeting encounters with screens are the situations in which commuters not only seek to re-work screen-mediations, but also to negotiate their travel space.

Negotiating a sense of place in the mediated travel space

One of the central patterns that emerged from this research relates to the uses the screens can serve in negotiating a sense of place. Traveling on the Underground involves passengers in complex spatial practices of reaching overground destinations by moving through underground corridors that orient one toward those locations. The Underground is, in that sense, directional space, promising through its orientations, to borrow from Ahmed, "the magic of arrival" (Ahmed, 2006, p. 16). Moreover, the practice and experience of travel itself is cross-referenced on the Underground: images of other places, such as those on adverts for tourist resorts, present themselves as locations already reached by mere looking, and take place during actual travel. If we historicize this connection, the conflation of actual and mediated travel on the Underground will appear not at all unusual. As we learn from Park *et al.*'s early observation, "transportation and communication ... are primary factors in the ecological organization of the city" (Park *et al.*, 1968, p. 2). Prioritizing "what communication and transportation *are*" over "what they *do*," Sterne reminds us that "[s]ocial reality is made not only at the level of symbols," but "is also built and organized, a world of motion and action" (Sterne, 2006, pp. 126, 118, original emphasis; see also Morley, 2011). In our case, as Brunsdon stresses, discussing the Underground as a cinematic representation, a map-image and a laboriously built physical space, "no electronic elsewhere can be understood without attention to its historical precedents and material bases" (Brunsdon, 2010, p. 198). From this standpoint, I want to consider the spatial dimension of circulation on the Underground.

Three different spatial sectors – being present *somewhere* (under the ground), in anticipation of reaching *elsewhere* (a location above ground), while already reaching various represented *imaginary elsewheres* by sight, complicate the sense of *here*. Augé has written about transportational places, standardized by the electronic signage, as "functional ... [and] non-symbolised" non-places (Augé, 1995, pp. 126, 118, original emphasis). As I will detail below, my respondents, conversely, make use of screens as augmentations and not annihilations of place. The Underground space references overground places by displaying names of lines, as well as by announcing "next" stations, and "east," "west," "south" or "north" directions. By fostering movement toward places, the Underground space does not negate but *postpones* place. The Underground space is neither anthropological place nor technological non-place, but an *intermediary space directed and directing toward place*. It invites anticipation of reaching place through its *transitionary someplace*, such as the train platform.

In this transitional space, commuters use images of more pleasant looking elsewheres as they negotiate their corporeal travel. Take Igor's and David's respective responses to posters with tourist offers seen in the corridors, "Icelandair.... Blue Lagoon visit...hmmm, I always wanted to go there.... Why is the 'tube' so dirty?" – and – "Flights to Glasgow...! I'd like to go there. I'd like to go anywhere...Oh, more incoming traffic!", they interacted with images of other spaces as potential getaways, not necessarily to those spaces but *away* from the space in which the images were perceived. Stating that he "would like to go anywhere," while already going somewhere, David made use of an image of Glasgow as a brief escape from the Underground. Engaging with the advert for travel complicated both his sense of place and his sense of *crossing* space, as we also hear from Alena: "I usually look for [posters promoting] cheap flights...beautiful pictures of Egypt and Greek islands or something like that, to take my mind away." In her diary produced on the platform, she paused by a "beautiful image of a mountain." She remained silent, enjoying the screening and explained in the interview, "you don't concentrate on the place where you are, but on the place where you want to be, the place shown to you." Alena, Igor and David, as other participants, rarely referred to the actual offers in advertisers' messages. "Blue Lagoon" and "beautiful mountains" appeared in their diaries not merely on screens placed in the "Tube" or solely as advertising, commonly defined as "the multiple and impersonal announcements of goods, services or commercial ideas" (Mattelart, 1991, p. 31). Participants referred to the imagistic elsewheres as spaces to which they projected their presences (the "Lagoon" and the "mountains") in contrast with the "dirty" and "busy" immediate physical space.

In the same way, the screen can appear to David as if it is connecting "to a camera pointing at [the shown] scene, and you feel like you're looking through, you're looking *outside*...You can go through it *somewhere else*" (David's emphasis). The informal name "Tube" for the Underground serves David as a practical way of making sense of the mediated elsewheres represented therein. He thinks of the screen before him as, in fact, one side of a photographic tube "pointing at a [projected] scene." His account echoes the modernist premise in architecture (most prominent in the work of Le Corbusier), which, according to Colomina, conceptualized "the window" in the house as "a lens" and "the house itself" as "a camera pointed at [the outside world]" (1994, pp. 311–312; *cf.* Colomina, Chapter 2). For the commuters, the screen seen in the space encased by walls, and codified by the imperative of looking, works similarly. It does not merely project images inside but is turned into a window for looking outside the tunnel. The long history of rail travel attuned passengers to the unique "panoramic" viewpoint offered through the windows of an (overground) train, cutting through the landscape as a "projectile" (Schivelbusch, 1986, pp. 52, 54), whereby a passenger "may be able to send their eyes out the window, thereby vicariously extending their personal space" (Goffman, 1972, p. 53). If interaction with technologically mediated elsewheres can inform their sense of place whilst on the Underground, passengers make the screens useful as "windows" that permit looking in a space that can otherwise show nothing (Figure 10.2).

Similarly, Emma studies the orientation panel, placed on each platform, which displays a portion of the Underground map pertaining to the stations in close reach. She thinks of the displayed stops as places to which she has already been, or would like to visit. The printed toponyms provide her with momentary gates to locations above ground, where she would prefer to be, while thinking of them underground. For the same reason, she fantasizes about train tunnels being covered in images, " 'cause I don't like the dark bit. If [the train] stops, and

Figure 10.2 Looking through the screen-window

I can't get out..." The sense of leaving the Underground space while viewing representations of other places serves for Emma, and the above respondents, as a form of "mobile privatisation" (Williams, 1990, p. 26) pursued in the travel space. Williams's discussion of visiting places through TV viewing may have been identified with the use of the remote control in postwar suburban living rooms, but it may now also be offering a way of understanding the consumption of moving images as a companion to corporeal travel through the Underground.

In summary, the research presented here shows commuters turning institutionally created forms of communication (the advertising posters and screens) to their own ends, without being allowed to use the "power switches" – that is, without being able to materially control or change them. Although appearing to progress silently, even uninterestedly, through the corridors, passengers make use of screens as resources for escapism, gathering information, assessing design, focusing their thoughts and managing interpersonal communication. As I will suggest below, these practices of appropriation are most "successful" if carried out routinely, without having to be worked out in each encounter anew.

Domesticating the screen-scenography

Claims such as "I don't care if it's imposed on me, I can escape it" were commonplace in my respondents' accounts of their daily encounters with screens in the Underground. As we saw above, commuters seek to repurpose the advertising screens as, among other things, more pleasant-looking elsewheres. However, encountering these screens every day requires commuters to engage in yet a different kind of labor. In order to maintain uninterrupted their daily movement through an environment filled with flickering screens and countless posters, commuters have to make their skills of resistance routine and their encounters with screens predictable.

Respondents explained that they incorporate the "situational uses of screens" (escapism, gathering information, focusing thoughts, assessing design) in a continuous shifting of their attention between the quickly changing inner and outer stimuli (a notion inaugurated by Simmel about a century ago (Simmel, 1990)). What commentators who have followed Simmel tend to ignore is that such practices now operate *routinely*. Respondents say they "zone" in and out of, or "scan" the screen-scenography, as well as "menu" its messages according to personal topical interests. As Alena explained, "it's not like 'oh, I definitely have to see [the adverts] now!' [Not]... if I have more important things to think about." Being "zoned out" of the space covered with screens does not conflict with David's navigation: "You're on some kind of an autopilot that's doing that for you . . . when you've become familiar with the route." In Alena's words, "you don't choose your carriage . . . you don't look at the map, because it's all already there, it's a machine-like procedure, you do the same route every day." On his way home, David finds himself "trying to solve a problem" (such as a work problem or a dispute with a friend), and he can spend the entire journey feeling he did "not see a thing." However, it would be misleading to infer from this corporeal disregard (i.e. not looking toward screens) that screens are insignificant in commuters' lifeworlds. Awareness of the ubiquitous screens is interaction of a different order. The taken-for-granted presence of screens for commuters is not a sign of their insignificance but of users' familiarity with Underground space. In providing users with signs of stability, as Ahmed puts it, "the familiar . . . is not allowed to reveal itself" (Ahmed, 2006, pp. 37, 33). Screens, materially positioned to address the forefront, can, in repeated encounters, experientially move to the background of attention (Figure 10.3).

While dealing with screens in the messy quotidian realities of moving through busy tunnels and corridors, respondents have developed

Figure 10.3 "Zoned out"

ethnomethods of "picking up" and then "disposing" of images "on the go," at will. As Alena explained,

> It's easy, isn't it? You take a photograph in your mind, and while you're pushing with other people, you're thinking about the image. It may have reminded you of something, or it told you something new, and then, most likely, if you're interested in it, you can have a second look, it will be [displayed again] only a few meters further [ahead] ... [Posters] are repeated, so when you see it again, you read more details.

As David explained, "I'm not necessarily thinking about each poster [wholeheartedly]." It can be "just a small detail that you will focus on, the logo, the trademark, the colors, it could be anything." Interacting with a message on the Underground is a matter of topical compliance with the personal topics of interest "already playing in your mind" (Peter). Alena perpetually glances at screens in her casual search for whatever might help her update her lists of socially "relevant" things. She finds it most practical to compare her hobby-like browsing of adverts in the corridors to "reading the [women's] magazines," which, as Hermes reports, is a similarly inattentive yet skilled practice (Hermes, 1995). In the corridor-galleries, passengers can be heard conveniently inserting adverts in their conversations as topics ("Have you seen [the film] *The Wolfman*?") – a practice carried out as routinely as clicking a link on an Internet browser.

Yet equally habitual is a converse practice of rejecting messages. As Igor explained, having encountered a new video for designer clothes, "I notice it and just say to myself 'not interested!' Just look around and start thinking about something completely different. It's a show, like a scene going on inside you, you know, left and right." The panoramic view from the personal "cockpits" allows passengers to see many, which, in a less familiar corridor, can be too many messages, experienced as "bing-bing-bing-bing... an *overload*" (David), or "bombardment" directed "in-your-face" (Igor). The Underground corridors can thus turn into mini communicational battlefields. Passing through can require from the "common hero" (Certeau, 1984) a laborious message-disposal, whereby passengers attempt to reject all, including potentially relevant information. For David, "advertising is guilty until proven innocent, and I'm gonna discard it before I've examined it properly. I would be edging towards just 'scanning' it and moving on" (Figure 10.4).

Figure 10.4 The corridor-gallery

"Moving on," as the key context of traveling on the Underground, is at once the central obstacle for advertisers in addressing "captive audiences," which is why adverts in the tunnels are repetitive. Returning to the point made earlier about the spatiality of the Underground (as a technological somewhere), we can ask: if, as we walk, we see the same images appearing here and there, have we then actually moved from here to there? Let us at this point recognize that rather than unique icons, the screens provide an *index* for the underground space. The presence of posters signifies familiarity with the space on the whole. One such articulation comes from the advertising industry itself.

An unsigned message, displayed for the purpose of promoting advertising on the Underground to potential clients, spoke the language of their target audiences' daily routines and depicted advertising posters as household items in the everyday travel space (Figure 10.5).

While crediting "the poster" ("taking your mind away") for what is actually the creativity of commuters in pursuing escapism ("there will be something here to read, transporting you away") and productive travel ("to fill those few empty moments"), the above message promotes the "poster" as a source of what Giddens calls "ontological

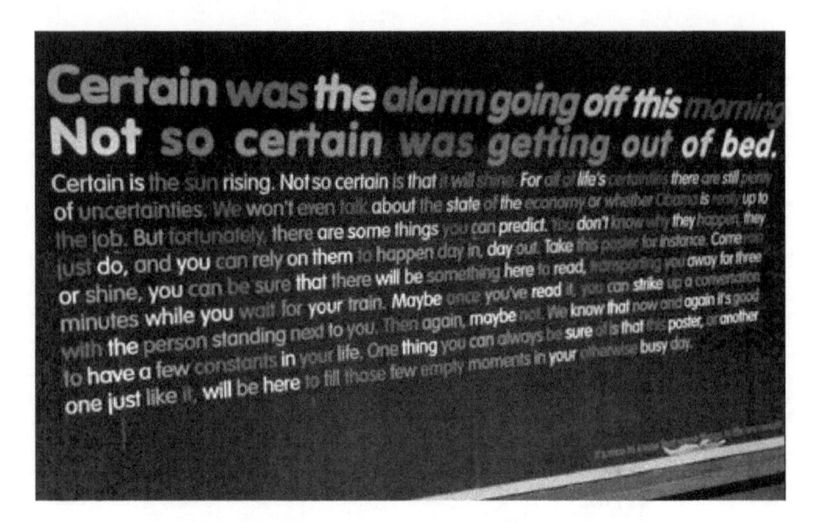

Figure 10.5 Advertising domesticity

security" (Giddens, 1990). The continued noticing of the presence of the poster in the space of everyday travel informs the sense of "constancy of the surrounding social and material environments of action" (ibid., p. 92). Similarly, "insider" participants were often quiet for long periods during their diary recordings and only sporadically referred to screens as common objects ("ummm ... very boring advertising today!"), rather than merely textual announcements brought in the underground space by dislocated broadcasters. As they pointed out later in interviews, "there was nothing to comment on" (Alena), "nothing I haven't seen" (Edward). However, in order to know the Underground as a space mediated by adverts, commuters must keep *making known* the portions of space that frequently change: the display surfaces. If, following phenomenological geography, familiarity with the everyday environment is one elementary prerequisite for inhabiting it (Tuan, 1977, p. 73), how is knowing the Underground, as the space of everyday travel, possible, given that some portions of its space, namely the screens, keep changing?

As Paul put it, "this place is timeless. This could be like [the] 60s, 70s, 80s, 90s ... *Until* you see the animated posters." Images that move, that is, change, as changing portions of space, do not merely "stand out" from the flux as distinguished visuals. What they *stand for* in the eyes of those familiar with the Underground is spatial novelty. Similarly, repetitive images inform familiarity with the space. Moving images on electronic screens, as opposed to stills on printed posters and billboards, complicate the work of familiarization for newcomer Nicola, because she has to "focus more in order to acquire more details." Her experience of moving cities for work taught her to keep looking around, because "in a new place you have to record everything. And you can't do this in one shot, you have to *practice the place*... Over time you need less and less new information." To Peter, a born Londoner, on the other hand, "every station looks very similar, because the posters are similar." Screens serve Peter as objects of orientation, which Ahmed termed "objects we recognize, so that when we face them we know which way we are facing" (Ahmed, 2006, p. 1). Commuters' familiarity with the Underground screen-space is part of their "intimate history" (Morley, 2006, p. 204) of living in London, and they can draw on that history when they encounter new screens.

At the time of research, in January 2010, the moving image cinematic screens at platforms were the latest piece of technology but they were already familiar. Alena's initial curiosity had already faded. "You get used to it and don't notice it any more," she said. "It's not that the magic is gone; you just go on looking for something new." Such changes of furniture in the known spaces require commuters to seek ways of "maintaining" the space as known. At his first encounter, David found himself studying with curiosity not so much the projection but the projector: "It was *new* in the environment... [it] could have been a *torch* up there, and I would have looked up!" After an initial assessment of the object (as to "whether it is safe or not"), David went on "try[ing] to figure out how [it] work[ed]." He tried linking the projecting machinery with the resulting images, thinking "it's [a] very good resolution... so the projector must be good!" This seemingly banal remark signals David's work of domestication – that is, the gradual inclusion of a new piece of media technology into his intimate repertoire of familiarity with different kinds of screens he encounters in various everyday contexts. Developing familiarity with the Underground thus involves both corporeal and technologically mediated interaction with its spaces.

Parallel with explorations done on foot, Nicola's experiences of the Underground also owe much to seeing images overseas, prior to arrival. "It's just like in the movies when you walk through the Underground. Like you are *in* the movie." Traveling on the Underground, for Nicola, means being in the wondrous space of a film set (Couldry, 2000), because "it all looks so similar, so real, like what you see on the TV." The sight of "[the] bouncing heads" under the low ceilings reminds David of "films of New York" he had watched as a child, before moving to

London. Commuting on the Underground gives him a flattering "feeling of being in a big city and public transportation system." Thus the "outsiders' " experience of the Underground does not proceed from a *tabula rasa* but is informed by previous representations. Londoners, on the other hand, negotiate the Underground spaces by referring to the temporal heterogeneity "engraved" on the screen-scenography. The "new" display technologies appear on side by side with the "old" posters.

Seeing screens within assemblages of "new" and "old" technologies allows the passengers to compare them. Commuters distinguish between species of screens (the "gimmick" of the pre-recorded advertising videos and the live TV broadcast in station foyers; Peter), genre of messages ("always the same" three key themes: "books, films, and exotic places," according to Mario), and sorts of layout (particularly "the color," according to Alena). This developing "screen literacy" informs the commuters' knowledge of the Underground. Mario practices his connoisseurship of adverts as he walks through the corridors by playing a game of guessing "is it going to be this, or that [advert]." His game implies that in familiar space one welcomes novelty. David's encounter with the new projectors at the platforms tells us something about the status of encountering novelty in familiar space: "it's *something you need* on 'the Tube'.... If you're taking the same journey 'day-in-day-out', that's exactly the same environment...nothing to make you think." Desirable novelty can be useful in *maintaining* the space as known.

As part of his research session, Mario entered a corridor that had just undergone reconstruction, and which had had all of its posters removed during the renovation. Documenting this encounter in his diary, Mario said "*This* is interesting... It feels very calm.... I could rest my thoughts, my eyes. It feels like diving into water. Which is frightening. Because it's just tiles" (Figure 10.6).

The unexpected encounter with the space devoid of its usual construction material – adverts – was a disturbance of his travel-lifeworld. Mario, like many other respondents, referred to adverts derogatorily. Rehearsing critical views of commercial activities in public space (with words such as "tacky," "selling," "everywhere" and "bombardment") seems to be a common response to the abundance of adverts in public space. At the same time, Mario's encounter with a space without adverts testifies to the ontological status of advertising in the space of the Underground: their disappearance made evident to the respondent that those screens do not, to quote Ihde, "usually occup focal attention" (1990, p. 111). How do we then make sense of David's acceptance of the

Figure 10.6 Encounter with change

new cinematic projectors as "something you need" and Mario's experience of a complete absence of adverts as something "unusual" and "frightening"?

To Peter, "seeing those moving posters for the first time" felt as though "there is something a bit different about the Underground, but it seems to stay the same." It is precisely at the intersection of "new" and "old" that one can helpfully, according him, "re-evaluate things." On the other hand, too much change can potentially disrupt, even harm, the lifeworld, as Mario's encounter with an empty corridor suggests. Peter's equivalent would be a change in design of the Underground map: "If they change[d] that, it would be a disaster... I've lived with that for many years." His suggestion is significant in part because the map is famously not a faithful representation of overground space. But even though it provides a "distorted" view of the city, it is reliable and durable because of the habit of relying on it and the need for it to remain the same. Since underground space is not only spatially less differentiated than the street but also separated from the atmospheric evidence of time, screens as "changing things" have for commuters the status of something "more vibrant" and "alive," because "it's not as much of a wall as it used to be," but rather, from time to time, "something else" (David). Encountering a periodic change of the interior "scenery" for David is important because "you get something new to look at." This is a "manageable" form of a novelty, "limited" in the scope of its impingement on the lifeworlds of its users. In the monotonous Underground space, commuters welcome seeing limited portions of its interior (such as screens) periodically change. The spatial organization (such as the orientation map and arguably the dense presence of screens) must remain the same. Dwelling in the technological space of transportation, invested with routines of practicing familiarity, thus requires what Heller called "a novelty *within the familiar*" (Heller, 1995, p. 8, emphasis mine). Habituating the screen-scenography, then, operates in between limited predictability and limited novelty.

Conclusion

In this chapter I have described ethnographic research investigating everyday interactions with screens on the Underground. In their everyday commute, passengers find themselves moving through a space designed to encourage continuous bodily flow and prevent blockage or deviance. At the same time, numerous advertising screens address passengers from the walls of tunnels and corridors. In response to this double institutional demand of moving straight and yet looking around, passengers carry out both activities complementarily. In anticipation of the real, passengers have at their disposal images of other spaces, which they find useful in altering the immediate circumstances of traveling in the city. Through a combination of observations, interviews and diaries, the research presented here suggested that encounters with screens are, essentially, situational. Interactions and encounters with screens occur alongside, and as part of, other activities, such as contending with the crowds, finding ways around and calculating "efficient" travel. Passengers develop myriad ethnomethods of appropriating screens as providers of up-to-date information on topics of interest, as images of more pleasant-looking elsewheres and as alternatives to the gaze of others. Those familiar with the Underground space can engage with screens habitually, "scanning" the environment, "zoning" in and zoning out. The presence of attention-seeking screens complicates habitual passages through the Underground, inasmuch as they present to everyday passengers changes of familiar space. Encountering new screens and messages requires novelties to be domesticated so that familiarity with the changing space can be maintained.

As I suggested in the introduction, public urban screens differ from household and workplace screens because they cannot be materially manipulated. They engage their incidental audiences, if not always in communication then at least in communication about the invitation. In that context, ignoring the screens, being aware of them and noticing them are all constitutive aspects of living with them. As advertisers strive to win passengers' attention by innovating technologically (e.g. through the introduction of dynamic LED screens), passengers strive to win a sense of stability and ordinariness by rendering the screens ordinary and even invisible on their repetitive trips. The creativity involved in the immaterial manipulation of screens requires us to study what citizens do, acting as sophisticated practitioners of public space, in which they inscribe their pleasures and struggles as they go on with their everyday lives in mediated cities. By excavating users' dynamic and intimate negotiations of space from the taken for granted, we can better understand the laboriousness of everyday life in technologically mediated urban environments.

Acknowledgments

This chapter is part of my PhD thesis "Negotiating the Mediated City: Everyday Encounters with Urban Screens" (Goldsmiths College, University of London). I am indebted to my supervisor, Professor David Morley, for immense intellectual support. I am grateful to my interviewees, and to Mira Armour, Monika Metykova, Liz Moor, Peter Taylor and Jelena Tomic Varosanec for assistance in various aspects of carrying out this research.

Notes

1. I adopt the term from Garfinkel's studies of verbal indexical practices of sustaining order in micro milieus. I refer to "ethnomethods" broadly as a name for "people's ways of doing" (Garfinkel, 1984).
2. I borrow the term "scenography" from McCarthy's observations of the placements of television sets in public spaces densely populated by other forms of signage, whereby "TV images become scenographic elements of the space that surrounds them" (McCarthy, 2001; see also Moor, 2007).
3. We must keep in mind that "[t]he saturation is increasingly global, though not irresistibly so" (Gitlin, 2001, p. 9). As Mattelart puts it, between "universalising modernity and territorial singularity" there is a "permanent dance of unequal exchange" (Mattelart, 1991, p. 38).
4. The quotidian work of domesticating technologies and texts is not "something which only takes place in the home" (Silverstone and Haddon, 1996, p. 46) but, with the spread of media technologies, increasingly also something that takes place "on the streets" (Berker *et al.*, 2006, p. 2).
5. I consider screens both as technologies and as texts. This has been found to be useful not only in studying TV in households (Morley and Silverstone) but also in "out-of-home" contexts where "ambient" TV operates as "at once a physical object in social space and a source of enunciations originating in, and displaying, other places" (McCarthy, 2001, p. 15).
6. As indicated above, I will take into consideration any form of display media – electronic and printed alike – that participants choose to interact with, which should also allow us to consider how participants distinguish between forms

of display and what such distinctions might say about their experience of daily commute (they may experience electronic screens as technological and imagistic forms of spatial change).

7. Historically, by focusing on objects that appear furthest away from train windows, rail passengers learnt to manage the inability to grasp the changing scenery from the moving carriage because "the more distant objects . . . seem to pass by more slowly" (Schivelbusch, 1985, p. 56). The LU passengers, similarly, look to the opposite side of the tunnel in seeking the perspective of distance.

Bibliography

Ahearn, Laura M. (2001) "Language and Agency", *Annual Review of Anthropology*, 30, 109–137.

Ahmed, Sara (2006) *Queer Phenomenology: Orientations, Objects, Others* (Durham and London: Duke University Press).

Althusser, Louis (1971) *Lenin and Philosophy, and Other Essays* (New York: Monthly Review Press).

Augé, Marc (1995) *Non-places: Introduction to an Anthropology of Supermodernity* (London, New York: Verso).

Augé, Marc (1999) *An Anthropology for Contemporaneous Worlds* (Stanford: Stanford University Press).

Augé, Marc (2002) *In the Metro* (Minneapolis: University of Minnesota Press).

Bausinger, Hermann (1984) "Media, Technology and Daily Life", *Media, Culture and Society*, 6(4), 343–351.

Berker, Thomas *et al.* (eds.) (2006) *Domestication of Media and Technology* (Maidenhead and New York: Open University Press).

Berry, Chris, Kim, Soyoung and Spigel, Lynn (eds.) (2008) "Introduction: Here, There and Elsewhere", in Berry, Chris, Kim, Soyoung and Spigel, Lynn (eds.) *Electronic Elsewheres: Media, Technology and the Experience of Social Space* (London and Minneapolis: Minnesota University Press).

Berry, Marsha and Hamilton, Margaret (2010) "Changing Urban Spaces: Mobile Phones on Trains", *Mobilities*, 5(1) (February), 111–129.

Bird, S. Elizabeth (2003) *The Audience in Everyday Life: Living in a Media World* (New York and London: Routledge).

Bloch, Alice (2004) "Doing Social Surveys", in Seale, Clive (ed.) *Researching Society and Culture*, 2nd edn. (London, Thousand Oaks, New Delhi: Sage).

Brunsdon, Charlotte (2010) "The Elsewhere of the London Underground", in Berry, Chris, Kim, Soyoung and Spigel, Lynn (eds.) *Electronic Elsewheres: Media, Technology, and the Experience of Social Space* (Minneapolis and London: University of Minnesota Press).

Buchanan, Ian (2000) *Michel de Certeau: Cultural Theorist* (London, Thousand Oaks, New Delhi: Sage Publications).

Buttimer, Anne (1976) "Grasping the Dynamism of Lifeworld", *Annals of the Association of American Geographers* 66(2), 277–292.

CBS Outdoor (2010) "XTP – Cross Track Projection", http://www.cbsoutdoor.co.uk/Our-Media/Digital/XTP---Cross-Track-Projection/?t=0, date accessed 17 February 2010.

Certeau, Michel de (1984) *The Practice of Everyday Life* (Berkley, LA and London: University of California Press).

Colomina, Beatriz (1994) *Privacy and Publicity: Architecture as Mass Media* (Cambridge: MIT Press).

Couldry, Nick (2000) *The Place of Media Power: Pilgrims and Witnesses of the Media Age* (London and New York: Routledge).

Couldry, Nick (2005) "The Extended Audience: Scanning the Horizon", in Gillespie, Marie (ed.) *Media Audiences* (Maidenhead: Open University Press).

Fiske, John (1989a) *Understanding Popular Culture* (London and New York: Routledge).

Fiske, John (1989b) *Reading the Popular* (London and New York: Routledge).

Friedberg, Anne (2006) *The Virtual Window: From Alberti to Microsoft* (Cambridge and London: MIT Press).

Gardiner, Michael (2000) *Critiques of Everyday Life* (London and New York: Routledge).

Garfinkle, Harold (1984) *Studies in Ethnomethodology* (Cambridge: Polity Press and Oxford: Basil Blackwell).

Giddens, Anthony (1990) *The Consequences of Modernity* (Cambridge: Polity Press).

Gitlin, Todd (2001) *Media Unlimited: How the Torrent of Images and Sounds Overwhelms Our Lives* (Metropolitan Books: New York).

Goffman, Erving (1972) *Relations in Public: Microstudies of the Public Order* (Harmondsworth: Penguin Books).

Hall, Stuart (1994) "Reflections on the Encoding/Decoding Model: An Interview", in Cruz, Jon and Lewis, Justin (eds.) *Viewing, Reading, Listening: Audiences and Cultural Reception* (Boulder, Colorado: Westview Press).

Heller, Agnes (1995) "Where Are We at Home?", *Thesis Eleven*, 41, 1–18.

Hermes, Joke (1995) *Reading Women's Magazines: An Analysis of Everyday Media Use* (Cambridge, MA: Polity Press).

Huhtamo, Erkki (2009) "Messages on the Wall: An Archaeology of Public Media Displays", in McQuire, Scott, Martin, Meredith and Niederer, Sabine (eds.) *Urban Screens Reader* (Amsterdam: Institute of Network Cultures).

Ihde, Don (1990) *Technology and the Lifeworld: From Garden to Earth* (Bloomington and Indianapolis: Indiana University Press).

Cetina, Knorr, D., Karin (1981) "Introduction: The Micro-Sociological Challenge of Macro-Sociology: Towards a Reconstruction of Social Theory and Methodology", in D., Karin, Cetina, Knorr and Cicourel, Aaron V. (eds.) *Advances in Social Theory and Methodology: Toward an Integration of Micro- and Macro-Sociologies* (Boston, London and Henley: Routledge and Kegan Paul).

Krajina, Zlatan (2009) "Exploring Urban Screens", *Culture Unbound: Journal of Current Cultural Research*, 1, Article 24, 401–430.

Larkin, Brian (2008) *Signal and Noise: Media, Infrastructure and Urban Culture in Nigeria* (Durham: Duke University Press).

Lull, James (1990) *Inside Family Viewing: Ethnographic Research on Television's Audiences* (London and New York: Routledge).

Lyons, Glenn and Urry, John (2005) "Travel Time Use in the Information Age", *Transportation Research Part A*, 39, 257–276.

Massey, Doreen (2005) *For Space* (London, Thousand Oaks and New Delhi: Sage Publications).

Mattelart, Armand (1991) *Advertising International: The Privatisation of Public Space* (London and New York: Routledge).

McCarthy, Anna (2001) *Ambient Television: Visual Culture and Public Space* (Durham: Duke University Press).

McQuire, Scott (2006) "The Politics of Public Space in the Media City", *First Monday*, Special Issue no. 4 (February), http://firstmonday.org/htbin/cgiwrap/bin/ojs/index.php/fm/article/ viewArticle/1544/1459, date accessed 14 June 2009.

McQuire, Scott (2008) *The Media City: Media, Architecture and Urban Space* (Los Angeles, London, New Delhi and Singapore: Sage Publications).

McQuire, Scott, Martin, Meredith and Niederer, Sabine (eds.) (2009) *Urban Screens Reader* (Amsterdam: Institute of Network Cultures).

Moor, Liz (2007) *The Rise of Brands* (Oxford: Berg).

Moores, Shaun (2005) *Media/Theory: Thinking About Media and Communications* (London and New York: Routledge).

Moores, Shaun (2006) "Media Uses & Everyday Environmental Experiences: A Positive Critique of Phenomenological Geography", *Particip@tions*, 3(2), Special Edition (November), http://www.participations.org/volume%203/issue%202%20-%20special/3_02_moores.htm, date accessed 6 February 2009.

Moores, Shaun (2007) "Media and Senses of Place: On Situational and Phenomenological Geographies", in *Media@LSE Electronic Working Papers*. Available at: http://www.lse.ac.uk/collections/media@lse/mediaWorkingPapers/ewpNumber12.htm, date accessed 1 February 2009.

Moores, Shaun (2012) *Media, Place & Mobility* (London: Palgrave Macmillan).

Moores, Shaun and Metykova, Monika (2009) "Knowing How to Get Around: Place, Migration, and Communication", *Communication Review*, 12(4) (December), 313–326.

Moores, Shaun and Metykova, Monika (2010) " 'I Didn't Realize How Attached I Am': On the Environmental Experiences of Trans-European Migrants", *European Journal of Cultural Studies*, 13(2), 171–189.

Morley, David (2006) *Media, Modernity and Technology: The Geography of the New* (London and New York: Routledge).

Morley, David (2011) "Communication and Transport: The Mobility of Information, People and Commodities", *Media Culture and Society*, 33(5), 743–759.

Park, Robert E., Burgess, Ernest W. and McKenzie, Roderick D. (1968) *The City* (Chicago and London: University of Chicago Press).

Poster, Mark (1992) "The Question of Agency: Michel de Certeau and the History of Consumerism", *Diacritics* 22(2) (Summer), 94–107.

Relph, Edward C. (1976) *Place and Placelessness* (London: Pion Limited).

Schivelbusch, Wolfgang (1986) *The Railway Journey: The Industrialization of Time and Space in the 19th Century* (Leamington Spa, Hamburg, New York: Berg).

Seamon, David (1979) *A Geography of the Lifeworld: Movement, Rest and Encounter* (London: Croom Helm).

Silverstone, Roger (1989) "Let Us Then Return to the Murmuring of Everyday Practices: A Note on Michel de Certeau, Television and Everyday Life", *Theory, Culture & Society*, 6, 77–94.

Silverstone, Roger and Hirsch, Eric (eds.) (1992) *Consuming Technologies: Media and Information in Domestic Spaces* (London and New York: Routledge).

Silverstone, Roger and Haddon, Leslie (1996) "Design and the Domestication of Information and Communication Technologies: Technical Change and Everyday Life", in Mansell, Robin and Silverstone, Roger (eds.) *Communication by*

Design: The Politics of Information and Communication Technologies (Oxford: Oxford University Press).
Simmel, Georg (1990) *The Philosophy of Money*, Frisby, David (ed.), (London and New York: Routledge).
Soja, Edward W. (2003) "Writing the City Spatially", *City*, 7(3) (November), 269–280.
Spigel, Lynn (2005) "Designing the Smart House: Posthuman Domesticity and Conspicuous Production", *European Journal of Cultural Studies*, 8(4), 403–426.
Sterne, Jonathan (2006) "Transportation and Communication: Together as You've Always Wanted Them", in Parker, Jeremy and Robertson, Craig (eds.) *Thinking with James Carey: Essays on Communications, Transportation, History* (Peter Lang: New York).
Tuan, Yi-Fu (1977) *Space and Place* (Minneapolis: University of Minnesota Press).
Vološinov, Valentin N. (1973) *Marxism and the Philosophy of Language* (Cambridge: Harvard University Press).
Williams, Raymond (1990) *Television: Technology and Cultural Form*, Williams, Ederyn (ed.) (London: Fontana).

11
Privatizing Urban Space in the Mediated World of iPod Users

Michael Bull

> What people most want from public space is to be alone with their personal network.
>
> (Turkle, 2011, p. 93)

> Street walkers are so engrossed in their conversations that they do not apprehend what is going on around them despite their eyes being wide open...the evidence does not suggest that these reductions in the human qualities of public space are likely to be mere transient adjustments.
>
> (Katz, 2006, p. 46)

This chapter investigates the meanings attached to the sonic mediated habitation of public urban spaces, through analysis of the experiences of Apple iPod and smartphone users as they navigate their way through the city accompanied by the music contained in their personal technologies. Urban subjects text whilst walking, attention focused on the screen of their phone; talk to absent others on their smartphones; sit in trains reading from their iPads whilst simultaneously checking their emails; or sit engrossed in the latest snippet from their *Facebook* accounts. These forms of technologically mediated behavior question what it means to inhabit public urban space for many city dwellers. Public space is increasingly turned into a utilitarian space of private mediated activity. Time is reclaimed in terms of its "usefulness" and multi-tasked in relation to the possibilities embodied in users' smartphones: "I'm not very good at doing one thing at once. I always feel that if I can do two things then it's better" (Samantha).[1] Streets walked through become secondary to the act of talking, texting, playing, listening or surfing. Awareness of others is equally recessed: "I work on the assumption that those people don't know me, and I don't know them. I'm not aware of any reaction I might be causing" (Lucy). Public space increasingly becomes a blank and neutral canvas on which to write one's personal activity and experience.

The sonic strategies analyzed below form an important part of the sensory re-organization of public space that has been furthered by the use of smartphones (Goggin, 2011). The sonic uniquely permits users to seamlessly reconfigure their relationship with urban space – to date, more than 50% of Western populations have the ability to create their own privatized sonic bubbles through the use of either dedicated MP3 players, such as the Apple iPod, or mobile phones with MP3 capability.[2]

The age of mechanical reproduction is an age of increasing sonic saturation in which urban space, both public and private, is colonized. Throughout the twentieth and twenty-first centuries, we have increasingly moved to music. This was originally supplied through Fordist technologies, such as those provided by the Muzak Corporation, which created a range of sonic uniformity for consumers. More recently, it has extended to the use of what I call the hyper-post-Fordist technologies of iPods and smartphones, through which – with the aid of a pair of headphones – users create individualized soundscapes. iPod use represents the culmination of more than a century of media use in which sensory filtering has become second nature to many (Geurts, 2002, p. 88), from early radio users who listened privately through headphones in their living rooms, through users of transistor radios, to those hermetically sealed listeners in automobiles.

The analysis moves from a Fordist understanding through which citizens experience the urban soundscape as largely given, to a hyper-post-Fordist soundscape whereby users actively create their own urban aesthetic experience of the city through privatizing strategies of iPod use. The development of this hyper-post-Fordist analysis of city spaces forces us to reconsider the nature and meaning that urban space and time has for many city inhabitants. In the chapter, the experience of public space is divided into three categories. Fordist appropriation is that which is experienced through traditional sonic technologies, such as those produced by the Muzak Corporation whereby all hear the same sounds simultaneously, from hotel lobbies to football grounds. This does not imply that all who are subjected to Fordist sounds respond in the same way, but merely that Fordist sounds ground the experience. A post-Fordist experience is one whereby specific sound enclaves are carved out collectively – for example the use of soundtracks in specific retail stores constructed to correspond to the cultural preferences of the consumer. Hyper-post-Fordist experience is indicative of the iPod user who wishes to individualize their experience of space and place. For example, the user might walk into a fashion shop with its chosen soundtrack but rather wish to experience the shop through their own soundtrack. Another example of this hyper-post-Fordism is found in gyms, where people work out to their own individualized soundtrack rather than to one that is experienced collectively. It is important to note that all three modes of apprehension co-exist in contemporary culture in parallel to other modes of media consumption.

Typical of the privatizing experience of the city is the following quote from a New York user:

> I enjoy having a soundtrack for New York streets. Having my own rhythm. I commute two hours a day. When I'm on the subway people listening to music on headphones often surround me. We each inhabit our own realities.
>
> (Karen)

Karen's experience of the city is one of technological mediation – the technology of the iPod and the music contained therein. It is indicative of the experience of many, whereby their urban experience has become increasingly mediated by an array of technologies that have both trained and conditioned the human sensorium (Benjamin, 1973, p. 216).

These mediating technologies need not be sophisticated in order to have dramatic effects. William Gibson understood the radical transformative possibilities that lay in a relatively simple everyday technological device when he remarked, "the Sony Walkman has done more to change human perception than any virtual reality gadget. I can't remember any technological experience since that was quite so wonderful as being able to take music and move it through landscapes and architecture" (Gibson, 1993, p. 4). He noted the radical transformation that technology can have upon the human sensorium. In essence, the technology empowers the auditory capacity of the user. Historically, the ears have been interpreted as both passive and democratic – passive inasmuch as the ears are open to all sounds, and democratic for this same reason. Walkman and subsequent iPod use is neither passive nor democratic but, rather, discriminating and distinctive. The passivity of the ears appears to be merely an historical effect, now technologically superseded through the development of earpieces, which empower users so that they can choose what they wish to hear, screening out the urban soundscape in order to create a private auditory universe (Sterne, 2003, p. 137). In doing so, users transform their relationship with the social world in which they live. Gibson is describing the experience of sonic immersion. Frances Dyson has recently commented upon the intimate relationship between sound technologies and immersion:

> Sound is the immersive medium par excellence. Three-dimensional, interactive, and synaesthetic, perceived in the here and now of an embodied space, sound returns to the listener the very same qualities that media mediates: that feeling of being here now, of experiencing oneself as engulfed, enveloped, enmeshed, in short, immersed in an environment. Sound surrounds.
>
> (Dyson, 2009, p. 4)

iPod use valorizes the "here and now." Sound both colonizes the listener and actively recreates and reconfigures the spaces of experience. Through the power of a privatized sound world, the world becomes intimate, known and possessed. Embedded in this sonic experience is the power of users to recreate the subjective nature and meaning of urban space at will, questioning the very nature of what it means to share urban space – one of the cornerstones of the very development of cities themselves – as shared social space.

Rethinking the experiences of urban space

City soundscapes have traditionally been understood as non-synchronous, anarchic and largely uncontrollable. Henri Lefebvre described the experience thus: "He who walks down the street...is immersed in the multiplicity of noises, murmurs, rhythms" (Lefebvre, 2004, p. 28). From this perspective, the urban citizen is primarily a "listening" subject, open, more or less, to the cultural diversity of the city. For Lefebvre, citizens actively immerse themselves in the sounds of the city, deciphering it in order to make sense of its multiplicity and confusion. The city soundscape is seductive, its chaotic and unrhythmic nature brought to order by the attentive ear, enabling the subject "to separate out, to distinguish the sources, to bring them back together by perceiving interactions" (Lefebvre, 2004, p. 27).

This kaleidoscopic image of sensory richness exists in earlier observations of the city centers of Paris (Benjamin, 1973; Certeau, 1988), Berlin (Simmel, 1997), New York (Sennett, 1990) and Vienna (Musil, 1995). It is the epistemology of the city center that has captured the imagination of urban and cultural theorists in their accounts of how the urban citizen experiences, copes and manages city life. However, technologies of sound reproduction could be placed and experienced virtually anywhere from villages to national parks. We take our technology wherever we go, making any space potentially an urban space (Lefebvre, 2004, pp. 3–4).

To illustrate this point of the stretching of the urban, during a recent visit to the ancient Buddhist sanctuary of Koyasan in Japan, I experienced the following sonic transformation of the site. The center is perched high up the mountains near to the city of Osaka, engulfed in ancient forests. Late one afternoon I took a walk through the old and rambling Okuno-in cemetery in the heart of the Koyasan complex with nothing but the sound of my feet and the birds to accompany my reveries. At 7.00 pm on the dot, my thoughts were interrupted by the all-encompassing sounds of what appeared to me to be celestial "shopping music" emanating from a concealed system of speakers attached to the trees throughout the graveyard. The serene and peaceful surroundings of the graveyard were suddenly transformed into a scene reminiscent of one in *Twin Peaks*, a suspense/horror television series shown in the early 1990s. This small personal anecdote illustrates the power of music in the transformation of our sense of place and space. It is a tale of Fordist "colonization," a Muzak-type moment to which I responded. The sound cannot be ignored – all people walking through that space will hear the same imposed sounds, to which they nevertheless respond individually.

If indeed my sonic experience of Koyasan was essentially Fordist in nature, then the privatizing aesthetic of the use of mobile technologies like the iPod represents a hyper-post-Fordist moment of urban culture in which the city is individually consumed and recreated. In the modernist urban world of the city it was the subject who was traditionally embedded in the electronic lights and billboards of the city, the subject becoming colonized by the enticements of the city, interiorizing the utopian dreams fabricated by the image. The representational spaces of the city were perceived as engulfing subjectivity:

> Illuminated words glide on the rooftops, and already one is banished from one's own emptiness into the alien advertisement. One's body takes root in the asphalt, and, together with the enlightening revelations of the illuminations, one's spirit – which is no longer one's own – roams ceaselessly out of the night and into the night.
>
> (Kracauer 1995, p. 332)

Kracauer's understanding of the urban colonization of the subject is essentially a Fordist one, in which the dominating rhythms of the city create the cadences within which all citizens walk. Urban experience becomes mediated through the advertising technologies of commodity culture and the empowered dreams associated with the very act of movement itself. iPod use reverses these phenomena. The user is rather saturated with the privatized sounds of the iPod – the cultural imperative, fully commoditized, lies in the contents of the iPod itself, not in the city street. The world is drawn into the user's "individual" narrative rather than the street drawing the user into its realm.

> It's as though I can part the seas like Moses. It gives me and what's around me a literal rhythm, I feel literally in my own world, as an observer. It helps to regulate my space so I can feel how I want to feel, without external causes changing that.
>
> (Susanna)

The experiences of the city described by Kracauer and those of the iPod user remain deeply mediated and commoditized. Both sets of descriptions are filmic in character, Kracauer's urban stroller lives in the polyrhythmic audiovisual world of the street, which presents itself to him as a spectacle in which the street becomes a commodified dream. iPod users, in contrast, construct a mono-rhythmic aesthetic narrative to the street deciphered from the sounds of the culture industry emanating from the iPod. Theirs is a hyper-post-Fordist street of potentially multiple audiovisual scenarios, with each iPod user constructing their own singular mediated dream world simultaneously. Whereas Kracauer's subject is diminished, made smaller by the enormity of the street and its illuminated signs, a marketing manager from London, Sophie, describes her iPod experience as "making the world look smaller – I am much bigger and powerful listening to music. The world is generally a better place, or at the very least it is sympathetic to my mood ... you become part of the music and can take on a different persona."

iPod users might be seen as uniquely individualizing social space, creating their own unique and unrepeatable audiovisual aesthetic of the city. Each journey is unique yet personal. Public space is made up of parallel individualizing trajectories as each user is absorbed in their own sound world.

For social and urban theorists from Augé to Sennett, this denuded and privatized social is thought to reside in the streets we walk through, the buildings we pass by, the modern shopping centers we are inevitably drawn to, the anonymous spaces of airports, train stations, parking lots and the endless motorways that many of us progressively live in as we shuttle backwards and forwards in our cars and on public transport. Augé, in his analysis of urban space, used the term "non-space" to describe an urban culture of semiologically denuded spaces of shopping centers, airports, motorways and the like (Augé, 1995). He thought of these spaces as if they had been dropped onto the urban landscape at random and as invariably architecturally bland. Who can tell one shopping center from another, for example? Urban spaces from this perspective increasingly functioned as the endless transit zones of urban culture, emblems of the increasingly mobile nature of urban culture.

Technologies like the iPod and many smartphones can enable users to transform any urban space into a non-space. The defining feature of the users' relationship to urban space is not necessarily how culturally situated they might be. For iPod users, urban "non-space" is not dependent upon the anthropological nature of the space itself but increasingly upon the technologically empowered subjective response to that space or, indeed, the prior negation of that space through the cognitive predilections of the subject. Just as the placing of earphones over the ears empowers the ear, so the urban subject is free to recreate the city in their own image through the power of sound:

> When I plug in and turn on, my iPod does a "ctrl+alt+delete" on my surroundings and allows me to "be" somewhere else.
>
> (Wes)

iPod use permits users to control and manage their urban experience. In doing so, time becomes subjectivized and speed brought into the rhythm of the user.

> I view people more like choices when I'm wearing my iPod. Instead of being forced to interact with them, I get to decide. It's almost liberating to realize you don't have to be polite or smile or do anything. I get to move through time and space at my speed [and] my pace.
>
> (Andrea)

iPod use potentially furthers the existing isolation of urban citizens. They are articulated and embedded in a range of technologies that enable them to carry out many traditionally public tasks with little or no interpersonal contact, which furthers the architecture of isolation articulated in the work of Augé, Bauman and Sennett (Augé, 1995; Sennett, 1977, 1990; Bauman, 2000). Exchanges are increasingly taking place between subjects and machines in urban culture, making interpersonal exchange obsolete. From self-service tills in supermarkets to hole-in-the-wall dispensing machines in banks, cognitively, consumers often expect, feel comfortable with and desire to avoid direct interpersonal communication whilst out in public. The construction of privatized sonic landscapes permits users to control the terms and condition of whatever interaction might take place, producing a web of asymmetrical urban relations that users strive to control.

Retreat has become a dominant urban metaphor to describe strategies whereby citizens attempt to maintain a sense of "self" through the progressive creation of distancing mechanisms from the urban "other." Richard Sennett describes urban space as "a bland environment [which] assures people that nothing disturbing or demanding is happening 'out there.' You build neutrality in order to legitimize withdrawal" (Sennett, 1990, p. 65). Urban retreat as a means to maintain a subjective sense of balance or equilibrium can be traced back to the work of Georg Simmel, who described the urban subject as constructing a blasé attitude toward the physical nature of the city in order to achieve this aim. The blasé attitude negated difference through distancing itself from that which surrounds it; "things themselves are experienced as insubstantial. They appear to the blasé person in an evenly grey tone, no one object deserves preference over any other.... The self-preservation of certain personalities is bought at the price of devaluing the whole objective world" (Simmel, 1997, p. 179). Simmel, in effect, became the first thinker to propose that a rich and full interiority was prefaced upon the negating of the urban environment that confronted the individual. Thus, the dystopian image of urban life is prefaced upon a rejection of difference and indeed of physical presence. Urban life, from this perspective, becomes a dialectical process of freedom and insecurity, whereby the urban citizen progressively retreats into their own cognitive or physical shell whilst simultaneously neutralizing the public spaces of the city. Urban retreat subsequently becomes the dominant metaphor in the dystopian image of urban life, whereby the urban citizen attempts to maintain a sense of "self" through the progressive creation of distancing mechanisms from the "other." Technology both comes to the aid of and furthers this management of urban space and cognition. iPod use becomes an habitual "mode of being in the world" (Geurts, 2002, p. 235) in which users choose to live in an increasingly privatized and "perpetual sound matrix" through which they "inhabit different sensory worlds" whilst sharing the same social space (Howes, 2003, p. 14).

City life is frequently understood through our understanding of surfaces. The superficial reading of the transitory clues involved in our observations of others, it is this phenomenon that has led theorists to understand urban culture through a recourse to the visual (Bull, 2000, pp. 135–146; 2007, pp. 24–37). Connectivity – if it occurs at all – is largely virtual for iPod users. The "personalization" of the user's sound world imbues the street and others with its own atmosphere in which the world appears intimate and endowed with significance.

The cosmopolitan image of city life is at least partially a function of life on the street (Simmel, 1997, p. 176). Through interacting with and being open to experience, the urban citizen contributes to the rich fabric of city life. Yet whilst many iPod users report enjoying city life, theirs is a mediated experience of the pleasures of the city. The city is frequently viewed through the products of the culture industry in the form of music and the iPod itself:

> I refer to my iPod as my pace maker, it helps me find that place. I almost exclusively travel to NYC when not in London. I have a dedicated playlist called "NY State of Mind." This includes a lot of New York rap music and NY/ East coast jazz – something with N.Y. in the lyrics, but also the sophistication, edge and energy of the place.
>
> (Sami)

> It makes NY City feel like a happy place – a place where taxi's don't honk... also, it always helps adjust my mood – if I'm listening to John Denver, I am happy go lucky – if it is AC/DC, I'm feeling like a New Yorker ....
>
> (Susie)

Cosmopolitanism, an urban cultural ideal, becomes a fictional reality existing in the often-eclectic mix of music contained in the iPod, in the user's music collection itself. For many iPod users the pleasure of the city comes from not interacting with others who "disrupt" and "distract" their energy but rather from listening to music, which might remind them of what it is to live in a city: a mediated cosmopolitanism encased and confined to the user's iPod itself.

The sonic training of the sensorium – an urban aesthetic

The imagination of the iPod user is mediated through the sounds of the iPod, which becomes an essential component of their ability to imagine at all. iPod users frequently construct an aesthetic narrative to the city deciphered from the sounds of music emanating from their earphones.

The world is brought into line through a privatized, yet mediated, act of cognition. iPod users often describe their city experiences in filmic terms. The world experienced as a movie script in which the user takes command is a common description of iPod users. The world and the user's experience within it gain significance through their enveloping and privatized sound world. This explains why iPod users invariably listen to their music with sufficient volume to provide them with an overwhelming sense of presence, whilst simultaneously blocking out any sound from the environment that might sully the heightened and empowering pleasure of use.

> The world looks friendlier, happier, and sunnier when I walk down the street with my iPod on. It feels as if I'm in a movie at times, like my life has a soundtrack now. It also takes away some of the noise of the streets, so that everything around me becomes calmer somewhat. It detaches me from my environment, like I'm an invisible, floating observer.
>
> (Berklee)

> I find when listening to some music choices I feel like I'm not really there, like I'm watching everything around me happening in a movie. I start to feel the environment in the sense of the mood of the song and can find that I can start to love a street that I usually hate, or feel scared for no reason.
>
> (Susan)

> I'll pick music that complements the weather, and that can alter the outlook on the world around me. I can take joy in otherwise gloomy, rainy, dank weather by putting on something wonderfully gloomy and dank, something I love to hear. It's a fine synergy of the visual and auditory environments. It makes me feel like I'm walking through my own movie, with my own soundtrack. The people around me look like extras on the set. I see myself in the third person.
>
> (Angie)

Whilst the conditioning of the filmic in the creation of a personalized audiovisual aesthetic is prominent in the above accounts of iPod use, it is useful to interpret the dynamic of aesthetic appropriation in some detail. For the most part, users claim that the aesthetic principle tends to be dependent upon the use of their iPods. Users will pick playlists or fast-forward to a music track that suits either their mood or their surroundings. In Berklee's account the environment is transformed by the music played, indeed the environment becomes a function of individualized sound. The listener becomes an auditory spectator. Yet, as in Susan's account, the iPod user is also dependent upon the music in order to recreate specific moods or images within their urban experience. Equally, Angie picks music that will enhance the environment and suits her mood. It is important to recognize the cognitive strategies being employed here. The world is being aesthetically reproduced in conformity to the user's mood or the mood of the music listened to. The iPod user's overriding aim is to create a privatized sound world which is in harmony with their mood, orientation and surroundings, enabling them to recreate their urban experience through a process that might be described as solipsistic aestheticization. iPod users, rather than reaching out to understand or see the "otherness" of the city as "otherness," as represented by the traditional practices of the *flâneur*, for example, aim to habitually create an aesthetically pleasing urban world for themselves in their own image. Theirs is a strategy of bringing the world in line with their cognitive predispositions, as an act of mimicry. This aesthetic appropriation of urban space is a prominent cognitive strategy in their attempt to create seamless webs of mediated and privatized experience in their everyday movement through the city, enhancing virtually any chosen experience in any geographical location at will.

Strategies of sonic transcendence are multi-faceted, but central to them is the construction of urban space as a "seamless space." iPod users possess the ability and have the desire to unify urban space as they move from home, to the street, to the automobile and to work, thereby denying the heterogeneity of the urban landscape passed through. The use of the iPod appears to bind the disparate threads of much urban movement together, both "filling" the spaces "in between" communication or meetings and structuring the spaces thus occupied. In the often repressive "realm of the ever-same" (Adorno, 1991, p. 78) or the "ever-always-the-same" (Benjamin, 1973, p. 146), iPod users attempt to achieve a level of autonomy over time and place through the creation of privatized auditory bubbles. iPod users often refer to the magical nature of carrying their entire music collection with them wherever they go, thus giving them an unprecedented amount of choice of music to listen to. In this de-routinization of time lies both the unalloyed pleasure of listening and the management or control of the user's thoughts, feelings and observations as they manage both space and time. Time and experience are increasingly micromanaged through the technological potential of the iPod. Jean, a 35-year-old bank executive, scrolls though her song titles looking for a particular song to listen to that suits her mood at that particular moment and, whilst listening to that song, scrolls through her list for her next choice. Her musical choices thus merge seamlessly into one another during her journey. She describes her journey time evocatively as possessing "no dead air." The ability whilst on the move to continually adjust music to moods with such sophistication and precision is relatively new, if indeed the desire to do so is not. Thus users "fine-tune" their relationship between cognition, space and music. This distinguishes iPod use from previous generations of personal stereo users, where they were confined to the fixed contents of the tape or CD. iPod users are more akin to sophisticated "listening selves" attuned to the transient nature of cognition whilst simultaneously attempting to "tune" their relationship to public space (Coyne, 2010, p. 16).

Tuning in/tuning out

iPod use offers a glimpse into the internal workings and strategies employed by users in their management of themselves, others and urban space by engaging in a series of self-regulatory practices through which they habitually manage their moods, volitions and desires.

iPod users, in describing their attentiveness to the flow of experience, appear to intuitively tune their flow of desire and mood to the spectrum of music contained in their iPods, beyond the scrutiny of others, existing in a naturalized urban heterotopia (Foucault, 1986). In the present age of instantaneous digital reproduction, iPod users manage their flow and flux of experience precisely through the technology of the iPod. Technologically mediated behavior increasingly becomes second nature to iPod users, habitual and unrecognized. Everyday behavior is mediated by, and constructed through, the omnipresent sounds of the products of music. Mediated behavior is transformed into an ideology of directness – of transparency – like so much in consumer culture in which appearance masks the production process. Transparency is suggested by the technological enclosing of the ears by headphones, enabling music to be played directly and immediately into the ears of users.

The fluid nature of music itself, coupled with the structure of choice offered by digital technologies like the iPod, complements the very nature of the user's consciousness, enabling them to construct an "individualized" relationship between cognition and the management of experience. iPods become strategic devices that permit users to shape the flow of experience, holding contingency at bay by either predicting future experience – the next song on the playlist – or shaping their own sound world in tune with their desire. Users are also able to adjust their privatized soundtrack whilst on the move, thus micromanaging their mood with great precision and skill. iPod users frequently demand an instantaneous response to the nuances of their mood, signifying a ratcheting up of expectations demanded of new technologies such as the iPod.

The technology of the iPod promotes the development of an "attentive" or "listening" self, embodied in rudimentary forms in previous analog technologies, such as the Sony Walkman. Earlier portable sound technologies provided less capacity for users, requiring prior and precise planning for the day's listening. For some users this was not a problem, as they would play the same tape each day for long periods of time, forcing their environment to mimic the straight jacket of their own auditory mindset. For most users, however, a hastily bundled selection of tapes or CDs would be carried in the hope that it would contain appropriate music (Bull, 2000, p. 76). The development of MP3 players, such as the Apple iPod, provided a technological solution to the management of the contingency of aural desire. Users now habitually take large portions of their music collection with them in their iPods. As one user describes, "it gives me the ability to carry my entire music collection in my pocket instead of a steamer trunk."

iPod users fully embrace the ideology that "more is better." The carrying of large slices or perhaps one's entire musical library in a small piece of portable technology appears to liberate users from the contingency of mood. They no longer have to predict what they will want to listen to or the vagaries of potential future moods. Whilst the personal stereo was commonly used as an "in-between" device – from door to door – the iPod expands the possibilities of use from the playing of music through attaching it to the user's home hi-fi device, plugging it into the automobile radio, and connecting it to the computer at work. Thus, it gives users an unprecedented ability to weave the disparate threads of the day into one seamless and continuous soundtrack. In doing so, iPod use extends a user's field of aspirational reorganization to include many more segments of daily life. The dream of living one's life to music becomes for some users a reality.

> I tailor my music and content by activity. Playlists allow me to create subsets of music that I can easily call up. I create playlists to

> tailor my music to my different moods. I label them as "Quiet" or "Exercise Tunes" or "Contemplative."
>
> (Jeremy)

iPod use permits users an unparalleled micromanagement of mood, environment and sound, permitting the successful management of the self through the contingencies of the user's day.

> There are times where I will put on one song, and then halfway through it I will change my mind and switch it to another song because my mood changed or the song wasn't capturing my mood correctly.
>
> (Heather)

> I almost always keep the setting on "shuffle" so that the songs come up randomly. If a song starts that doesn't suit my mood at the moment, I just hit "next."
>
> (Karen)

The mundane world of the city becomes more adventurous within a privatizing sound world. The contingency of the street in which one moves with the others, dependent upon the ebb and flow of others, becomes manageable and potentially pleasurable. The subject is simultaneously "passivized" and "energized" as they wend their way through the street. Walter Benjamin, in his analysis of city life, was attentive to the role that technology played in the navigation of the urban subject through the city. iPod users become reminiscent of the urban subject he described as "[plunging] into a crowd as into a reservoir of electric energy... a kaleidoscope equipped with consciousness" (Benjamin, 1973, p. 171). The iPod user has moved on technologically, accompanied by music, which drives both their mood and their relationship with the spaces passed through. Enhancement relates to the mood of the user and sometimes also the environment passed through, which in turn feeds back into the cognition of the user.

Whether subjects live in New York, London or Paris, there is a similarity of description as to how the iPod functions to manage mood and experience, and a similarity of desire to micromanage experience through the use of the iPod and to construct a mediated and privatized auditory world through which experience is seamlessly filtered. This filtering aims not just at enhancement but also at mimesis, by bringing the world into line with cognition through music.

Epistemologically speaking, following Herbert Marcuse, the audiovisual forms of aestheticization enacted by iPod users are largely transcendent. To aestheticize is to simplify, to strip reality of its inessentials (Marcuse, 1978, p. 46). The aesthetic principle is inherently one of transcendence. An essential component of this transcendence for the urban citizen is to replace the multi-rhythmic and hence unmanageable nature of urban life with their own manageable audiovisual mono-rhythms. In enacting these practices, iPod use embodies a dialectic of utopian and dystopian impulses. Aestheticization is an active mode of appropriating the urban, transforming that which exists by making it the user's own. The desire to engage in these processes derives partly from the habitual predispositions of users located in wider media use. For are not TV and film viewers equally in positions of imaginary omnipotence whilst they watch from the comfort of their own home (Morley, 2000, p. 185) and of the movie theaters? It is also a response to the nature of urban space itself, and the dislocation from it felt by the urban subject (Sennett, 1990, p. 212). Yet in this denial of contingency lies a liberating moment whereby the city is re-enchanted through the individualizing of each journey – the city as "aura" is reclaimed through the sonic "tactics" of iPod users (Certeau, 1988, p. 103). The price of this aesthetic enhancement, paradoxically, is the collective life of public space.

This chapter represents a moment in the sensory reorganization and framing of the way in which public space is managed largely through the sonic. Furthering Benjamin's observation that technologies rearrange our sensory experience and continue to do so, then, we may ask, what further re-organization exists with the next range of portable technologies embodied in the new generation of personal technologies, such as the Apple iPhone? The possibilities and demands embodied in smartphones are multi-faceted. One can search the internet, or update one's *Facebook* account to the sounds of one's own music through the use of its iPod function, thereby remaining largely in control of one's sound world. To receive calls, one's private sound world must be switched off, returning the user to the contingency of the world. Yet underlying the multiplicity of possibilities is a further transformation of our sensory selves and our relationship with the public spaces of the city. The use of a smartphone re-organizes the senses of the user. The haptic, the visual and the sonic are reconfigured as they scroll down the screen using their fingers to do so; the screen responds to the users' fingers, which, in their manipulation of the images on the screen, simultaneously miniaturize and globalize the subjects' reach. Touch, vision and sound are reconfigured in an increasingly managed simultaneity of experience immersing the user in a reconfigured here and now. Public spaces thus become instantaneous spaces of private engagement, pleasure and work.

Notes

1. The primary data used in this chapter derive from a series of interviews and questionnaire responses carried out with iPod and smartphone users in 2006 and 2011. The earlier data were carried out primarily through qualitative worldwide Internet responses to requests in *The New York Times*, *Wired News* and *BBC Online News* whilst the most recent data derive from qualitative interviews carried out in the UK by me.
2. The latest figures for active broadband subscriptions in "developed nations" is 56.6%, which covers North America, Europe and Australia. In numerical terms, mobile phone subscriptions in China and India outstrip those of the developed nations but with a much smaller percentage having access to mobile broadband services (International Telecommunication Union, 2011).

Bibliography

Adorno, Theodor (1991) *The Culture Industry: Selected Essays on Mass Culture* (London: Routledge).

Augé, Marc (1995) *Non-places: Introduction to Anthropology of Supermodernity* (London: Verso).

Baudrillard, Jean (1989) *America* (London: Verso Press).

Bauman, Zygmunt (2000) *Liquid Modernity* (Cambridge: Polity).

Benjamin, Walter (1973) *Illuminations* (London: Penguin).

Bull, Michael (2000) *Sounding Out the City: Personal Stereos and the Management of Everyday Life* (Oxford: Berg).

Bull, Michael (2007) *Sound Moves: iPod Culture and Urban Experience* (London: Routledge).

Certeau, Michel de (1988) *The Practice of Everyday Life* (Berkeley: University of California Press).

Coyne, Richard (2010) *The Tuning of Place. Sociable Spaces and Pervasive Digital Media* (Cambridge: MIT Press).

Debord, Guy (1977) *Society of the Spectacle* (Detroit: Black and Red).

Dyson, Frances (2009) *Sounding New Media: Immersion and Embodiment in the Arts and Culture* (Berkeley: University of California Press).

Foucault, Michel (1986) "Heterotopias", *Diacritics*, Spring, 22–27.

Geurts, Kathryn Linn (2002) *Culture and the Senses: Bodily Ways of Knowing in an African Community* (Berkeley: University of California Press).

Gibson, William (1993) *Time Out* (London), (6 October), 4.

Goggin, Gerard (2011) *Global Mobile Media* (London: Routledge).

Howes, David (2003) *Sensual Relations: Engaging the Senses in Culture and Social Theory* (Ann Arbor: University of Michigan Press).

International Telecommunication Union (2011) Key Global Telecom Indicators for the World Telecommunication Service Sector, http://www.itu.int/ITU-D/ict/statistics/at_glance/KeyTelecom.html, date accessed 20 April 2012.

Katz, James Everett (2006) *Magic in the Air: Mobile Communication and the Transformation of Social Life* (New Brunswick: Transaction).
Kracauer, Siegfried (1995) *The Mass Ornament: Weimar Essays* (Cambridge: Harvard University Press).
Lefebvre, Henri (1991) *The Production of Space* (Oxford: Blackwell).
Lefebvre, Henri (2002) *The Urban Revolution* (Minneapolis: University of Minnesota Press).
Lefebvre, Henri (2004) *Rhythmanalysis: Space, Time and Everyday Life* (London: Continuum Press).
Marcuse, Herbert (1978) *The Aesthetic Dimension* (Boston: Beacon Press).
Morley, David (2000) *Home Territories: Media, Mobility and Identity* (London: Routledge).
Musil, Robert (1995) *The Man Without Qualities* (London: Picador).
Sennett, Richard (1977) *The Fall of Public Man* (London: Faber and Faber).
Sennett, Richard (1990) *The Conscience of the Eye* (London: Faber).
Sennett, Richard (1994) *Flesh and Stone* (New York: Norton).
Simmel, George (1997) *Simmel on Culture* (London: Sage).
Sterne, Jonathan (2003) *The Audible Past: Cultural Origins of Sound Reproduction* (Durham: Duke University Press).
Turkle, Sherry (2011) *Alone Together: Why We Expect More from Technology and Less from Each Other* (New York: Basic Books).
Twin Peaks (1990–1991) Created by David Lynch and Mark Frost. Produced by Lynch/Frost Productions.

12
Publics and Publicity: Outdoor Advertising and Urban Space

Anne M. Cronin

This photo essay reflects on mediatized public space, "publicity" and their relationship with the outdoor advertising industry and its products – billboards, panels, and adverts on buses and taxis. Excerpts from ethnographic research on the industry and images of advertising's impact on urban space are placed in dialog to offer insights into the forms of publicity created.[1] This series of snapshot urban views aims to echo people's apprehension of advertising texts, and to signal how people and advertising panels inhabit city spaces. It shows how the advertising industry's research on its targeted consuming publics is folded into this urban encounter. This performs a publicity that is mediated not just by the adverts but by commercial knowledge practices and the intense semiotic "noise" of contemporary cities.

From Henri Lefebvre's perspective, the advertising industry would take its place alongside architects and town planners as a key actor in shaping cities and in channelling capitalist ideologies. This, for Lefebvre, is the production of abstract space:

> It is here that desire and needs are uncoupled, then crudely cobbled back together. And this is the space where the middle classes have taken up residence and expanded.... Not that this space "expresses" them in any sense; it is simply the space assigned them by the grand plan: these classes find what they seek – namely, a mirror of their "reality", tranquillizing ideas, and the image of a social world in which they have their own specially labelled, guaranteed place. The truth is, however, that this space manipulates them, along with their unclear aspirations and their all-too-clear needs. As a space where strategies are applied, abstract space is also the locus of all

> the agitations and disputations of mimesis: of fashion, sport, art, advertising, and sexuality transformed into ideology.
>
> (Lefebvre, 1991, p. 309)

This is a dystopian view indeed in which urban space and its publics are molded and tranquilized into compliance. It is a perspective that attributes great power to manipulators of space, such as the advertising industry, while also assuming that space is passively amenable to such action. But is this the reality of outdoor advertising's impact on urban space? How does the industry attempt to wield such spatial powers? How does it imagine and speak to its viewers?

Outdoor advertising is far less glossy and glamorous than the advertising industry claims in its pitches to its potential client firms. It jostles for street space and for people's attention; competition for both is intense (Figure 12.1).

Street signs, building structures, roadworks, rubbish and graffiti all form part of the textual and material fabric of place. Views are partial, overlaid and obscured (Figures 12.2 and 12.3).

Figure 12.1 The messy reality of outdoor advertising
Source: All photographs by Anne Cronin.

Figure 12.2 Urban perspectives on consumption

Figure 12.3 The city speaks to us in many voices

How should we read such spaces? Such visual noise and material clutter confounds a simple textual analysis and offers interesting problems for academic study. But it also presents problems to the outdoor advertising industry, and particularly to media-owning companies that aim to sell advertising space on their billboards and panels. These companies must offer up such spaces to client firms that wish to speak to urban publics – "buy this," "remember this brand." Knowing public spaces and the people who move through them is crucial for media-owning companies – but even more crucial is their ability to persuade potential clients that these understandings will translate into increased sales of their product. But advertising campaigns often do not deliver, consumers refuse to be impressed, sales are unpredictable, commercial research on people and spaces is tenuous and even the industry is skeptical of its accuracy. Yet research is continually commissioned, shaped, refined, presented and pitched to clients:

> **About this fantastic audience**
> Huge commuter base
> 85% of journeys are during the week
> 50% of commuters are AB
> The means to spend – family incomes 46% higher than the UK average
> Half the regular commuters represent the top 30% of consumer spenders[2]

This "captive audience" of commuters is amalgamated into a commercial object – a particular consuming segment – and presented as attention to be captured, money to be tapped. Commercial research promises much to the potential advertiser, who is keen to understand this public of unpredictable consumers:

> Recognize the evolution of the "nuclear family"
> Helps in rationalizing recommendations to strategies and briefs
> Delve into their lifestyles, values and general attitudes[3]

"Publics as consumers" are investigated through market research surveys and questionnaires, reformed into quantifiable responses, and shaped and categorized through purchasing histories. Views and values are corralled into market segments – do you agree strongly, agree, disagree, disagree strongly?

I usually find outdoor advertising informative
My work is a career not just a job
I often notice outdoor advertising
I tend to work weekends
Outdoor advertising gives me something to look at whilst I'm traveling
There are not enough hours in the day to do all the things that I want to do
I couldn't deal with a company that I didn't trust
Life is far more stressful these days
I find a great deal of advertising patronizing
There is little I can do to change my life
It is wrong for the government to ignore public opinion between elections
When I am shopping for groceries I often decide what to buy when I'm in the store
If I had the technology I would stop watching adverts
I am a vegetarian
I am willing to spend money to save time
Friends always seem to be asking me for advice on what to buy
I am optimistic about life
I always read the labels on packaging before I buy food
It is important to continue learning new things throughout your life[4]

Such accounts of consumers are recognized even within the industry as partial, provisional and flawed. The connection between researching consumers, placing outdoor adverts, and increased product sales is understood as complex at best and random at worst. Firm relations of (advertising) cause and effect (on sales) get redefined and quantified by media owners as "opportunity to see" an advert on a particular billboard (e.g. OTS "200,000 adults per week").[5]

Lefebvre argues that "desire and needs are uncoupled, then crudely cobbled back together," by the actions of powerful spatial actors, such as architects and planners (Lefebvre, 1991, p. 309). But an ethnographic focus on the advertising industry's practices also reveals that unpredictable market relations, and imprecise causal links between adverts and sales, create their own commercial needs and desires for stable markets and predictable, quantifiable consumers. Commercial research, and how it is fed back into the practices of placing adverts, cobbles together spaces, people and potential purchasing actions following its own logic.

This reflects what some would consider to be a more general desire for space as a ground or orientation:

> I would like there to exist places that are stable, unmoving, intangible, untouched and almost untouchable, unchanging, deep-rooted; places that might be points of reference, of departure, of origin... Such places don't exist, and it's because they don't exist that space becomes a question, ceases to be self-evident, ceases to be incorporated, ceases to be appropriated. Space is a doubt: I have constantly to mark it, to designate it.
>
> (Perec, 1999, p. 91)

Media-owning companies wish for spaces that are mappable, quantifiable and populated by saleable segments of consumers. But space and people-in-space remain doubts for them, although the companies continually mark and designate places. This doubtful quality derives from the character of urban spaces – these marks are necessarily in dialog with structures, spaces and moments that are beyond the control or predictive power of the advertising industry. Even a city's buildings and roads cannot act as the unchanging material backdrop for placing ads and for capturing urban publics. Buildings decay and are reformed, flows of people alter, sightlines change: cities are transitive and their ground shifts continually. People glance at fragments of texts, blurs of color or impressions of shapes that do not cohere into the "advertising message" as it was conceived (Figures 12.4 and 12.5).

Even industry research shows that people do not "read the space" as discrete textual units or engage in one-to-one dialogs with the advert. They experience urban spaces as three-dimensional, as messy, as inhabited, not as the flat world in the planes of text on the face of a billboard (Figures 12.6 and 12.7).

Advertisers want to speak to consumers in context – they tap into the shape and movement of spaces in order to frame and target people who inhabit those spaces (Figure 12.8).

Adverts speak to (and of) people's bodies as they move around public spaces – sensations of movement, eyes flitting across texts, bodily feelings of fatigue, boredom and excitement. As Sennett notes, "urban spaces take form largely from the ways in which people experience their own bodies" (Sennett, 1996, p. 370). These experiences shift and may not be easily anticipated.

Figure 12.4 Material conversations

Figure 12.5 Visual sound bites

Figure 12.6 Three-dimensional commercial

So, if outdoor adverts are vehicles for the "tranquilizing ideas" that Lefebvre notes, then their delivery is patchy and their message scrambled (Figure 12.9).

Advertising texts and structures are woven into the fabric of the city – and indeed into the very history of cities. And histories get re-inscribed and re-spatialized in regenerated urban areas where history is offered back to the public as images (now detached from the original invitation to buy a product) (Figures 12.10 and 12.11).

What does this mediatization of public space perform? On one level, it shapes an experience of a dreaming city, where snatches of

Figure 12.7 Behind the commercial

Figure 12.8 Mimesis

Figure 12.9 Join in

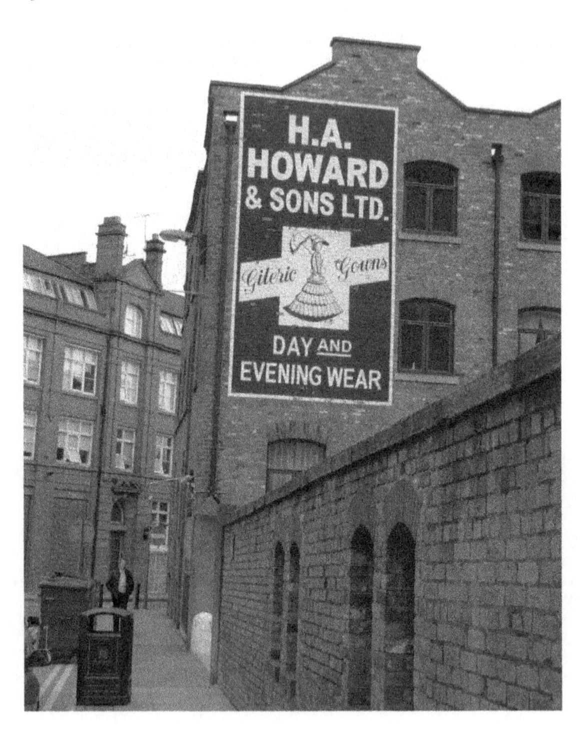

Figure 12.10 Reinstated advert in regenerated urban zone

Figure 12.11 Addressing the public

images, text and advert structures form a mass of non sequiturs, a clamorous semantic backdrop to people's material encounters with urban places. The messages of advertising are disrupted. If outdoor advertising attempts a kind of "call and response" engagement with people, it is a dialog that is often resisted, ignored or reworked. The grammar of desire and ownership marked on spaces by advertising is one which is fractured by the everyday messiness of people's visual and material encounters with cities.

On another level, the commercial research practices that feed into the placement and form of advertising structures act to perform a publicity. Indeed, "the 'public' is the product of mass media and their relationship to authority" (Street, 2001, pp. 41–42). But in the case of outdoor advertising, it is a kind of "publicity" that engenders a relationship between people and space that is embodied and hard to control, and slips away from the commercial authority of the advertising industry. The public address of outdoor advertising may act to call into being a virtual viewing collective, but it is unable to fix its parameters as a *consuming* public.

Notes

1. The research was funded by an ESRC grant (RES 000221744). The project is written up fully in Cronin (2010). It comprised ethnographic work at a UK media owner's offices, and also interviews with practitioners in other media-owning companies, media agencies, specialist poster agencies, trade associations, research companies and one client company. The data collected included client briefs, research questionnaires, research project results and PowerPoint presentations. A complementary section of the project involved a case study of the visual impact of outdoor advertising in Manchester, UK.
2. Excerpt from a PowerPoint presentation produced by a media-owning company to sell advertising space to potential clients.
3. Composite from media owners' promotional materials aimed at potential clients.
4. Composite of questions from a major market research questionnaire used by the UK outdoor advertising industry.
5. Taken from a media owner's promotional material selling a particular roadside billboard site.

Bibliography

Cronin, Anne M. (2010) *Advertising, Commercial Spaces and the Urban* (Basingstoke: Palgrave Macmillan).

Lefebvre, Henri (1991) *The Production of Space*, Donald Nicholson-Smith (trans.) (Oxford: Blackwell).

Perec, Georges (1999) *Species of Spaces and Other Pieces*, John Sturrock (trans.) (London: Penguin).

Sennett, Richard (1996) *Flesh and Stone: The Body and the City in Western Civilization* (New York: W.W. Norton & Company).

Street, John (2001) *Mass Media, Politics and Democracy* (Basingstoke: Palgrave Macmillan).

Index

Printed and bound in Great Britain by
CPI Antony Rowe, Chippenham and Eastbourne